CONCEPTUALIZING AND PROPOSING QUALITATIVE RESEARCH

SECOND EDITION

Thomas H. Schram
University of New Hampshire

PEARSON

Merrill
Prentice Hall

Upper Saddle River, New Jersey
Columbus, Ohio

Library of Congress Cataloging-in-Publication Data

Schram, Thomas H.
   Conceptualizing and proposing qualitative research : mindwork for
fieldwork in education and the social sciences / Thomas H. Schram.-- 2nd ed.
      p. cm.
   Rev. ed. of: Conceptualizing qualitative inquiry. c2003.
   Includes bibliographical references.
   ISBN 0-13-170286-6
   1. Education--Research--Methodology. 2. Social sciences--Research--Methodology.
3. Qualitative research. I. Schram, Thomas H. Conceptualizing qualitative inquiry. II.
Title.
   LB2326.3.S38 2006
   370'.7'2--dc22
                                                        2005018782

Vice President and Executive Publisher: Jeffery W. Johnston
Publisher: Kevin M. Davis
Editorial Assistant: Sarah N. Kenoyer
Production Editor: Mary Harlan
Production Coordinator: Lea Baranowski, Carlisle Publishers Services
Design Coordinator: Diane C. Lorenzo
Text Design and Illustrations: Carlisle Publishers Services
Cover Design: Jason Moore
Cover Image: Corbis
Production Manager: Laura Messerly
Director of Marketing: Ann Castel Davis
Marketing Manager: Autumn Purdy
Marketing Coordinator: Brian Mounts

Pearson Education Ltd.
Pearson Education Singapore Pte. Ltd.
Pearson Education Canada, Ltd.
Pearson Education–Japan

Pearson Education Australia Pty. Limited
Pearson Education North Asia Ltd.
Pearson Educación de Mexico, S.A. de C.V.
Pearson Education Malaysia Pte. Ltd.

ISBN: 0-13-170286-6

For Cindy, Cody, and Jesse

Preface

Truth be known, the real work of qualitative research lies in mindwork, not fieldwork.

Harry F. Wolcott (2001, p. 96)

How to move yourself and your ideas through the process of conceptualizing and proposing a field-based qualitative study is the focus of this book. The text has evolved, naturally and over time, from the questions and concerns of students as they think through ideas for an inquiry and then generate a written proposal for research. It has emerged, not as a source of clean or conclusive answers, but as a means to address practical questions and formulate your own judgments about how to proceed as a qualitative researcher. Students seeking guidance on how to design a qualitative study or prepare a proposal for a doctoral dissertation or master's thesis should find this book especially helpful.

My goal throughout the text is to catch real people at teachable moments, to focus on essential concepts and questions that reveal their significance in episodes that challenge the hows and whys of their efforts. Noticeably absent are the pristine and polished offerings of "old hands" whose exemplary monographs and journal articles—while something to aspire to—are often too far removed from the student more immediately concerned with how hunch begets purpose begets question begets worthwhile study. Front and center are the questions, frustrations, anxieties, and achievements of graduate students and others who are trying their hand at qualitative research for the first time.

Any attempt to deliver what a text like this promises risks reducing the complexity of thinking about, justifying, and engaging in field-based research to a series of how-to offerings. Some reduction is inevitable in the shift from actual experience to written text, but with an eye toward practical applications, my aim is to help you recognize and work through the messy uncertainties that pursuit of the qualitative entails.

THE MATTER OF CONCEPTUALIZING

The matter of *conceptualizing,* to which the book's title refers, reflects a twofold emphasis. First, a procedural emphasis regards conceptualizing as an essential prelude to the formulation of a workable and worthwhile field study. How do you transform hunches or personal concerns into something that can drive a purposeful inquiry? How do you develop a mind-set that is conducive to good research? This aspect of conceptualizing, the clarifying mindwork[1] that precedes and informs a research proposal and the start of fieldwork, is a primary emphasis throughout this text.

---

[1]As far as I have been able to determine, use of the term *mindwork* in the context of qualitative research was coined, or at least popularized, by Harry Wolcott (2005), who stressed, "Fieldwork is a state of mind. And something you put your mind to. Whatever goes on in your mind as you prepare for it, engage in it, reflect back on it, and report from it, constitutes its essence" (p. 147). I have highlighted the term for this text to emphasize the importance of your mental set as you anticipate and prepare for fieldwork.

Second is conceptualizing in the sense of organizing one's thinking around selected orienting concepts. Examples include addressing the basic conceptual concerns of *focus* and *locus* as a means to clarify your research purposes (Chapter 2); drawing upon concepts of *authority, ownership, purposefulness,* and *credibility* to formulate an argument for your study (Chapter 4); or considering your approach to fieldwork through the lens of fundamental concepts such as *intent, involvement,* and *familiarity* (Chapter 7). My aim is to use such concepts as a means to translate the multifaceted dialogue that is research into practical matters of application and choice about how to proceed as a researcher.

POSITIONING THE TEXT

Perspective, suggests anthropologist James Peacock (1986), is a matter of questioning both *how* one sees and how *one* sees. I have written this text from the perspective of one whose own introduction to qualitative inquiry reflected an acute awareness that what a researcher chooses to attend to, and how, is necessarily a trade-off in considering other matters of concern and ways of attending. This awareness is coupled with an understanding that qualitative research requires not only practical strategies for how to pursue an inquiry but also particular standards for what is worth knowing and how that knowledge is to be applied.

Together, these ideas direct attention to the premise that no single perspective encompasses the variety of viewpoints, practices, and traditions that are conveyed by the label *qualitative inquiry,* except at a general level. As I address in Chapter 1, certain major themes and concepts recur in the understandings set forth by qualitatively oriented researchers, and these can helpfully (if not exhaustively) convey some of what it means to claim a qualitative stance.

Field-Oriented Perspective

As someone coming to qualitative research from the social sciences, I have, by training and inclination, a different perspective than those coming to qualitative research from, say, the arts and humanities. Fieldwork, in particular, is not necessarily a defining characteristic of inquiry for those approaching research from an aesthetic or philosophical perspective. This book focuses on the significant proportion of qualitative pathways within the social sciences that are field-oriented and that involve actual interactions with people and experiences in natural settings.

Decision-Based Applications

This book is not intended to serve as a comprehensive and detailed methods text; instead, it is a focused guide through some of the options novice researchers face as they work to develop ideas for a qualitative field-based study and generate a written proposal. Throughout the text, therefore, I have emphasized critical decision-making points that shape the process of conceptualizing and proposing a field-based study.

I draw upon specific questions and examples from students with whom I have worked, as well as a few from my own research. The primary experiential threads that serve to connect Chapters 2 through 9 are represented by Patrice, Jayson, Julie, and Carolyn, actual students whose initial forays into qualitative research reflect the types of anticipated challenges and unanticipated insights encountered by newcomers to the field. Their preliminary drafts, thoughtful reflections, and honest appraisal of their evolving inquiries provide a cumulative and in-depth means to explore the processes of conceptualizing and proposing a study. Patrice's case unfolds as the central, ongoing example throughout the text. Jayson, Julie, and Carolyn revisit the discussion with illustrations from their work in a number of chapters. Patrice is introduced at the start of Part One, the others in Chapter 2. Selected experiences of other students introduced throughout the book provide even more opportunities to apply concepts and practices across a range of topics and disciplines.

Methodological Emphases

A single text simply cannot address all the methodological options you face as a qualitative researcher. My decision to focus on certain research perspectives and approaches but not others boils down to the priority I place on conceptual clarity rather than methodological comprehensiveness. In particular, my aim in Chapters 3 and 6 is not to account for an extensive range of options but to clarify how particular approaches predispose you to see things in particular ways and position you to achieve certain aims. Coming to terms with how you might decide to proceed in one or two instances provides a basis, or at least a point of comparison, for understanding how you might play out your options in other situations. In short, I want to foster a mind-set of informed decision making around methodological choices so that you are thinking, "If I do this—or something *like* this—then I need to consider these possibilities and implications."

My coverage of research approaches encompasses frequently used forms of ethnography, phenomenology, and grounded theory. This coverage has been expanded in this second edition to include narrative research and a discussion of case study. Overall, I try to make explicit the distinctive emphases within various research approaches, but also suggest how different approaches can complement and enrich each other. In this regard, I am joining those who invite and challenge us to consider the benefits of thinking across methodological boundaries to inform and enhance our research. (See, for example, the discussion of grounded theory in ethnography by Charmaz & Mitchell, 2002; narrative in ethnography by Cortazzi, 2002; and ethnography and conversation analysis by Silverman, 2004.)

My own graduate-level courses in qualitative design, ethnography, and field methods are based in education, but over the past 15 years have included students from sociology, anthropology, family studies, nursing, outdoor education, policy studies, occupational therapy, social work, and natural resources. Most of the examples in the text are drawn from the experiences of students engaged in research in education and the social sciences, but the ideas addressed are by no means limited to the needs of students, scholars, and practitioners in these fields.

Voice

The issue of voice is pivotal in qualitative inquiry in that it expresses one's stance relative to the distance and relationship between researcher and researched, and between author and reader. I write throughout the book in a voice and tone reflective of the directness and candor that I seek to foster in discussions with my students and advisees. I directly engage you, the reader, much as you would hear me talking with students about their research while seated around a table in a seminar room, in my office, or in the local coffee shop. Conceptualizing an inquiry, like fieldwork itself, is a human endeavor in which personal contact and straight talk can carry you further along than academic posturing and heaped jargon. You cannot, of course, discuss qualitative inquiry without encountering some pretty heady notions, and there are many in the chapters that follow. It is my intent to bring you to a practical understanding of these notions by revealing how they pertain to people who have faced the types of questions and difficulties you likely face as a newcomer to the field.

ORGANIZATION OF THE TEXT

The chapters that follow are organized in ways that reflect my dual commitment to convey the iterative and interconnected nature of conceptualizing and designing a qualitative study and to consider particular aspects of that process in depth. I do not treat in detail either the deeper historical or theoretical underpinnings of qualitative inquiry or the actual carrying out of a fieldwork project after the proposal stage. Rather, this text complements existing overviews of research foundations and methods by looking specifically at practical issues involved in conceiving and connecting the ideas that guide a field-based qualitative study.

I use as my point of entry a broad brushstroke characterization of qualitative inquiry as a complex and contested work in progress. Chapter 1 sorts through competing assumptions and recurring themes in qualitative inquiry, ultimately building a case for the distinctive contributions that enable researchers to claim they are proceeding from a qualitative stance.

The chapters in Part One, Positioning Yourself for Inquiry, narrow the scope of discussion and direct attention to discrete aspects of conceptualizing and generating a study. Chapter 2 works through the initial complexity of positioning yourself relative to a researchable problem and clarifying your intent in doing so. Chapter 3 poses both guidelines and challenges tied to the construction of your intellectual orientation and moral stance as a researcher. Chapter 4 discusses how you make a case for how and why your ideas matter relative to the work and ideas of others. The key point in this chapter is that you need to make an argument for your inquiry, not simply present your ideas along with other people's ideas and hope for the best. Chapter 5 focuses on how you move your inquiry toward a point of clear definition in the form of a research question. This chapter points toward the heart of your eventual research proposal, the section in which you bring the focus and logic of your inquiry into clearest definition through your questions. Chapter 6, the concluding chapter in Part One, presents an overview of selected research approaches and offers guidelines for your decision to lay claim to a particular type of field-based research.

The chapters in Part Two focus on the need to anticipate aspects of your inquiry in action. Chapter 7 highlights key strategic and relational issues you need to consider as you approach fieldwork. Chapter 8 prepares you to respond to the practical and ethical issues involved in establishing the integrity and ultimate trustworthiness of your study.

The multiple dimensions of conceptualizing a study find expression in specific parts of a research proposal, the actual document you construct to communicate and justify to a particular audience how you have conceptualized your inquiry (Maxwell, 2005). Chapter 9 highlights how you might draw upon elements of your conceptualizing work to inform and shape a written proposal for your study. You might benefit from perusing this chapter right after reading Chapter 1 in order to gain a sense of the product you hope to produce from the overall design process. With that image in mind, you might have a clearer sense of direction as you work through the discrete challenges of generating a study that Chapters 2 through 8 address. A brief concluding section addresses what it means to come full circle in this process and offers some practical advice about pursuing field-based qualitative research.

NEW FEATURES IN THIS SECOND EDITION

In response to reader feedback and the ongoing development and exchange of ideas in qualitative circles, I have extended my discussion of selected issues in each of the chapters and have incorporated updated references throughout the book. I continue to hope that this text will provide a user-friendly source of practical guidelines, probing questions, real-life experiences, and conceptual guidance about how to proceed as a field-based researcher, all placed in the context of significant issues that help define qualitative inquiry. Among the new or substantially enhanced features in this second edition are the following:

- Throughout the text I have included more, and more detailed, examples based on the actual experiences of students with whom I have worked to help illustrate practical applications of concepts discussed in the text. In this way, readers will have more options to play off the primary case illustrations provided by Patrice.
- Chapters 2 through 8 now include brief exercises designed to focus your attention on selected aspects of your own developing inquiry. Although primarily intended as a means for you to reflect upon and organize your ideas with no audience other than yourself in mind, some of the writing you generate for these exercises may feed directly into your actual research proposal. All of these exercises stem directly from the suggestions and practical needs students have expressed over the years.
- I have attempted to provide a greater degree of guidance regarding supplemental resources that could be important to you as you develop your own research. Recommended readings and resources focused on key aspects of the text now appear at the end of each chapter.
- I have expanded Chapter 1, updating and adding to my discussion of qualitative conversations and assumptions.
- I have made a couple of substantial additions to Chapter 2. First, I have expanded upon my discussion of memos by including additional practical guidelines and exercises for memoing, as well as a detailed example of how one of my students used the process to help generate ideas for her study. Second, I have added a new section on the role of pilot studies.
- Chapter 3 now includes practical illustrations of how to position yourself as an interpretive or critical inquirer, expanded treatments of feminist and systems thinking, and new information on critical race theory.
- In Chapter 4 I have expanded my explanation of how to formulate an argument for your study, including specific strategies and additional examples from students. I have also added guidelines for working through your ideas with others.
- Chapter 6 has new sections on narrative and case study, as well as more detailed strategies for linking your research questions and methods.
- Chapter 8's treatment of ethical considerations in anticipation of fieldwork includes current debates about the nature of rapport and engagement with study participants, an expanded discussion of informed consent, and a new section on building and sustaining relationships with study participants.
- Chapter 9 includes additional options, with expanded examples, for how you can present parts of your proposal.
- A new concluding section offers some practical advice for pursuing a qualitative research project.

ACKNOWLEDGMENTS

My acknowledgments begin where the first edition of this book began, with my students in EDUC 904, Qualitative Inquiry in Education, along with the master's and doctoral students I have advised in the course of their research. Special thanks to Patrice Hallock, Jayson Seaman, Julie Simpson, and Carolyn Shepard, who share the details of their experiences with the highs and lows of research in the pages of this book. For those of you who came to know Patrice in the first edition of this text, I am pleased to confirm that she indeed completed her study, presented a top-rate dissertation, and is currently an assistant professor at a college not far from where she grew up. Other students who have shared their insights and allowed me to bring their experiences into this second edition include Sara Cleaves, JoAnne Malloy, Chris Teague, Barbara Tindall, Leigh Zoellick, and Rosemary Zurawel.

I would like to thank the reviewers of the initial manuscript and the completed first edition, who invested valuable time and generated thoughtful critique during the development of this book. These reviewers include James H. Banning, Colorado State University; Donald Blumenfeld-Jones, Arizona State University; Renee Falconer, The University of Southern Mississippi; David S. Flinders, Indiana University; Peter A. Hessling, North Carolina State University; Barbara Kawulich, Georgia State University and Mercer University; Helen Kress, San Jose State University; Hanne Mawhinney, University of Maryland, College Park; Joseph Maxwell, George Mason University; Patrick McQuillan, Boston College; Maria Piantanida, University of Pittsburgh; Marcia L. Rosal, Florida State University; David Williamson Shaffer, University of Wisconsin; and Michelle D. Young, University of Missouri. Coming to terms with qualitative inquiry is an inherently argumentative and incomplete process, and I am grateful to these individuals for their insightful and balanced perspectives. The responsibility for any misperceptions or shortcomings in the text is entirely my own.

I would also like to acknowledge the wonderful staff at Merrill/Prentice Hall who ushered the book along with grace, skill, and professionalism. In particular, I wish to thank Kevin Davis, Publisher, for continuing to believe in my ideas and in my writing. I also thank Lea Baranowski, Project Editor at Carlisle Publishers Services, for her organizational savvy and remarkable attention to detail; and Karen Bankston, copy editor, for once again affirming my voice while honing my presentation.

I was originally drawn into this project through the encouragement and collaborative energy of my good friend and colleague, Geoff Mills (Southern Oregon University). He has remained a steady source of advice and feedback throughout the development of this book, and I am deeply indebted to him. I would also like to thank my friend and mentor, Harry Wolcott, for his editorial assistance and detailed comments on early drafts of the manuscript. Irv Seidman (University of Massachusetts–Amherst) has been an ongoing source of inspiration and support.

Finally, for their help in countless ways, including generous portions of patience and good humor, I thank my sons, Cody and Jesse. For keeping all of us focused on what's important and for her enduring love and support, I thank, foremost and always, my wife, Cindy.

Tom Schram

Educator Learning Center:
An Invaluable Online Resource

Merrill Education and the Association for Supervision and Curriculum Development (ASCD) invite you to take advantage of a new online resource, one that provides access to the top research and proven strategies associated with ASCD and Merrill—the Educator Learning Center. At **www.educatorlearningcenter.com**, you will find resources that will enhance your students' understanding of course topics and of current educational issues, in addition to being invaluable for further research.

HOW THE EDUCATOR LEARNING CENTER WILL HELP YOUR STUDENTS BECOME BETTER TEACHERS

With the combined resources of Merrill Education and ASCD, you and your students will find a wealth of tools and materials to better prepare them for the classroom.

Research

- More than 600 articles from the ASCD journal *Educational Leadership* discuss everyday issues faced by practicing teachers.
- A direct link on the site to Research Navigator™ gives students access to many of the leading education journals, as well as extensive content detailing the research process.
- Excerpts from Merrill Education texts give your students insights on important topics of instructional methods, diverse populations, assessment, classroom management, technology, and refining classroom practice.

Classroom Practice

- Hundreds of lesson plans and teaching strategies are categorized by content area and age range.
- Case studies and classroom video footage provide virtual field experience for student reflection.
- Computer simulations and other electronic tools keep your students abreast of today's classrooms and current technologies.

LOOK INTO THE VALUE OF EDUCATOR LEARNING CENTER YOURSELF

A four-month subscription to Educator Learning Center is $25 but is **FREE** when packaged with **any** Merrill Education text. In order for your students to have access to this site, you must use this special value-pack ISBN number **WHEN** placing your textbook order with the bookstore: 0-13-225963-X. Your students will then receive a copy of the text packaged with a free ASCD pincode. To preview the value of this website to you and your students, please go to **www.educatorlearningcenter.com** and click on "Demo."

Brief Contents

Contents

CHAPTER 4

Constructing a Conceptual Argument   58

CHAPTER 5

Forming Research Questions   74

CHAPTER 6

Choosing a Research Approach   92

PART TWO

CHAPTER 7

Strategic Considerations for Fieldwork   120

CHAPTER 8

Establishing Your Inquiry's Integrity   132

CHAPTER 9

Writing Your Proposal   150

NOTE: Every effort has been made to provide accurate and current Internet information in this book. However, the Internet and information posted on it are constantly changing, so it is inevitable that some of the Internet addresses listed in this textbook will change.

List of Exercises

Chapter 1

FINDING A POINT OF ENTRY

Where is my point of entry into qualitative inquiry? What underlies my claim to be proceeding as a qualitative researcher? What sort of mind-set contributes to my ability to proceed from a qualitative stance? What do qualitative researchers have in common? How do features of qualitative inquiry inform the way I might conceptualize a study and develop a research proposal?

The introduction to qualitative inquiry presented in this first chapter highlights these key points:

- Qualitative inquiry is a work in progress.
- There is no one best way to be a qualitative researcher.
- We cannot usefully discuss how to do qualitative research without attending to competing assumptions about how qualitative research can and should be done.
- Recurring themes in qualitative inquiry enable us to speak of its distinctive contributions.
- These distinctive contributions can inform the way we conceptualize and generate a study.
- When you engage in qualitative research, you take on responsibility for making some part of the social world "readable" to an audience of others. This is expressed initially in your written research proposal.

In starting with a broad view of qualitative inquiry, I hope to establish a means for you to place the parts that follow in context. My implicit aim, reflective of a qualitative bent, is to invite consideration of how parts and whole interact in a way that conveys the process of generating an inquiry as more, rather than less, complex. The chapters in Part One will get you working from the ground up soon enough, directing your attention to discrete aspects of generating a study. For now, let the broad brush strokes of this chapter serve as a reminder that you can never really attend to any one aspect of the qualitative research process in isolation from the others and without an appreciation of the big picture.

ENTERING INTO QUALITATIVE CONVERSATIONS

We find neither definite nor conclusive answers to the question of what makes a qualitative study qualitative. Like a friend's face in a crowd, we recognize a qualitative study when we see one; its features seem unmistakable, but few of us can explain why. That familiar face, the melody of a song, or the aroma of food are among the many aspects of everyday life that we learn to recognize from repeated, firsthand experience. Our knowledge is largely tacit, and so, it would seem, is our knowledge of qualitative research. (Flinders & Mills, 1993, p. xi)

One point on which most researchers would agree is that qualitative inquiry is much more difficult to define than it is simply to identify. The myriad forms of qualitative research—each with its own perspective, conventions, disciplinary alliances, and internal divisions—leave many of those who seek a common defining thread in a state of despair. The task is akin to entering a crowded room and trying to listen in on a number of ongoing conversations. How do you decide where you should focus your attention? What are the consequences of listening in on just one conversation to the exclusion of others? What if one circle of talk sets you up to be at odds with the one right next to it? Do certain conversations absolutely demand your attention? These are important questions, but first you need to consider the possibilities that lie in front of you: What conversations are you likely to encounter, and what can you learn from them?

The Labeling Conversation. As you edge toward this conversation, it appears a comfortable enough place to start: People are simply discussing what to call this or that type of inquiry. It is relatively straightforward, you reason, to draw distinctions among various types of qualitative research—certainly more so than to define qualitative inquiry as any sort of coherent whole. Then you get your first earful and realize this conversation can carry you in any number of directions. Some of the terms being tossed around appear to be synonymous or to overlap with others; other terms used in tandem are not on the same conceptual level. Still others that you had assumed to be popular fail to meet criteria as an actual qualitative "type" according to one viewpoint or another.

You step back and consider the possibilities. A qualitative research designation may refer to a perspective ("interpretive," "naturalistic"), a disciplinary tradition ("ethnography," "phenomenology"), an epistemological stance ("feminist," "hermeneutic"), a type of strategy ("participant observation," "focus group"), or even a location ("field study"). Given such a range of possibilities, at what conceptual level do you compare, for example, a feminist study and a grounded theory study? For that matter, how should you regard a designation like *grounded theory,* which can be considered both a set of assumptions about the production of knowledge and a set of guidelines for data collection and analysis? Or try wrapping yourself around the term *phenomenology.* Depending on what you read and to whom you listen, it can refer to a philosophy (Husserl, 1967), an analytical perspective (Schutz, 1970), a research tradition (Creswell, 1998), an interpretive theory (Denzin & Lincoln, 2000), or a research methods framework (Moustakas, 1994). And what about the eclectic case study—is it better regarded as a strategy for conducting research (Merriam, 1998; Yin, 1994), a choice of *what* is to be studied (Stake, 2000), an analytic framework (Seale, Gobo, Gubrium, & Silverman, 2004), or simply a form of reporting (Wolcott, 2001)?

Adding to this complexity is the common practice among researchers of combining perspectives. For example, you could do a critical ethnography, combining elements of ethnography and critical theory. Or you could apply a postmodern feminist lens to a grounded theory study, as one of my students did, designating the components of her approach as methodological (grounded theory) and philosophical (postmodern feminist).

In short, more is at stake in this part of the crowded room than simply the sorting and labeling of methods and strategies. What you can draw from this qualitative conversation is an awareness of the choices that surround you and an appreciation of how these choices express oppositions as well as agreements.[1]

---

[1]Some qualitative scholars, notably Tesch (1990) and Patton (2002), have generated detailed explanations of qualitative research types. Tesch's typology groups the various types of qualitative research within four areas of research interest: characteristics of language, discovery of regularities, discerning meaning, and reflection. Patton, in contrast, summarizes 16 common theoretical and philosophical perspectives that can inform qualitative inquiry. An especially helpful aspect of Patton's work is the identification of central questions that provide the focus of inquiry for each of the perspectives.

The Disciplinary Conversation. You wander over to this conversation as you hear the familiar names of well-established disciplines. Sociology, anthropology, psychology, history, sociolinguistics, ethnic studies, and so on all promote their own traditions of qualitative inquiry, often with identifiable favorites to which researchers are drawn. But disciplinary boundary work and border crossings start to complicate matters of definition and distinction. Some ethnographers, for example, who trace their roots in anthropology, are not hesitant to claim methodological ties to grounded theory (Agar, 1996). In turn, some grounded theorists invite ethnographers to apply and adapt grounded theory methods to enhance their work (Charmaz & Mitchell, 2002). Some researchers claim common philosophical ground between grounded theory and phenomenology (Stern, 1994), others argue the importance of phenomenological ideas for ethnography (Jackson, 1996), and still others assert the importance of distinct disciplinary boundaries (Wolcott, 1999, in the case of ethnography). Then you encounter something like narrative inquiry, to which at least five disciplines lay claim (Clandinin & Connelly, 2000; Cortazzi, 1993; Daiute & Lightfoot, 2004). Even if you are not yet familiar with the research approaches just mentioned, you get the point: Clear-cut distinctions and "pure" disciplinary approaches are often the exception rather than the rule.

At another level of disciplinary border work, you may encounter an exchange in which the terms *interpretivist, constructivist, phenomenological,* and *naturalistic* are bantered about in synonymous fashion, reflecting one or another's grounding in sociology, philosophy, or anthropology. Such examples of overlap and similarity abound across disciplinary lines. The good news is that this qualitative conversation is typically characterized less by discord than by polite acknowledgment of differences and, increasingly, exploration of cross-disciplinary possibilities.

The Postmodern Conversation. Intriguing claims of advocacy and self-appraisal draw your attention here, as well as the critical questioning of terms used to describe what researchers are actually up to in their work. Qualitative researchers of all types have responded in various ways (including feeling lost, as you might at first) to ethical and representational challenges posed by the postmodern context. This tends to be a lively interdisciplinary conversation, reflecting wide disagreement as to what exactly the term *postmodern* means, except perhaps that it represents a reaction to, critique of, or departure from conventional styles of academic discourse rooted in so-called "modernism" (Schwandt, 2001). For example, to the extent that modernism emphasized what is universal, what is permanent, and what can be generalized or simplified, postmodernism shifted emphases to what is local, what is tenuous, and what is irregular, contradictory, or complicated (Clarke, 2003).

Your easiest point of entry for this conversation might be in assessing postmodernism's impact rather than ascertaining its precise meaning. For example, postmodern influences have directed more explicit attention to how local and global concerns are linked together as well as how individuals can be linked morally and practically in the collaborative construction of a research agenda and product. The postmodern attitude has also prompted researchers to debate the basis for the authority of qualitative research claims, including how and to what end researchers can represent others in their studies. Researchers are now challenged to communicate how their perspectives and actions, and those of study participants, express social, political, and moral values (Schwandt, 2000).

Fundamentally, the postmodern conversation is about the positioning of inquiry and the inquirer amidst contradictory and complicated issues of power, ownership of knowledge, and political and economic contexts. To whatever degree you become actively engaged in this conversation, it is a good idea to keep an ear attuned to it as a way to position your own inquiry within the broader qualitative dialogue. (For insightful discussions of qualitative inquiry in the postmodern era, see Denzin, 1997; Dickens & Fontana, 1994; Esteva & Prakash, 1998; and Fontana, 2002.)

The Social Responsibility Conversation. A rather animated circle of conversation dominates the next section of the room. The pivotal question seems to be about how to balance the conventional research aim of questioning what seems to be going on in social settings with the activist aim of challenging what might be wrong with what's going on. The growing number of researchers in this circle of talk are intent on foregrounding a critical, feminist, or otherwise highly participatory and activist stance as part of their decisions about research design, implementation, analysis, and write-up. The stated expectation here is that one's research will serve in some way as a vehicle for reform and heightened awareness of inequities or oppression. An underlying message is that the researcher's view of the social world matters.

Especially for novice researchers, it can be rather daunting to make that step from the aim of understanding to the aim of potentially unsettling the social realities they encounter. Precisely where you locate yourself on a continuum that stretches from knowledge seeking to activism is the question that will probably keep you returning to this circle of talk. At the very least, what you should carry with you from this conversation is the importance of attending to how and where your perspective is made apparent in your research. Chapter 3 will revisit the complementary aims of understanding and change as part of the larger responsibility you bear in clarifying your perspective as a researcher.

The Moral Conversation. Either branching out from the postmodern and social responsibility conversations or emerging on its own as one of the focal points for discussion among qualitative researchers today is the question of what ethics in research is all about (de Laine, 2000; Lincoln, 1995; Mauthner, Birch, Jessop, & Miller, 2002). Everyone in the room finds reason to contribute to this exchange of ideas at some point. The trend in contemporary fieldwork toward more participation and less observation is making it an especially problematic but necessary conversation in which to be engaged. References to moral deliberation, choice, and accountability punctuate this discussion.

As you enter this circle of talk, be prepared to confront dilemmas, not simply about the consequences of looking at study participants but also the responsibilities tied to being with and even for them (Birch & Miller, 2002; Denzin, 1997). This prospect can be particularly intimidating to the newcomer, reflecting as it does a broadening of the ethical conversation from traditional, easily codified concerns about what researchers might *do* to study participants (raising issues of informed consent and confidentiality, for example) to the moral implications of simply being a researcher.

An especially noticeable influence on this conversation in recent years is the catalytic work of those who urge us to consider how feminist theorizing can inform research ethics. The many debates and disagreements among feminist researchers bring to the fore helpful distinctions between justice-based and care-based ethical models, among others, as well as more definitive understandings of the play of power and context in the formation of research relationships. (For examples and practical guidelines pertaining to these issues, see Edwards & Mauthner, 2002; Miller & Bell, 2002; Porter, 1999; Sevenhuijsen, 1998.) You may not have the means or experience to connect with all these notions at this point, especially if you are extending an ear into this conversation for the first time. Just remember that filtering through most of these debates among feminist thinkers is the persistent notion that ethics should be about how to deal constructively with the conflicts and dilemmas of research practice rather than simply attempting to eliminate them.

Chapters 3 and 8 will revisit some of the practical and procedural implications of the moral conversation for your work in establishing both an intellectual identity and moral presence as a researcher.

The Dichotomizing Sub-Conversation. The other Q word catches your ear in a far corner of the room, where you overhear a group of researchers speaking of qualitative inquiry as the "unquantitative." Here you encounter a debate built largely upon deficit viewpoints that, unless you are careful, can chip away at the generative and forward-moving tone of the other conversations to which you have been listening. It has been three decades since Cronbach (1975) tried to put to rest overly dichotomizing perspectives on quantitative and qualitative, but apparently it remains a restless issue.

In a recent commentary on the tendency of many researchers to establish either/or positions, Watkins (2001) draws upon this instructive paradox: "Actually, there *are* two kinds of people in this world: those who believe there are two kinds of people in this world and those who are smart enough to know better" (quoting from Robbins, 1980, p. 82). In highlighting our very human inclination to make everything dichotomous, this paradox directs attention to what is arguably the least productive type of conversation in our crowded qualitative room. It is so frustrating because it is often not a conversation at all, but rather, to use Watkins's terms, a "talking past each other."

I confront this issue most every day. When students and colleagues describe me as "you know, a qualitative type," I am left to wonder how accurately those prefacing words "*you know*" reflect agreement that we all know what we are talking about. Employing the designation *qualitative type* to mean simply that one is not a quantitative type usually leaves those in the qualitative camp to be defined by what they're not or defensive about what others say they should be.

You have to decide how useful this type of bipolar talk is for defining what you are up to as a researcher. The reality is that, with the highly visible exception of current "scientifically based research" agendas manifested in federal initiatives like the No Child Left Behind Act, the classic qualitative-quantitative debate, while still alive, is not what it used to be. There is less need to argue the value of qualitative research by differentiating it from the work of quantitative or experimental researchers. This means that we qualitative inquirers can turn our attention more to each other and the types of questions that can expand our own and others' understanding of what we do. For example, from the social responsibility conversation: How do you balance *understanding* and *action* as aims of inquiry? From the postmodern conversation: How do you distinguish among recording, constructing, and co-constructing data, and how is that important? Or, an overlapping concern of several conversations: Does the characteristically qualitative engagement with notions of subjectivity obligate you to discount objectivity at any level, or are there ways to consider how both notions inform your thinking?

The primary lesson from this undercurrent of talk is to regard either/or pronouncements with a discerning eye. In each instance where patterns of resistance to others' way of doing research might be constructed, keep in mind the potential offered by trying to make sense of difference and investigating a range of research stances. (For guidance on how to respond to overly dichotomizing perspectives on qualitative and quantitative research, see Eisenhart, 1995; Maxwell, 2004; Miller, Nelson, & Moore, 1998; Newman & Benz, 1998).

Qualitative Conversations and Your Own Research

As soon as you start generating ideas for your own research, you add to the ongoing necessity of listening to these conversations the responsibility of being a contributor to at least some of them. You cannot simply affix a label to your efforts—"I'm doing a critical ethnography!"—and expect to proceed unchallenged, even (or especially) among those who espouse similarly labeled approaches. You need to be informed sufficiently enough to articulate how the substance of debates—in this example, about what it means to be *critical* and *ethnographic*—might pertain to your particular inquiry. Situating your work in this way is not an option; it is a responsibility you bear as a participant in the conversations that help to define your research approach.

In the course of reading, class discussion, and your preliminary steps toward fieldwork, you will naturally come to view a particular approach as a preferred way of conducting research. Such choice amidst variety is the spice of the qualitative life, but it also precludes a generic vision that could be labeled as *the* qualitative approach. So what *do* qualitative researchers have in common? And what might underlie the claim that your approach to inquiry is qualitative?

CHOOSING TO THINK QUALITATIVELY

Your eventual choice of a preferred way of conducting inquiry will reveal in some measure the professional socialization you have undergone in your graduate studies—that is, the ideas, perspectives, and people to whom you are exposed. It will also reflect a case-by-case determination of what is an appropriate approach (a "good fit") for the research questions you are pursuing (see Chapters 5 and 6). At a more implicit level, the way you choose to proceed as a researcher will reflect your natural and acquired predispositions, the mind-set you bring to the task of inquiry.

Start now to identify and acknowledge the fundamental inclinations that inform your decisions about inquiry. Ask yourself: Am I predisposed as a researcher toward achieving some sort of closure, toward seeking knowledge that can be replicated and reconfirmed and therefore held with considerable certainty? Is it important that my data enable me to explain, predict, or even control the outcomes of similar future events? Do I feel the need to eliminate plausible competing explanations for findings that I obtain through my research? Am I uncomfortable with uncertainty?

Alternatively, while acknowledging the need for some level of assurance, ask yourself: Am I more inclined toward uncovering multiple (sometimes even conflicting) interpretations of the phenomenon or experience I am investigating? Am I comfortable with the prospect of furnishing more than a single meaning to features of an experience? Am I predisposed toward the generation of questions that invite rather than reduce complexity? Am I comfortable with uncertainty?

The first grouping of questions reflects the degree to which qualitative inquiry is still responding to strict interpretations of "science" as applied to social scientific research (Barone, 2001; Page, 2000). "Yes" responses to those first several questions suggest that you might yet be uncomfortable challenging some of the tendencies reflected in biomedical, evidence-based models of research. Affirmative responses to the second grouping of questions reflect, in rather broad terms, a predisposition to think in qualitative terms. Do not worry; this is not a test of your viability as a qualitative researcher. Think of it more as an initial positioning of yourself along a continuum that encompasses the varying tendencies and emphases that each of us brings to the process of inquiry. (For an engaging debate on the place of science in educational research, examine the series of arguments and responses presented by Eisner, 1997; Knapp, 1999, Eisner, 1999; Mayer, 2000; and Barone, 2001).

A Qualitative Predisposition

As a qualitative researcher your position on the continuum will indicate a predisposition toward working with and through complexity rather than around or in spite of it. You will embrace the challenge of turning familiar facts and understandings into puzzles. You will see value in seeking out your subjectivity as a means to explore how your assumptions and personal biography may be shaping your inquiry and its outcomes. From an enlarged awareness of how your own assumptions may be informing or affecting your understanding will emerge a still greater appreciation of complexity.

You will undertake inquiry not so much to achieve closure in the form of definitive answers to problems but rather to generate questions that raise fresh, often critical awareness and understanding of problems. Your distinctive contribution will lie in raising questions about ideas otherwise taken for granted or left unasked (Barone, 2001; Page, 2000).

In this way you might begin to identify yourself as a qualitative researcher: embracing complexity, uncovering and challenging taken-for-granted assumptions, feeling comfortable knowing your direction but not necessarily your destination. If we view the nature of qualitative inquiry in these terms, it becomes even more apparent that, while there are numerous ways to construct qualitative understanding, there is no one way to be a qualitative researcher. What, then, can we add that allows us to group a range of approaches and methodologies under the rubric *qualitative?*

PROCEEDING FROM A QUALITATIVE STANCE

To speak of qualitative inquiry as being coherent, as most of us instinctively do, is not to claim that its practitioners are the same, know the same things, use the same methods, or ask the same types of questions. Instead, the coherence of qualitative inquiry finds form in the suggestion that those who are committed to it share an understanding that certain issues are pivotal in the conduct of their research. The dialogue around these concerns has been a defining one in that it has cultivated an awareness of key features and assumptions that distinguish what it means to proceed from a qualitative stance.

In a commentary on the evolution of qualitative inquiry across disciplines, Page (2000) notes distinctive features of qualitative methodology that appear to have been retained over the years:

> . . . chiefly a research focus on "one human being trying to figure out what some others are up to" (Agar, 1996, p. 2), the ancient and seemingly ordinary method of fieldwork, and a research logic that is both empirical *and* imaginative as it works to portray how people are simultaneously unique and connected, often in ways they only partially comprehend. (p. 28)

Building upon these basic notions, we can portray the perspective of qualitative inquiry writ large as grounded in assumptions about the social world, and implications of those assumptions for field-based research, that include the following.

Guiding Assumptions of Qualitative Inquiry

We gain understanding of the social world through direct personal experiences in natural settings.

What This Means for You as a Qualitative Researcher

Qualitative inquiry finds its strength in the opportunities made possible by being there and getting close to people and circumstances, either through physical proximity and participation over time or in the social sense of shared experience, empathy, and confidentiality (Patton, 2002). The focus of a qualitative study unfolds naturally in that it has no predetermined course established or manipulated by the researcher such as would occur in a laboratory or other controlled setting. Researchers get personally engaged where the action is and in a way that draws upon all their senses, including, as Patton (2002, p. 49) emphasizes, "the capacity to experience affect no less than cognition." The well-known but awkward term *participant observation* is typically associated with this aspect of the qualitative. In its most basic sense, participant observation represents the assumption that the raw material of field-based research lies in people's activities, and the best way to access those activities is to establish relationships with those people, participate to some degree in what they do, and observe what is going on (Agar, 1996).

To immerse yourself in the naturally occurring events of everyday life calls for your ability to let go of control of possible confounding variables (for example, who in the setting is willing to talk to you about particular issues) and to be prepared to go with the flow of changing circumstances. In keeping with an approach that at various times has been described as naturalistic or discovery-oriented, you engage study participants as much as possible in places and under conditions that are comfortable for and familiar to them. Correspondingly, and in contrast to a laboratory setting, it is more often the study participants rather than the researcher who dictate the timing and tone of interactions. Being open and pragmatic to this degree requires that you possess a high comfort level with ambiguity and uncertainty as well as trust in the ultimate value of what an emergent and largely inductive analytical process will provide.

Among the many practical implications of getting personally engaged in real-world settings, perhaps the toughest strategic challenge is how to make your research needs and preferences known without disrupting the natural flow of experience. There can be quite a difference between passively accepting information in the course of experiencing something and making your presence felt in a directive manner by getting nosy. Your decision to reveal some issues or topics as more consequential than others in the course of your fieldwork—for example, through the questions you pose in an interview—imposes your agenda onto what might naturally be said or done. This, in turn, may impact the substance and persuasiveness of what you put forth as data. Chapter 7's discussion of involvement and role awareness will address these implications in more detail.

The nature of our engagement with others filters and affects what counts as meaningful knowledge for our inquiry.

What This Means for You as a Qualitative Researcher

Developing qualitative understanding through field-based research means that you engage in personal encounters and exchanges with self and others. Simply stated, qualitative methods work through you. Your presence, manifested through talking, listening, looking, reading, and reflecting in greater or lesser degrees of engagement with study participants, filters and affects what counts as meaningful knowledge for your inquiry.[2] Several essential aspects of qualitative fieldwork frame these considerations (Glesne, 1999; Patton, 2002; Rossman & Rallis, 2003):

- The perspectives and subjective lenses that the researcher and research participants bring to a qualitative study are part of the context for the findings.
- The negotiation of research relationships is ongoing, with the potential for the perspectives and understandings of both researcher and participants to be changed in the course of the inquiry. Part of your responsibility is to monitor and account for how these changes influence your fieldwork and interpretation of events.
- Developing self-awareness—that is, examining *what I know* and *how I know it*—is essential to determining the influence of research relationships on your inquiry and to constructing an authentic understanding of what's going on.

Together, these considerations point toward an acquired sensitivity, a simultaneous awareness of self and other and of the interplay between the two, that has become a defining feature of qualitative inquiry. Typically conveyed by the term *reflexivity,* this self-questioning reminds the qualitative inquirer that making perspectives and assumptions explicit serves to inform, not undermine, a study's credibility. How do I know what I know? How do study participants know what they know? How do I perceive them? How do they perceive me, and how might they respond to my interpretations? How and why is that important? These types of questions define part of the work of qualitative inquiry and affirm the centrality of real, live, individual human beings in that work.

Chapter 7's consideration of involvement and Chapter 8's discussion of presence, selectivity, and subjectivity provide an opportunity to revisit these issues in the context of decisions you will face as you prepare for fieldwork.

Inquiry into the social world calls for sensitivity to context.

What This Means for You as a Qualitative Researcher

Qualitative inquirers seek to make phenomena more complex, not simpler. For this reason, qualitative research is context sensitive or context specific—that is, it proceeds from the assumption that ideas, people, and events cannot be fully understood if isolated from the circumstances in which and through which they naturally occur.

As Patton (2002) instructively reminds us, "taking something out of context" is to distort it, to change its meaning by omitting consideration of how a gesture, a conversation, or even a word occurs in a context that locates it in time, space, and circumstance. The scientific or quantitative ideal of generalizing across time and space places a premium on identifying qualities or "truths" that do not depend on context. Broadly conceived, generalization refers to an ability to demonstrate the wider relevance of one's research and findings beyond the specific context in which the study was conducted (Schwandt, 2001).

---

[2]I deliberately avoid describing this in terms of the self as research instrument, the phrase of choice among researchers for many years now. Self as instrument tends to convey making use of the self simply as a means to an end, particularly in the sense of imposing oneself on or applying oneself to a situation.

In contrast, qualitative inquiry seeks to preserve, or at least maintain the relevance of, natural context. This means that, as qualitative researchers, we are not in the business of separating out variables or taking things apart to see how they work across a range of settings. Nor is our goal to produce a standardized set of results that any other careful researcher in the same situation or studying the same issue would have produced. Rather, we are in the business of embedding, of putting things in relation to the circumstances, both immediate and broad, of which they are a part.

This last statement deserves a brief word of caution and clarification. Even as you acknowledge context as a central concern in qualitative inquiry, take care to avoid the presumption that *context* is simply an objective, static set of circumstances or some sort of detached independent variable that "determines" this or "causes" that. Context is more complex, variable, and unsettled than that. Think of it as something that is "worked" and "worked within" by those actors who inhabit it and by those researchers who seek to understand its play in social interactions (Holstein & Gubrium, 2004).

Inquiry into the social world calls for attentiveness to particulars.

What This Means for You as a Qualitative Researcher

Qualitative inquiry's emphasis on context and its attentiveness to particulars hold complementary positions as two sides of the same coin. They work off and depend on each other. Let me clarify what I mean by this. Providing specific details about an experience, in and of itself, does not necessarily mean you are conveying what is important to know about the circumstances in which that experience is embedded. In a worst case scenario, it could mean that you are haphazardly writing as much as possible in your fieldnotes, patting yourself on the back for your incredible level of detail but losing sight of the aims of your inquiry. Conversely, simply attending to the general character and overall distribution of events or cases cannot help you understand how an experience is situated in time and space.

The complexity we seek to uncover as qualitative researchers demands that we attend to the particular (and unpredictable) nature of events and experiences. This means that we rely on depth, richness, and detail to provide the basis for our qualitative account's claim to relevance. Anthropologist Clifford Geertz (1973) coined the wonderful term *complex specificness* to convey the understanding that a researcher's findings can be both specific and circumstantial. For several years in the early 1990s I undertook a study of Laotian refugee students in a rural high school that accounted for the experiences and perspectives of scores of disparate family, school, community, and public agency members within the portrayal of a single case. In confronting the "complex specificness" of a particular teacher's experience with a particular group of students, I presented a means to think realistically and concretely *about* broader problems of cross-cultural adjustment, home-school relationships, and the like. This is not a claim to see the world in a grain of sand, but a characteristically qualitative acknowledgment that small aspects of experience, conveyed in sufficient depth and detail, can speak to large issues.

Qualitative inquiry's avowed focus on the particular is often at the center of debates about how generalizations work or do not work in the qualitative arena. Broadly understood, *generalization* refers to the wider relevance of one's research beyond the specific context in which it was conducted—an act of reasoning from a particular instance to all instances believed to be like the one in question (Schwandt, 2001). As you delve further into the literature, you will discover that some researchers claim generalization in qualitative research is possible, some argue it is not, and others simply assume it is irrelevant. Still others maintain that generalization in the conventional sense is unrealizable and suggest alternative ways you can talk about the applicability of findings to other cases with similar circumstances. For example, some qualitative researchers believe what really matters is the question of "fit" or transferability between the specific situation studied and other situations to which someone else might apply the concepts and conclusions of that study (Schofield, 2002). But this only works if the researcher provides sufficient detail about the context of the situation that was studied. Such detail enables readers to make an informed judgment about whether the findings are applicable to other, similar situations with which they are already familiar (hence my earlier statement about how context and particularity complement each other). Chapter 9's discussion of how you convey your study's significance and implications in your research proposal will offer some practical tips on how to address the generalizability issue.

Qualitative inquiry is fundamentally interpretive.

What This Means for You as a Qualitative Researcher

Experiences do not speak for themselves; nor do features within a research setting directly or spontaneously announce themselves as worthy of your attention. As a qualitative fieldworker, you cannot view your task simply as a matter of gathering or generating "facts" about "what happened." Rather, you engage in an active process of *interpretation*, noting some things as significant, noting but ignoring others as not significant, and missing other potentially significant things altogether (see Chapter 8's discussion of presence, interpretive necessity, and selectivity). Those things you note as significant either become data or somehow inform and shape data for the purposes of your research.

A practical understanding of interpretation starts with some basic definitions of data and what you do with them in the course of fieldwork. Qualitative data can be thought of as the objects and events that a researcher perceives and describes. By *perceive* I mean you obtain an impression of an object or event by use of your senses; you see, hear, smell, touch, or taste it. By *describe* I mean you give an account of that which you perceive. For example, you observe two students in a classroom exchanging notes and record that flow of action in your fieldnotes. That seems straightforward enough, *if* you are satisfied with the notion that what you are doing is simply collecting data *and* that those data simply represent the way things are. But how do you decide that those pieces of paper are "notes" or that the act in which the students are engaged is an "exchange"? How is your account affected by the conception you already have of classrooms, students, and the way you classify this particular action among the various kinds of acts in which students engage? How is it that you are abstracting "facts" from this slice of experience?

It is quite easy, as Silverman (2001) cautions, to become smug about such naturally occurring data and simply assume that what you are seeing or hearing is the way things are. This assumption, he points out, disregards the inevitable way in which all data are filtered through your own reasoning and that of your research participants. The descriptions you construct to support your interpretive work are more accurately *factual claims* about what you perceive (Schwandt, 2001). In the case at hand, you are claiming that these students you are observing are passing notes. Interpretation kicks in, in the sense that you are not simply providing an account of what you perceive but also making a claim that this is in fact the case

(Gubrium & Holstein, 1997; Schwandt, 2001). With regard to the two students in the classroom, your reasoning might look like this:

> "Given what I've observed of these particular students and this particular classroom, and given what I already know of student behavior and classrooms like this, it makes sense to claim that what I'm observing is an exchange of notes."

In other words, what you do when you interpret is build upon factual claims (what you and others perceive and select as important and meaningful) and incorporate them into a line of reasoning (formed by linking your claims with other actions or circumstances). The credibility of this interpretation rests on others seeing and accepting the relationship between your factual claims and your reasoning—a matter of persuasion, not proof (Peshkin, 2000). And because you are operating from a particular point of view, other interpretations and understandings are possible and may compete with your own.

Too often overlooked in discussions of interpretation in qualitative research is the deceptively straightforward task of transcribing a taped interview. Given the common lack of clearcut endings in ordinary speech, how do you determine when and how to punctuate to indicate a completed phrase or sentence? Is it a function of *how* the interviewee said what she said? How do you determine *how* something was said? How does your decision affect the intent or meaning of what was actually spoken? And ultimately, how do you determine the degree of trust you should attach to what was said? In other words, even a transcript is the product of ongoing interpretive and ethical decisions about the significance you give to what other people convey as meaningful.

All of the preceding considerations point to the fundamental assumption that qualitative inquiry is not a search for knowledge for knowledge's sake (or for knowledge that is simply "out there"), but a search for the *significance* of knowledge (Edson, 1988). In this sense, interpretation really has nothing to do with proving things right or wrong, predicting, or controlling. Interpretation demonstrates its worth through how effectively it explains things and whether it impacts or inspires the practice of others (Peshkin, 2000; Wolcott, 1994).

Qualitative research is an inherently selective process.

What This Means for You as a Qualitative Researcher

As a qualitative researcher, you cannot presume to be in the business of replicating the complexity of everyday life—approximating or reducing it, perhaps, but certainly not replicating it. You simply cannot be everywhere at once, nor can you possibly take note and make note of everything amidst whatever circumstances you happen to find yourself as a researcher. Whether by choice, chance, or ignorance, you talk to some people, not others, engage in some activities, not others, and write down some observations, not others. In the end, you sacrifice a lot of lived experience to feature a little on the printed page.

Justifying what you select as potentially meaningful data is a hefty responsibility to bear. You cannot depend on the experience of fieldwork, in and of itself, to somehow bestow upon you an unassailable claim to authority and accuracy. Despite what I have already stated about the importance of direct personal experiences in field-based qualitative research, "being there" does not automatically translate into "being right." (See Chapter 8's discussion of the relationship between presence and credibility.) You draw upon your research purposes and questions, as well as intuition and the thoughtful integration of others' ideas, to help guide your selection of those bits of experience to which you attach particular significance as data. Inevitably, you end up giving significance to some things that, apart from your efforts to make sense of them, might not be especially significant to anyone else, especially those in the setting. The key point is this: To understand the selective nature of qualitative inquiry is to acknowledge that data need your help to gain significance and meaning; data as data do not exist apart from the intentions you bring to them as a researcher.

ASIDE: The Importance of Meaning

Understanding how we distinguish data and their meaning is an essential aspect of qualitative inquiry. Qualitative researchers tend to adhere to the basic claim that human or social action is considered meaningful in the sense that it "cannot be adequately described in purely physical terms" (Schwandt, 2001, p. 153). Schwandt illustrates this point with the example of observing the same motion of raising one's hand as performed by a woman on a busy street as she steps to the curb, by a student in a classroom, and by a witness taking the stand in a court room. The meaning of the identical physical movement is different in each instance. That is, when we attribute significance to raising one's arm, or any such action, we need to look to its situation or context as well as to the positions and perspectives of different observers (Dey, 1993; Shank, 2002).

It's a similar matter with language and word meaning. When my youngest son shouts down the stairs, "Dad, I don't have a shirt to wear today!", I have come to understand that it doesn't necessarily mean he has no shirts in his dresser (or more often lying scattered about his room). What it likely means is that he doesn't have his preferred tee shirt to wear for that afternoon's soccer practice. Gee (1999) describes such patterns of experience in terms of understanding the many *situated meanings* of a word. My point is that meaning is not self-evident in your data, and data never speak for themselves. Meaning, constructed each time you seek to understand something, is always meaning for someone.

When you make distinctions, you are in a basic sense making meaning. As Dey (1993) explains, "Meaning is bound up with the contrast between what is asserted and what is implied not to be the case" (p. 11). For example, when conducting fieldwork you hear some of your study participants assert that the local community in which you are researching is "tightly knit." The meaning of this bit of data plays off one or more distinctions, not simply off your own sense of what *tightly knit* means. That is, you have to understand how *tightly knit* might mean that the community is *not* divisive or *not* competitive or *not* porous or *not* loosely integrated. In so doing, you give greater definition to the meaning you finally attribute to *tightly knit*.

In short, your work as a qualitative researcher is not focused on the intrinsic meaning of actions and words, but on what they are *made* to mean, particularly in terms of what they accomplish for those who engage in or use them (Jackson, 1996). The communication of this meaning through your interpretation is always negotiable and incomplete. In the end, it is a matter of how plausible your ideas appear to others and how persuasively you make your case for their significance.

Keeping Matters in Perspective

I caution you to keep these general assumptions and qualities in perspective. On the one hand, they are not absolutely definitive in the sense they say all there is to say about a qualitative stance. On the other hand, all they say does not account for the fact that when people use the designation *qualitative inquiry*, they can mean different things depending on the qualitative conversations to which they are most attuned. With this mind-set we start to come to terms with how we define ourselves as qualitative researchers: walking together on separate, sometimes overlapping paths, recognizing that we address concerns differently but appreciating the fact that we have common concerns to address.

USING QUALITIES TO INFORM CONCEPTUALIZATION

Immersing yourself in naturally occurring complexity. Acknowledging the interactive and intersubjective nature of your sense making. Proceeding with sensitivity to context. Attending to particulars. Employing an interpretive frame of reference. Attending to some things but not others. All of these qualities and considerations find expression through the process of conceptualizing and generating a qualitative study, as well as in the subsequent conduct and presentation of the research. As we proceed through the chapters of this book, we will see how each quality finds particular definition and significance within discrete aspects of the conceptualization process.

Table 1.1 provides a way to view how the qualities described in the previous section find emphasis in the particular tasks and processes described in Chapters 2 through 8. I realize that using a table to display how qualities are expressed within particular processes may oversimplify

Table 1.1

Qualitative Features Informing Conceptualization

Qualitative Feature	Finds Particular Emphasis in...
Direct personal experience in real-world settings	Problem finding and entry-level theorizing (*Chapter 2*) Clarifying your practical purposes (*Chapter 2*)
Interactive and intersubjective nature	Considering ways of being a researcher (*Chapter 3*) Anticipating fieldwork relationships (*Chapter 7*) Establishing practical and ethical integrity (*Chapter 8*)
Sensitivity to context	Situating the problem (*Chapter 2*) Constructing a conceptual context (*Chapter 4*)
Attentiveness to particulars	Distinguishing focus and locus (*Chapter 2*) Clarifying your research purposes (*Chapter 2*) Forming research questions (*Chapter 5*)
Interpretive nature	Making decisions about methodological distinctions (*Chapter 6*) Anticipating fieldwork strategies (*Chapter 7*) Establishing practical and ethical integrity (*Chapter 8*)
Inherent selectivity	Moving toward your research question (*Chapter 5*) Focusing attention through your approach (*Chapter 6*) Attending to some things but not others (*Chapter 8*)

matters, particularly in terms of suggesting clearly defined one-to-one relationships. Keep in mind that this table is not a representation of absolute or exclusive linkages, but a way to introduce the relative emphasis of qualities within and across features of conceptualization.

Consider, for illustration, the first feature displayed, that of direct personal experience in real-world settings. Although by no means limited to the concerns described in Chapter 2, the interplay and input of direct experience and personal concerns are especially significant in how you engage and shape a sense of problem and purpose for your inquiry. It is at this preliminary phase of problem finding and initial theorizing that firsthand knowledge and experience play a major role in your determination that "we have a problem" or "something is missing in my understanding of this situation."

In the subsequent delineation of the various aims of your inquiry, your direct personal experience likewise feeds substantially into the practical purposes of your research. These purposes, distinct from your researchable aims (see Chapter 2), pertain to real-life applications directed at change, improvement, or advocacy that your research will inform. When you reach the point of developing your written research proposal, the contextual background provided by your personal experiences can also be used to frame your Introduction (see Chapter 9).

Again, keep in mind that all such considerations are matters of emphasis. Direct personal experience plays into nearly every facet of conceptualizing a qualitative study, as do the other features introduced in this chapter and portrayed in Table 1.1. For now I am merely drawing attention to topics upon which these features have an especially significant or defining influence. Taken together, the features and topics portrayed in Table 1.1 can provide points of reference to mark your progress through the chapters of this book.

SUMMARY OF KEY POINTS

- Qualitative inquiry is a complex and contested work in progress, an approach to research that is much more difficult to define than it is simply to identify.
- The coherence of qualitative inquiry rests upon persuasive principles and guiding assumptions rather than absolute rules and clear-cut distinctions. Accordingly, there is no single, agreed-upon way to be a qualitative researcher.
- The decision to proceed from a qualitative stance reflects a predisposition toward working with and toward complexity, rather than seeking knowledge that can be replicated and reconfirmed. Qualitative researchers are careful about, even dubious of, the possibility or meaningfulness of generalization across time and circumstances.
- Competing claims about how qualitative research can and should be done preclude a generic vision that could be labeled as *the* qualitative approach. At the same time, several recurring themes enable us to speak of qualitative inquiry's distinctive features.
- These guiding themes or assumptions include a commitment to direct experiences with people, situations, and ideas as they naturally occur; an acknowledgment of the interactive and intersubjective nature of constructing knowledge; the need to be sensitive to context as a means to understand the complexity of phenomena; the value of attending to the particular, unpredictable, and complex nature of specific cases; the logic and necessity of an interpretive frame of reference; and the selective nature of qualitative research.
- These assumptions find expression within and across the various dimensions of conceptualizing a qualitative study and developing a research proposal.

RECOMMENDED READING

At this early stage you need to explore further where and how various qualitative conversations are taking place. To find out what researchers are actually doing and saying, start familiarizing yourself with some of the key journals that focus on methodological issues raised by qualitative research as well as those that present actual studies. Here are some recommendations:

International Journal of Qualitative Studies in Education (QSE)
Published by Taylor & Francis, *QSE* is published quarterly and typically includes two or three research articles, a couple of articles on methods and ethics, and book reviews.

Anthropology and Education Quarterly (AEQ)
The journal of the Council on Anthropology and Education, a section of the American Anthropological Association, *AEQ* focuses primarily, but not exclusively, on ethnographic research and publishes scholarship on schooling in social and cultural contexts and on human learning both inside and outside of schools. Periodic "Reflections from the Field" offer insights into the thinking of researchers. The journal lists the latest book reviews available on the Web at www.aaanet.org/cae/aeq/br/index.htm.

Qualitative Inquiry (QI)
Published by Sage, *QI* offers the latest developments in and discussions of methodological issues across the qualitative and disciplinary spectrum.

Qualitative Research (QR)
Also published by Sage, *QR* provides an interdisciplinary forum through research articles, research notes, reports on new techniques and technologies, and review essays.

International Journal of Qualitative Methods (IJQM)
IJQM is an online, peer-reviewed journal published quarterly by the International Institute for Qualitative Methodology at the University of Alberta, Canada, and its international affiliates. It is a multidisciplinary, multilingual journal, free to the public. *IJQM* can be accessed at www.ualberta.ca/~ijqm.

Finally, if you are serious about moving in a qualitative direction, pick up a copy of Schwandt's helpful second edition of the *Dictionary of Qualitative Inquiry* (2001), a thorough and reader-friendly guide to terms, phrases, and key references pertaining to qualitative research.

Part One

Positioning Yourself for Inquiry

A STRATEGY TO HOLD IT ALL TOGETHER

During the period of her graduate work in education, Patrice directed an infant and toddler program that provided early intervention services to families in the state. Drawing upon her professional ties with Early Head Start programs throughout rural northern New England, she hoped to conduct a study of infant well-being from the perspectives of families impacted by poverty. Her preliminary research aims reflected a twofold emphasis, addressing both the concept of infant mental health and the experience of participation in a program that provided services for families with infants. Her following reflection describes the mix of, in her words, "giddy excitement" and "painful cognitive dissonance" that characterized the search for ways to conceptualize a research design.

I began the semester seeking a way of conceptualizing my proposed study that was "solid," much like a scaffold or blueprint to a house. From the start, however, I was cautioned that I needed to take into account my changing understanding of concepts and that, if I visualized my framework for inquiry as a scaffold or similar image, it would likely be too rigid. "It's a dynamic process, not a static blueprint," I was reminded by my advisor. My discomfort around such a notion of research design rose rapidly—how could I hold on to something that was fluid?

I looked to the literature on research design. My reading led me to identify sources for the "modules" of a theoretical framework: experiential knowledge, existing theory and research, pilot and exploratory research, and thought experiments (Maxwell, 1996). I revisited an exercise I completed for an earlier seminar that tracked the origins and evolution of my research perspective through the succession of proposed titles for my study (Peshkin, 1985a). I systematically unpacked the "subjective I's" that were contributing to the shape and direction of my research ideas (Glesne & Peshkin, 1992; Peshkin, 1988). I completed a writing exercise in which I identified my biases, made explicit my identity and experience, and wrote an "experience memo" (Maxwell, 1996). I identified existing theory I was likely to draw on for my research, and I thought about how I might use my ideological stance as part of a framework for my inquiry (Creswell, 1998). The pieces, as discrete entities, were beginning to make some sense, but my biggest challenge remained: How could I maintain the coherence of all of these elements in a way that allowed for the dynamic, changing process inherent in qualitative inquiry?

This was the point at which I realized I had been confusing my desire for a solid framework with a need for a strategy to hold it all together—a way to maintain coherence while allowing for fluidity. If I could come up with a way to visualize my research design, I would have a way spatially to organize myself. I needed a way to hold on to and organize the inquiry process so that I could pay attention to bits of it at a time and not lose sight of it as a whole. I likened my experience at this point to visiting an unfamiliar city, an adventure that I could enjoy as long as I knew where I was on the map. I needed a way to spatially represent the pieces of my research design, see where I was in relation to them, and find my way around the landscape of my inquiry.

THE DYNAMIC WITHIN THE DESIGN

Patrice's reflection provides a useful starting point for considering what is conveyed by the notion of *research design*. Her expressed need for a sense of coherence amid fluidity suggests a dynamic within the design process that is often glossed over by those seeking a straightforward and structured pattern for framing their inquiry.

Marshall and Rossman (1999) suggest the term *cycle of inquiry* to conceptualize one's design. It is arguably an even messier and less well-defined process than that connoted by cyclical movement, although this image does move us closer to a key point: Qualitative research design does not begin from a fixed starting point or proceed through a predetermined sequence of steps (Maxwell, 2005). It might appear so from the organization of this book's chapters, but that structure is more a practical limitation of trying to convey in written text what is in reality an interactive and accumulating set of experiences. As a researcher, you grab a hold of the research process at any number of entry points created or highlighted by personal, professional, and political influences in your own life. Patrice, as illustrated further in Chapter 2, was driven by a deep emotional commitment to infants and an intrigue with her professional relationship as a middle class service provider working with families impacted by poverty, an interest she could trace back to particular memories of material differences among classmates during her primary school years. That professional relationship—and, in particular, the questions it prompted about how such relationships influenced the practice of others—was the spark that ignited her research interests. Other students you will meet in the following chapters found their points of entry along a spectrum of experiences—from immersion in prior research and existing theories, to questioning how they might advocate more effectively for their students, to pursuing contradictions they perceived between policy and practice.

The five chapters in Part One play off this variability and reflect what sociologist Howard Becker describes as a distinguishing feature of qualitative research, namely, that it is "designed in the doing" (1993, p. 219). This notion suggests that you do not frame and follow a research design as much as you create *connecting conversations*, or arguments, among the various experiences, ideas, and perspectives that feed into your inquiry. Your research question, traditionally viewed as the necessary starting point for design efforts (Janesick, 1994; LeCompte & Schensul, 1999), is in this way of thinking a logical and creative outcome of the connections you have made (Marshall & Rossman, 1999; Maxwell, 2005).

In practice, giving shape and substance to a process that is designed "in the doing" means that you are never really attending to any one aspect of that process in isolation from the others.

My own favorite analogy for this is to think of the manner in which you attend to aspects of research design as similar to the way that you try to focus on the shifting patterns within a kaleidoscope. All of the same basic elements—fragments of colored glass—are present all the time, but the pattern of shapes and colors that comes into focus at any one time depends on how your shaking and twisting of the whole instrument position the contents. (Of course, to realize the full potential of this analogy, we must assume that you also have made the effort to gather the fragments of glass, determine which ones go into the mix, affix a lens, and actually construct the kaleidoscope.)

ASIDE: A Cautionary Note on Pairing 'Emergent' and 'Design'

It is common in discussions of qualitative research to apply the term *emergent design* to convey the responsiveness of a researcher's plans and strategies to changing circumstances. Like Schwandt (1997), however, I have come to view emergent design as "an unfortunate term for an important idea" (p. 34). As he later explains,

> If we use the strict sense of the word *emergent* (i.e., arising unexpectedly), it would be reasonable to say that the fieldworker does encounter emergent issues or emergent circumstances or both that call for a response and, hence, the plan for fieldwork should be flexible and adaptive. As a modifier for the term *design*, however, the term *emergent* can suggest that the design arises unexpectedly or that the fieldworker has no design or plan at all at the outset of the study. This kind of complete laissez-faire attitude of seeing 'what happens' is ill advised. (Schwandt, 2001, pp. 63–64)

The primary downside to the now instinctive use of *emergent* is that it glosses over the dynamic and deliberate cognitive processes that make you, the researcher, the prime mover in the inquiry you are trying to develop. The assumption that your research design is out there waiting to be freed and that you will, of course, recognize it when you see it is not justified. As illustrated in the preliminary efforts of Patrice, Julie, and other students you will meet in Chapter 2, some lines of inquiry and problem posing reflect the play of relevant theoretical or conceptual work done by others against the critical input of the researcher's own experience, intuition, and hunches. Other conceptualizations of the research problem change in response to researchers' developing understanding of and exposure to events and ideas. You should not regard this proactive stance of allowing for and anticipating adjustments in one's plans as synonymous with the passive, come-what-may attitude conveyed by a literal rendering of the term *emergent*.

THINKING AHEAD TO YOUR RESEARCH PROPOSAL

Chapters 2 through 6 direct your attention to discrete aspects of conceptualizing and then establishing the coherence and fluidity of your planned inquiry. Each chapter focuses on key processes and decisions that feed into the development of an actual research proposal. You may want to look ahead to Figure 9.1 in Chapter 9 to help you anticipate the role of the following processes in shaping the presentation of your ideas for a written proposal.

Engaging Problem and Purpose (Chapter 2)

This chapter works through the initial complexity of positioning yourself relative to a researchable problem and clarifying your intent in doing so.

Clarifying Your Perspective (Chapter 3)

This chapter helps you come to terms with who you are and what you bring to the process of developing a qualitative study, specifically by giving shape and substance to your intellectual orientation and your moral stance as a researcher.

Constructing a Conceptual Argument (Chapter 4)

This chapter gets you situated conceptually and theoretically and then helps you make the case for how and why your proposed inquiry matters relative to other people's ideas about what's important.

Forming Research Questions (Chapter 5)

This chapter addresses three major aspects of getting at and working with research questions: (a) moving toward your question, (b) justifying your question, and (c) going somewhere with your question.

Choosing a Research Approach (Chapter 6)

This chapter presents strategies for determining when and how it matters to distinguish your approach to inquiry as a particular type of field-based research (e.g., ethnography, grounded theory, phenomenology, narrative, case study).

Chapter 2

ENGAGING PROBLEM AND PURPOSE

How do I transform what seems to be just an informed hunch or nagging concern into something that can drive a legitimate and purposeful inquiry? How do I know whether the purposes driving my inquiry are appropriate and workable? What strategies can I use to develop a clear sense of problem and purpose? What if I want to try out some of my preliminary ideas before I fully commit to them?

The clean, linear presentation of statements of problem and purpose that are typically found in scholarly chapters and journal articles provide a thin basis for understanding the initial mess and frustration of finding and fine-tuning a problem for your inquiry. For that matter, it is probably misleading to suggest that you simply "find" a problem or question, as if all you have to do is reach into that mess and pull out a researchable idea. Problem posing in qualitative inquiry demands more of you than simply hunting, gathering, and then displaying.

This chapter invites you to experience the creative discomfort of working from a fuzzy concern toward a researchable aim. It directs attention to what it means to pose a researchable problem and how you meaningfully engage a topic of inquiry. Figure 2.1 gets us started with a schematic description of the dynamic process encompassed by the phrase *engaging with a sense of problem*. As a means to conceptualize a strategy for holding on to and making sense of the ideas that are prompting your inquiry, it suggests a dynamic between personal or immediate concerns that drive an inquiry and systematic considerations that orient an inquiry. The former concerns represent a complex mix of direct experience, professional insight, intellectual orientation, intuition, emotional investment, and common sense. The latter considerations can be approached along more readily defined pathways that include:

- how and why you are choosing to position yourself relative to a particular problem or issue you have defined
- why you are looking at issues in a particular way
- when and how you are linking up your inquiry with the work and ideas of others
- how you are developing and then justifying the questions that focus your research
- how you are deciding on your approach to real-world observations and data gathering

Thinking Ahead to Your Research Proposal. This aspect of your work takes shape in your eventual research proposal most prominently in your Introduction and in sections that address the Background, Significance, and Implications of your study. In a practical sense, your definition of problem and statement of purpose serve as crucial points of reference whenever you encounter moments of doubt and decision in the course of developing your inquiry. In research, just as in architecture, form must always follow function; purpose must always precede method or format.

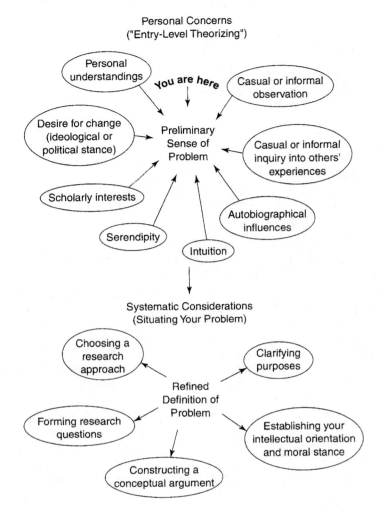

Figure 2.1
Engaging with a Sense of Problem from Personal Concerns to Systematic Considerations

SHAPING A PRELIMINARY SENSE OF PROBLEM

Initially, the interplay and input of your direct experience and personal concerns feed into the shaping of a sense of problem. At this stage, you're working with any number of hunches, nagging concerns, compelling interests, and curiosities. Casual observations, informal inquiry into others' experiences, political commitments, scholarly or professional interests, intuition, and even serendipity are playing off each other to bring into question how you are viewing an issue or set of circumstances. Consider the various ways in which these students grabbed onto a personal, professional, or political motivation to initiate a research project:

Carolyn. Carolyn was a doctoral student in education who, in the fall of 2003, initiated long-term fieldwork with a small population of Cambodian immigrants in a rural northern New England town. Well before she had committed herself to this research, when she was still working as an English as a Second Language (ESL) teacher for adults, Carolyn had become sensitive to how Cambodian learners in her classes seemed to feel powerless and distanced from most English speakers they encountered. Immersed as she was in the practicalities of her everyday work, Carolyn had not yet placed these preliminary feelings in the context of any formal understandings or theories of social interactions between second language learners and target language speakers. She was merely at the point of questioning what seemed to be going on in specific situations and expressing concern (to whomever would listen) that there might be something wrong with what was going on. The emotional "grab" for Carolyn, in others words, stemmed from her professional concerns and inclinations as a teacher and advocate for her adult students. This was enough to get her started. When she then began her graduate work, she transformed these concerns into more systematic questioning of what second language theorists were saying about power relationships and social structures inherent in formal educational contexts like adult ESL classes.

In sum, Carolyn was driven by a concern for change and a desire to raise awareness of the social, economic, and other forces impacting the lives of adult ESL students.

Jayson. Jayson was a doctoral student in education who, in the summer of 2004, initiated fieldwork focused on how group activity is mediated in experiential, adventure-based workshops (e.g., four-day programs built around small group initiatives, physical challenges, guided debriefings, and the like). A long-time practitioner in the field of outdoor experiential education and a voracious reader of the professional literature, Jayson had for years been questioning commonplace views about what it means to "learn through adventure." His motivation stemmed from a feeling that outdoor education practices had become over-idealized, and that the simple equation "learning derives from doing" too easily disregarded the powerful guiding influence of the workshop leader. "Contradictions in the way we view the role of these group leaders are rarely being noticed," he wrote early on, "because our theories do not require us to notice them." He sought through his research to disrupt what he regarded as faulty assumptions about the role practitioners actually play in facilitating group experiences. This focus fit within his broader concern that research had for many years addressed *what* is learned in adventure programs, but had left open to question *how* adventure experiences contributed to learning.

In sum, Jayson was driven by the intellectual aim of complicating what he considered to be oversimplified explanations of experiential learning. He sought to represent more accurately the role of the practitioners in adventure-based programs.

Julie. Julie was a doctoral student in education who was in the midst of generating her research proposal during the 2004–2005 academic year. Prior to and during that time she worked in the university's Office of Sponsored Research, where she managed the flow and compliance of research proposals submitted to the university's Institutional

Review Board. Julie had noted for some time that members of the Review Board were often in the position of having to reconcile regulatory requirements grounded primarily in the biomedical research model with qualitative research activities based in the social sciences. This was especially troublesome in matters involving the principle of informed consent. (The principle of informed consent forms the basis of what institutions like universities require of researchers in order to protect their research participants from harm. For more on this issue, see Chapter 8.) It had become apparent through her own work on matters of compliance that researchers and participants who engaged in qualitative fieldwork developed different and even contradictory understandings of what it means to consent to participate in research. She wondered how the apparent certainty of the informed consent process—it did, after all, require research participants to agree to and sign a document—played against the apparent uncertainty of qualitative fieldwork (specifically participant observation studies) in which perceptions, questions, and relationships seem to shift constantly. She wondered whether informed consent was an unattainable ethical ideal in the context of such fieldwork. She puzzled over what *informed* actually meant. She especially worried over the moral obligations of researchers to participants regarding informed consent.

In sum, Julie was driven by practical and ethical concerns that stemmed from incongruities she perceived between the nature of certain qualitative research activities and guidelines used to regulate those activities.

As these examples suggest, a sense of problem may take shape simply as a questioning of why something is one way and not another. Or, it may emerge as a hunch that something is missing in your understanding or interpretation of a situation. Or, it may stem from a heartfelt sense that something is simply unfair, out-of-balance, or dysfunctional. In any case, a sense of problem can, but need not, imply that something has gone wrong and must be fixed. As suggested in Chapter 1, qualitative studies typically do not aim at problem solution, but are exceptionally well suited to *problematizing* phenomena to reveal their complexity (Piantanida & Garman, 1999; also see this chapter's section on research purposes and practical purposes). By problematizing, I mean inviting consideration of other plausible interpretations of phenomena and inviting attention to their complexity. A more detailed look at a single case will help to illustrate some of the practical aspects of problematizing, or productively complicating, an issue or topic. In the following experience described by Patrice, a casual observation fed into a preliminary articulation of a problem for inquiry.

Sitting in a local restaurant as part of a recent off-site management meeting recently, I was distracted by a young man—presumably the father—cradling in his arms what looked to be a five-month-old infant. The baby had the attention of another adult who had positioned her body close to the man's side and was interacting with the baby by making gleeful, animated faces to which the infant clearly responded with pleasure.

As this social interaction unfolded, the threesome attracted the attention of other bystanders, and the group grew. Within minutes, there were at least five adults in awe of this beautiful infant who knew how to charm the group with quick smiles, dancing eyes, and vocalizations that engaged everyone's attention. I interpreted all of this as healthy behavior that reflected the notions I held about what constitutes healthy development for infants. The social and emotional responses and interactions were as they should be and I assessed the infant to be delightfully "developmentally age-appropriate."

The bothersome piece for me, however, was the contrast between the social situation I had just witnessed and informally assessed and the social situation of many of the infants for whom I am called upon to make similar, more formal assessments. When an infant is born into a context of poverty, what opportunities exist to facilitate what I know to be healthy social and emotional development? The families that I know who live in poverty do not have these same experiences; the restaurant scene would in many cases be an unfamiliar context for such interaction. Do I produce a valid assessment of infant social and emotional development when I apply my middle class constructs of infant well-being to infants and families who live in poverty?

Patrice's firsthand knowledge and experience as an early intervention home visitor gave rise to her consideration that "we have a problem" or that "we need to question what appears to be going on." In this case, her sense of problem emerged from the discomfort she felt when she observed infants and adults in "classic" social engagement situations (such as the restaurant episode) that leading child development experts would describe as "normal." Her discomfort stemmed, as she stated,

. . . from knowing full well that not every baby has the opportunity for these experiences but has different experiences that may or may not promote optimal development. It is observing the emotion on a mother's face when a home visitor explains to the mother what will happen if her child "fails" a screening. Although I understand the intent and meaning of the home visitor, I also conclude that this mother has a history of negative emotions associated with failing, and a barrier between the home visitor and the mother has likely been erected.

Entry-Level Theorizing

Such observations and accompanying insights contributed to the play of ideas, emotions, and experiences that enabled Patrice to move toward an increasingly refined sense of problem. She engaged in a fluid and dialectic process of focusing her inquiry by alternately grasping and letting go of notions, interests, and questions like those described previously, situating herself relative to a problem that I equate to *entry-level theorizing* (Wolcott, 2005). Entry-level theorizing refers to "a well-thought-out position from which the researcher as inquirer feels drawn to an issue or problem and seeks to construct a firmer basis in both knowledge and under-standing" (Wolcott, 2005, p. 178). Patrice subsequently conveyed her well-thought-out posi-tion in this way:

> Professionals in the field of infant development apply concepts of emotional health that have likely been created outside the context of poverty. If I adhere to the notion that what we know is socially constructed, then I question (a) the idea of what constitutes an emotionally healthy infant as determined by middle class researchers and practi-tioners, and (b) how we apply this definition to families who live under different cir-cumstances, such as those families who live in poverty.
>
> If I am going to evaluate effectively and fairly the social and emotional development of infants in the context of poverty, I need to understand infant development from the perspectives of those who live in poverty. How do families who live in the context of poverty view infant well-being?

Taken together, the incorporation of personal experience and professional insight repre-sented in these three excerpts from Patrice's preliminary reflections might take the practical form of a *researcher experience memo*, or *analytic memo* (Maxwell, 2005, building upon Mills, 1959). Making the effort to identify and explicitly take into account how your identity and ex-perience are informing your sense of problem, and documenting that effort in a written memo, is a valuable and necessary strategy in the development of your inquiry. Keep in mind, as well, that this is not a one-time exercise. Although crucial at this early stage of problem finding, memos should resurface to inform, spur systematic reflection, and provide reality checks throughout the course of your inquiry. (For illustrations and practical guidelines on how to use memos to move your research ideas forward, see "Mining Your Memos" later in this chapter).

Situating Your Problem

With her increasingly refined sense of problem, Patrice gradually positioned herself to con-sider in more systematic fashion how she might link up with the work and ideas of others by addressing issues of purpose, theory, perspective, and method—in effect, *situating her problem*. This entails linking up with the ideas of others and considering the relationships among the key issues within one's design. These links, identified in the bottom half of Figure 2.1, will be discussed more thoroughly in Chapters 3, 4, 5, and 6.

When moving on from the personal and experiential emphases of entry-level theorizing, you continue to position yourself relative to a problem. However, as you engage with the sys-tematic considerations of situating your problem, the generative flow of inquiry is from a re-fined definition of problem rather than toward a preliminary sense of problem. (Note the reversed direction of the arrows in Figure 2.1.) This is a decisive shift: You must now consider your inquiry as something constructed in relation to ideas, contexts, and purposes beyond the immediate scope of your direct experiences and observations. It is time to expand your notion of positioning to include how you identify, distinguish, and justify your research purposes; how and why you decide to look at the world and your particular problem in a certain way;

how you link your thinking with the work and ideas of others; how you develop and justify your research question(s); and how you decide on strategies and methods for data collection, generation, and analysis.

Some words of caution: As I noted in the introduction to Part One, positioning yourself systematically demands that you consider all of these key issues at the same time and over a period of time. They are interconnected in such a way that the manner in which you respond to any one issue, taken in any order, affects how you respond to the others. This is another way of saying that, as a qualitative researcher, you work through complexity rather than around or in spite of it.

The preceding words of caution still beg the question of where and how to find a point of entry into the multiple tasks of situating your problem and establishing systematic links among the various components of conceptualizing and designing your study. Taking that step is often a function of individual circumstances or serendipity—finding yourself drawn initially to the play of some intriguing concepts, for example, or perhaps feeling pressed to clarify your assumptions before you can proceed further. If there isn't a pull toward one component or another, experience suggests that clarifying one's intent or purpose is a logical and practical way to get on with situating your problem and, more broadly, your inquiry.

CLARIFYING PURPOSES

Do you have a solid, justifiable aim or set of aims to guide your inquiry? The task here is to make the connection between positioning yourself relative to a problem and clarifying your intent in doing so. This represents a subtle shift in emphasis, particularly if you regard the individual concerns and entry-level theorizing discussed in the previous section as tacit expressions of the personal or experiential purposes motivating your inquiry. It is important that you take into account your purposes at this personal level and acknowledge how they may be shaping your inquiry. At the same time you need to distinguish them from the more public and systematically generated statements of purpose that help to guide and justify your study— namely, research purposes and practical purposes (Maxwell, 1996).

Research Purposes and Practical Purposes

Consider the ways that Patrice could proceed depending on how she focuses the purpose of her inquiry. She might describe her aims in terms of understanding something or gaining insight into what is going on in a setting—that is, a *research* purpose (Maxwell, 1996). For example: "The purpose of this study is to understand the experience of families who participate in early intervention programs," or "The purpose of this study is to explore infant well-being as described by families who are impacted by poverty." Either of these purposes can be addressed directly by an empirical field study.[1]

---

[1]The word *empirical* has been widely misused to refer only to quantified data. Used correctly, as Metz (2000) reminds us, it refers to "information that has been gathered in any systematic way about the world around us as it is available through experience rather than through mere deduction" (p. 68). Qualitative data, in Metz's view and according to the presentation of ideas in this text, are "profoundly empirical."

Contrast this researchable aim with a statement of purpose focused on accomplishing, changing, or evaluating something—that is, a *practical* purpose (Maxwell, 1996). For example: "The purpose of this study is to generate program changes that will improve the experiences of families impacted by poverty," or "The purpose of this study is to identify ways that home-visiting human service providers can more effectively partner with families as a way to promote healthy infant development." Neither of these purposes can be directly addressed by empirical research even though each reflects a valuable aim—highlighting the point that practical goals are especially valuable as you later attempt to justify your research (Maxwell, 2005). Patrice acknowledged both emphases within her efforts early on and described her concern for maintaining the "authenticity" of her research:

> It seems that what I want to do is some sort of "transformative" research . . . but I'm not sure I want to claim that because I would have to go into my site assuming, for example, that the relationships [between the early intervention service providers and the families] serve to perpetuate poverty. However, I think I can go in saying, "If that, then this," meaning, "If I see behaviors and interactions that perpetuate poverty, then I will take an approach that could lead to some sort of action." My caution remains, however, that if I go into a site with an agenda [to change the situation], my research won't be authentic.

By maintaining the distinction between her research purposes and practical purposes, Patrice can establish as a legitimate part of her design a discussion of how her inquiry may, and perhaps should, create opportunities for social action, change, or advocacy (Marshall & Rossman, 1999). This complementary discussion of practical aims would flow from, but certainly not substitute for, her primary focus on research purposes that can feed directly into the framing of questions answerable by an empirical study. Chapter 3 will return to this issue in terms of where and how you make known your perspective as a researcher.

Exercise 2.1
Distinguishing Research Purposes and Practical Purposes

Write a memo about some research you might be envisioning in which you try to distinguish between those things you want to understand through your inquiry (research purposes) and those things you might want to accomplish or change, but are not directly researchable through an empirical field study (practical purposes). Since you are likely just stepping into the qualitative arena for the first time, you may want to seek additional feedback on the question of what is researchable, but I encourage you to take a stab at it. Keep in mind that this exercise is to help clarify your own thinking, not to impress anyone else.

Are the distinctions you are making between research and practical purposes clear and consistent? If not, what seems to be confusing matters for you? Is one set of purposes dominating rather than complementing the other? If you are having difficulty distinguishing your aims, try this: For each preliminary statement of purpose, draft a tentative question suggested by that statement. Then ask yourself if that question appears to be answerable by an empirical study. (Sometimes it's easier to see the distinction when viewed through the lens of a question rather than a statement.)

If you are having a difficult time getting your head around any sort of purpose statement at this point, try the strategy of listing what your proposed inquiry is *not* about (see Wolcott, 2001). Be reasonable, however, in that what you want to address in a "weeding out" process like this is not every possible delimitation for a study, but just those purposes and considerations that are close to, but clearly do not encompass, your key concerns and motivations in pursuing your inquiry. For example, Patrice might have listed that her envisioned research was *not* about comparing Early Head Start to other family service programs or *not* about the criteria used to determine family participation in Early Head Start. Once you work through a number of such delimitations, it may be easier to state what you *do* want your proposed aims to address.

Distinguishing Focus and Locus

The task of homing in on research purposes directs attention as well to the important distinction between the focus and locus of your inquiry. I was first alerted to the significance of this distinction during my own graduate studies in anthropology and education when I encountered these cautionary words from Clifford Geertz: "The locus of study is not the object of study. Anthropologists don't study villages (tribes, towns, neighborhoods . . .); they study *in* villages" (1973, p. 22). In other words, when considering how to convey the purposes of your research, do not confuse where you are looking (or what you are looking at) with what you are looking for.

Why is this so important? It is easy to become captivated by what you perceive to be the intrinsic value or appeal of a particular situation, such as a stellar classroom teacher who weaves her pedagogical magic with a group of students or an exciting cross-cultural teacher exchange program. Such an opportunity, if construed to be the focus of inquiry, may set you up to provide an engaging, descriptive, even affirming (pat-on-the-back) account. However, it falls short of identifying a conceptual issue or concern that effectively orients you to attend (or not to attend) to certain things in the conduct of your research. Keep yourself appropriately focused by continuing to revisit these questions: "What's at issue here? What's going to convey the broader conceptual significance of this study?"

The focus of Patrice's study was not the Early Head Start program per se; rather, the Early Head Start program was the context in which she embedded her concern for how people in different socioeconomic and cultural circumstances perceive infant well-being. Your study's *focus*, as ultimately reflected in your statement of research purpose, should direct attention to conceptual concerns and point toward an inquiry into the meaning of something. Your study's *locus* is where you locate these concerns, in the sense of situating them in a specific social process or set of circumstances. Consider the following examples of research focus and locus generated by some of my students:

For a research project on how student-to-student discussions around text relate to their development of self and identity as readers:

Focus: students' sense of self and identity as readers
Locus: spontaneous and teacher-directed conversations between students about text

For a research project on the experiences of students with emotional and behavioral disorders within a high school:

Focus: students' sense of personal agency
Locus: the interactions between the students and institutional structures (e.g., decision-making processes around student placement; student responses to discipline and academic policies)

For a research project on how student writers "position" themselves, their texts, and their readers in response to current practices and curricular influences in high school English classes, including systemic influences like standardized assessment of writing:

Focus: how students position themselves and their texts for writing
Locus: classroom discourse about writing (e.g., student and teacher conversations and conferences about their writing; formal statements of expectations by teachers about student writing)

For a research project investigating the roots of pro-environmental behavior and action:

Focus: how ecological consciousness is manifested and given meaning in individuals' behaviors and actions
Locus: the process of their involvement in decision making around a local environmental issue

These examples also help to illustrate the important distinction between a study's locus and simply its location (e.g., in a particular high school) or one's data sources (e.g., a particular group of students or teachers). One's locus in field-based qualitative research is generally found within social action of one sort or another, such as peer interactions in the classroom, a curriculum implementation process, or decision making around a particular issue. In the first example of research on students' developing sense of self as readers, the locus of inquiry is not the students, it is a particular set of behaviors and interactions in which they engage.

Your focus and locus find their clearest expression in the statement of purpose you construct for your research proposal. Remember that your research purpose directs attention to what you want to understand and identifies your aim as an inquiry into meaning. This means that your focus, the seed of your study's broader conceptual significance, is what stands at the core of your statement. Your locus, also reflected in your statement, helps to ground that conceptual concern in the specificness of a social process or set of circumstances.

Purposes and Going Qualitative

Another important connection in the design process is the compatibility of your purposes (personal, research, and practical) and your reasons for pursuing a qualitative approach. Historically, qualitative researchers have claimed the following as major purposes for inquiry:

- **descriptive aims** to document and describe what is happening in a setting, event, or set of circumstances

Exercise 2.2
Clarifying the Focus and Locus of Your Inquiry

Write a brief memo about how you are distinguishing, at least in a preliminary sense, between the focus and locus of your envisioned inquiry. Keep in mind that your focus

- should direct attention to *conceptual* concerns
- is most directly reflected in your statement(s) of *research* purpose
- is the initial indicator of the *significance* of your study

Your locus, in turn, should direct attention to social action within particular circumstances; it is where you situate your conceptual concerns.

You are not after style points in these early writings to yourself, so try to get right to the point: "The focus of my study is . . . ". If terms included in this preliminary statement need further clarification, then certainly do so. For example, Sara, the student in the preceding list of examples who was interested in exploring pro-environmental behavior and action, drafted the following explanation of her focus in an early memo:

> The focus of my study is how ecological consciousness is manifested and given meaning in people's actions and behaviors. For now, I define ecological consciousness as a way of thinking, feeling, and making meaning of the world through environmentally friendly lenses. For someone with ecological consciousness, for example, being an "environmentalist" is not understood as a job but as a way of life. I expect this definition will change and get more complicated the further I get into this, but I needed an initial point of reference. The point is that I hope to be able to understand and describe how people shift from one way of thinking or meaning-making to another—from a less to a more sustainable way of being.

Sara then devoted a page or so of her memo to exploring questions and concerns suggested by her focus. Here's a brief excerpt:

> What does this shift in perspective and thinking feel like and mean for those who go through it? Do people involved in environmental issues see a process through which their thinking, feeling, and actions toward the environment became what they are today? My focus entails understanding how people perceive and interpret their own ecological consciousness. How do they make sense of their current values, beliefs, and assumptions toward the environment? What does their environmental awareness and action mean to them?

Next she expanded upon various aspects of her locus, for example, by clarifying what she meant by her use of the terms *active* and *involvement:*

> By active I mean involved to at least some degree in discussing and trying to settle with others ongoing local environmental issue. Involvement could include actions like the following: attending town meetings or other community meetings where the issue will be discussed or addressed; writing letters to the editor; writing or calling town officials, state agencies (including environmental agencies), or environmental groups to discuss the issue; or actively supporting a lawsuit initiated by a local group.

She then devoted a page or so to further justifying her locus, highlighting questions it suggested and the practical and conceptual challenges it posed.

As I followed Sara's progress toward her proposal, I noted that some of her wording changed, emphases shifted slightly, and points became clearer. You, too, will hone your ideas over time, so be patient and don't hassle with fine-tuning preliminary memos like this one. They are works-in-progress and potential entry points to the ideas that will eventually shape your research proposal.

- **interpretive aims** to investigate important categories of meaning, to understand how the particular context in which participants act influences their behavior and actions, or to uncover and/or generate questions or hypotheses for further research
- **explanatory or theoretical aims** to identify and analyze patterns, including unanticipated influences, related to what is happening, and to identify plausible relationships shaping what is happening (Erickson, 1986; Marshall & Rossman, 1999; Maxwell, 1992)

In the past couple of decades, studies grounded in critical, postmodern, or feminist assumptions have extended consideration of research purposes to include an emphasis on action, advocacy, or empowerment. Brantlinger (1999), Lather (1991), and Marshall and Rossman (1999) exemplify a substantial body of scholars who account for this and strongly promote the following category:

- **emancipatory aims** to raise awareness, foster self-understanding and self-determination, and create opportunities to engage in social action and seek social justice

Patrice's research purposes appear to emphasize the interpretive (addressing how participants give meaning to the concept of infant well-being) and the descriptive (documenting the experiences of participants in the program). The practical purpose embedded within her research (to somehow improve the experience of families served by the program), especially when considered in light of the personal concerns motivating her inquiry, suggests an implicit emancipatory emphasis.

These categories, while helpful to Patrice for clarifying the compatibility of her aims with an intended ethnographic approach (see Chapter 6), should not be construed as a way to measure her decision to "go qualitative" against some minimum requirements or optimum combination of stated (and unstated) purposes. (Imagine going to your thesis advisor to defend your qualitative approach by claiming, "My proposed study will be 50% descriptive, 35% interpretive, and 15% emancipatory!") Instead, think of these categories less as a standard and more as one of a number of strategies for ensuring that the various elements of your research design inform, and are consistent with, each other.

It is also important to recognize that your purposes are influenced by the way you look at the world, interpret what you see, and decide which things you see are valid and important to document. In this respect, your orchestration of connections within the design process continues to work you simultaneously through greater complexity and toward finer focus. This is the work of positioning yourself relative to a problem and clarifying your intent in doing so, as discussed in this chapter. It also entails building an orientation and a context for your inquiry, in terms of which your inquiry, and your reasons and strategies for pursuing it, make sense. Chapter 3 focuses on how you construct an intellectual orientation and moral stance for research. Chapter 4 addresses how you construct a conceptual and theoretical context for your inquiry.

STRATEGIES TO HELP CLARIFY YOUR IDEAS AND AIMS

Mining Your Memos

Before closing out this discussion of problem and purpose, I want to return to some practical considerations around the use of memos as a tool for pulling together ideas around your inquiry. Like Maxwell (1996), my students and I have found that "memos do for ideas what fieldnotes and transcripts do for perception: they convert thought into a form that allows examination and further manipulation" (p. 12). The "examination and further manipulation" piece is the key consideration. Memos are eminently practical as a source of "data" for your developing sense of problem and direction for inquiry. My students have found them to be invaluable as a means to focus, reflect upon, and refine their understanding of concepts and ideas that may eventually feed into their preliminary research proposals.

To illustrate, let's consider the case of Julie, one of several students introduced at the start of this chapter. As you recall, Julie was in the initial stages of developing a study on the nature of informed consent in participant observation research. She aimed to look closely at the interactions between researchers and their study participants and to focus specifically on the communication of intentions between them. Approximately a year prior to submitting her actual research proposal, Julie encountered literature on research ethics that questioned what informed consent looks like when the relationship between researcher and participant is that of "being with" rather than the traditional biomedical notion of the researcher "looking at" the subject of investigation. If she was going to come to terms with participant observation research in a way that acknowledged current thinking in the field, she realized she needed to construct a better understanding of what "being with" meant. She grappled with this notion in an early memo (presented in its entirety in Example 2.1). As you read this memo, consider the following questions:

- Broadly speaking, how is Julie using this memo to open up further possibilities for framing and presenting her ideas?
- More specifically, how is Julie using this memo to explore the range of potential meanings derived from "being with"? What is she accomplishing through her exploration of this notion?

- How do Julie's reflections on "being with" lead toward the formulation of questions that might help guide her inquiry?
- Who appears to be the intended audience for this memo?

EXAMPLE 2.1 An Analytic Memo on *Being With* for a Study on Consent in Participant Observation Research

---

In general terms, *being with* connotes someone existing in close proximity with another being. Examples include "I like being with my dog" and "I like being with my brother." Both of these denote that I like their company, that I like to be close to them, and that my interactions with them bring me satisfaction. I think that *being with* implies some type of relationship with this other being, but does not describe anything about this relationship, such as that I trust or am friendly with the other being. *Being with* my dog is different from *being with* my brother, both of which are different from what is implied by the statement, "Being with my client all day tomorrow will be exhausting." In each case there is a relationship, but each type of relationship is different. The relationship between my dog and myself is based on companionship, human-canine interaction, and hopefully obedience (from the dog!). The relationship between my brother and myself is based on love, kinship, and personal traits. My relationship with my client is based primarily on professional interests, although it might also include a personal element, such as friendship. In other words, the context seems to be important in order to understand the type of relationship involved. It could be just an issue of proximity (i.e., "I am uncomfortable being with her, and not just when she talks about politics"). Here the intimation is that there is no relationship, unless one counts dislike as a bad relationship. So far, then, I see the major components of *being with* as proximity and type of relationship.

Relationships are complex phenomena involving multiple attributes. These include nature (reciprocal/collaborative vs. exploitive), power differentials (equal vs. asymmetrical), purpose (means to an end vs. end in itself), authenticity (truth vs. deception), type of interactions (affective vs. intellectual), nature of affective interactions (regard vs. animosity), physical involvement (distant vs. intimate), level of trust (none to complete), and level of emotional involvement (detached vs. fully involved). These attributes might be grouped so that they are delineated along a continuum that ranges from professional to personal. When I think of a professional relationship, I think of it in terms of making someone a means to an end, self-interest, objectivity, or maybe adhering to a code of conduct. This is in contrast to a personal relationship that may involve love, trust, friendship, care, emotion, empathy, or physical intimacy. Although these are only crudely defined, these attributes help to illustrate the continuum of relationships between professional and personal and the multidimensional framework that characterizes the notion of relationships.

With regard to participant observation, what does it mean to *be with* rather than to *look at*? One could employ the professional-personal relationship continuum here, where *look at* is toward the professional end of the continuum (e.g., objective, intellectual interaction, little physical involvement, means to an end) and where *being with* is further toward the personal end of the continuum. This interpretation of *being with* as characteristic of attributes such as trust, care, emotion, and friendship is in line with the general tenets of the ethic of care and the perspectives of many feminists. As such, *being with* would require a researcher to develop and maintain a relationship based on care, empathy, emotional commitment and responsiveness to the needs of others, trust, and friendship. However, wouldn't the purpose of research be antithetical to a *being with* relationship if so defined toward the personal end of the continuum? If so, we would need to define how a researcher-participant *being with* relationship, or for that matter any *being with* relationship that has a purpose other than the relationship itself, differs from that of a non-research *being with* relationship.

The complex nature of relationships makes me realize how important it is to define the characteristics of the intended researcher-participant relationship; simply stating that it is a *being with* relationship is not adequate. Exactly what attributes does the researcher want the relationship to reflect? How should the researcher take into account power differentials, authenticity, type of interactions, and nature of affective interactions? The researcher would need to think about the different dimensions of the relationship with regard to the research aims. What information is needed and how do the attributes of the relationship relate to the collection of that data? Then there is difference between intentions and results. The researcher might set out to establish a *being with* relationship (that is, one built on attributes such as trust, friendship, and emotional involvement), but can a researcher really establish such relationships with everyone who is a potential participant? How are these intentions communicated to participants? What do such relationships require of participants? How do the researcher's intentions regarding the relationship play out? What factors contribute to shaping the relationship?

As you can see, there is nothing mysterious, complicated, or theoretically formal about Julie's memo. There are certainly playful, analytical, and speculative aspects to what she has written. A memo like this reflects work in progress, and so can hold contrasting or even incompatible perspectives in creative tension. You will discover that such fluidity and openness to apparent contradictions are among a memo's most valuable qualities. Likewise, there are no hard and fast rules about a memo's structure, style, or aim. The most consistent benefit of good memos is that they are generative and often conclude, like Julie's, with questions that reposition you relative to a researchable problem and help to identify and prioritize your research aims.

As Julie did, you might construct a memo in order to explore the various properties and dimensions of a single term or concept that seems to be central to the development of your inquiry. Such microanalysis can help you uncover new relationships among your ideas, in some cases by jolting you out of your taken-for-granted modes of thinking. As Julie learned, there was a lot more packed into the notion *being with* than she had initially reckoned; problematizing its meaning, as she liked to say, helped to reveal its complexity and range of application. In other cases, memo writing can push you to consider a broader range of conceptual possibilities and thus help you to avoid taking an exclusive, unexamined stance toward the topic at hand. Or, as illustrated in some of Patrice's reflections presented earlier in this chapter, memos can help you to explore the significance of a personal experience or an insightful reading, or simply to pour out a stream of consciousness response to a colleague's comment. In any case, keep in mind that all this memoing precedes the type of formal writing that goes into your research proposal. This means that you do not have to worry quite yet about grasping the significance and place of this concept or that idea in the bigger scheme of things. You are getting your ideas down, playing them off each other, and developing their potential to help you come to terms with your problem or topic.

Ultimately, just as with the fieldnotes and interview transcripts you will be dealing with in your actual research, you face the practical necessity of reducing the complexity and volume of lived experience and spur-of-the-moment ideas into something you can grasp. Reexamined *out of the moment* and in the context of additional "data," once familiar and taken-for-granted ideas captured in your memos can take on new significance. Contradictions or connections in your thinking may start to become apparent: "Look at this: all this time I've been claiming that *this* is the focus of my inquiry. So why have so many of my reflections directed attention to *that?* I need to rethink this." "Aha! There, within those two previously unconnected phrases, I can begin to see a way to state my purpose." Such considerations affirm the need to revisit your memos, build connections within and between some of them, and allow yourself to wonder what in the world you were thinking when you wrote others. But you should hold on to and file all of them. (As you will see in Chapter 9, reconfigured bits and even large chunks of your memos can productively find their way into your research proposal.)

Your best insights are often garnered through sharing your written memos with others. In my research classes I regularly encourage such sharing, or collaborative "mining" of memos, but always predicate it upon the following caution: "[T]hinking of memos primarily as a means of communicating to *other* people will usually interfere with the kind of reflective writing that you need to do to make memos most useful to you" (Maxwell, 2005, p. 13). Memos are cumulative and meant to be personally useful; they should reflect thinking in progress rather than polished ideas intended for others. Make them your own.

Exercise 2.3
Generating an Analytic Memo

Analytic memo writing can be a challenging process to initiate, especially if qualitative research is relatively new to you. You may wonder what to focus on, where it should lead, and whether you really can "make it your own." Particularly vexing to some students is the frequent experience of not reaching a sense of closure with a memo, but instead coming to a point of more and varied questions. Others embrace this possibility from the start.

A helpful type of analytic memo that you might attempt early on is one that focuses on trying to come to terms with a single term (like Julie's memo in Example 2.1). Start by identifying a central idea or concept that continues to pop up in your current thinking about a research focus. Write a memo that explores that concept's characteristics (those aspects that define and give it meaning) as well as the ways in which those characteristics might vary in different contexts. Don't shy away from being speculative, introducing conflicting perspectives, and simply playing with your ideas. See, as Julie did, if your writing itself becomes a method of inquiry (Richardson, 2000), a way of discovering new aspects of your topic and generating further questions about it.

Pilot Studies

A well-conceived pilot study can complement and feed directly into the process of generating memos. A pilot study in the context of qualitative inquiry is a modest probe of some aspect of your ideas or methods with the aim of clarifying how you will proceed with your proposal for a more full-scale investigation. It can be an effective way to get your bearings and thus be able to make better-informed decisions about the substance or direction of your research. I encourage students to do a pilot study when:

(a) they need to clarify their understanding of how a particular concept might help them position their inquiry,

(b) they need to uncover assumptions and biases that might be at play in their thinking,

(c) they need to gain a preliminary sense of the meaning that experiences have for the participants involved in them, or

(d) they need to try out a particular research method.

Some researchers insist that you complete some fieldwork prior to writing a research proposal and further caution that designing a study without preliminary observations or interviews can lead to unfocused armchair theorizing or overly speculative frameworks to which you become prematurely committed (Bogdan & Biklin, 2003; Strauss, 1987). This, I think, is more a caution about how you use (or misuse) prior research than about your decision to conduct a pilot study, but the underlying concern about embracing a theory too soon is important to keep in mind (see Chapter 4's discussion of seeking theoretical legitimacy).

Like memos, pilot studies are formative. They are intended to be useful to you and should emphasize the further development of your ideas rather than a definitive presentation of their significance. This does not mean that pilot studies are haphazard; to the contrary, they are typically well focused and clearly bounded in time (relatively brief), circumstance (easily accessible and manageable), and size (a small, purposeful sample). Their modest aims do not preclude the need to proceed as you would with a larger study in terms of submitting a proposal to an institutional review board, obtaining participants' consent, delineating methods, and so on.

With regard to immediate practical outcomes, a pilot study can play an important role in how you decide to use or modify a particular fieldwork strategy, how you position yourself as a participant in a setting, or how you phrase interview questions, to name just a few possibilities. Tailor your aims appropriately. One of my students, Rosemary, had generated remarkably well-conceptualized ideas for a study of teacher interactions with students in comparable Japanese and American contexts, but was tentative about her skills as an interviewer. She accordingly designed a modest pilot study that involved several Japanese and American teachers like those she would engage in her eventual dissertation study. She focused this preliminary probe around the specific aims of identifying potentially effective interview questions and practicing her own interviewing techniques. She was open to additional and unanticipated insights from the pilot study, but deliberately centered her efforts on these method-related concerns.

In the course of this brief fieldwork, she became aware of the degree to which her interviewing practices were being constrained by her reluctance to step outside the structure of her preestablished questions. Part of this reluctance stemmed from her understandable feeling (especially as a novice to qualitative fieldwork) that such adherence to structure, in and of itself, might contribute to the rigor and legitimacy of her efforts. The reality, however, was that she was increasingly stymied by her questioning procedures and realized that she was stifling both the responses of her participants and her own ability to probe more deeply into those responses. Her previous readings and coursework in qualitative research and field methods did not automatically translate into certainty about what she should do or say when she found herself in actual interview situations (a good lesson for all of us). She brought her concerns to me and also shared them with some of her fellow students. In time, with feedback and further experience, she loosened up and developed into a more responsive and confident interviewer, adept at introducing follow-up probes, following the leads of her interviewees, and fostering a more conversational stance. Her eventual dissertation research was well served by the heightened awareness and abilities she developed in this pilot study.

SUMMARY OF KEY POINTS

- The process of engaging with a sense of problem encompasses the dynamic interplay between personal or immediate concerns that drive an inquiry and systematic considerations that orient an inquiry.
- Positioning yourself relative to a researchable problem is the preliminary task. At this level of engagement, you try to construct a basis of knowledge and understanding, a well-thought-out position from which you can develop a more refined definition of problem.
- With a definition of your problem in hand, you are positioned to consider in more systematic fashion how your inquiry makes sense in relation to ideas, contexts, and purposes beyond the immediate scope of your direct and personal experiences. This entails linking up with the work and ideas of others by addressing issues of purpose, theory, perspective, and method.
- In addressing purpose, you need to distinguish (a) between research purposes and practical purposes, (b) between the focus and locus of your inquiry, and (c) among the descriptive, interpretive, theoretical, and emancipatory aims that, in varying levels of emphasis, can characterize a qualitative approach.
- Two strategies that are especially helpful in clarifying the focus, aims, and emphases of your inquiry are memo writing and pilot studies.

RECOMMENDED READING

A complementary perspective on the interactive connections between research purposes and other components of qualitative research design can be found in Maxwell (1996, and his expanded second edition, 2005), my source for the distinction between practical and research aims and one of several helpful sources on the use of analytic memos. For fuller explanations of how you might incorporate memos into all phases of the research process, see Emerson, Fretz, and Shaw (1995) and Strauss and Corbin (1998). Richardson's (2000) insightful discussion of writing as a method of inquiry includes a useful compendium of writing suggestions and exercises that can help you become a more productive writer in the context of coming to know both your research topic and yourself as a researcher.

Chapter 3

CLARIFYING YOUR PERSPECTIVE

What perspective, or intellectual orientation, am I bringing to this research? Why is that important? What does it mean to be a social inquirer, not only in intellectual terms but also in a moral sense? Where and how should I make my perspective apparent in my work?

When the research opportunity first arose in the early 1990s to "look at what was going on" in the lives of Laotian refugee students in a rural New England high school, I did not pretend to be naïve or clueless about what might or could be happening in the setting. Like any qualitative researcher, I carried my "intellectual set of foreshadowed problems" (Delamont, 2004, p. 224): a mix of vaguely theoretical ideas and commonsense notions informed, in this case, by my prior research and familiarity with the literature on immigration and schooling. I made a genuine claim to open-mindedness, knowing as well that my previous experiences and readings had sensitized me to the potential significance of particular concepts and perspectives that I might encounter in the course of my fieldwork. I also carried basic assumptions about what I could possibly come to know through my research. For example, I did not believe I would uncover a single "true" perspective on the refugee student experience. I was correspondingly predisposed to go about acquiring that knowledge in particular ways—ways that, among other considerations, favored my direct engagement in the lives of those students, teachers, and others whose experiences I was hoping to understand.

Less straightforward was how I would handle my concerns about whose interests were being served in the setting. Personally and professionally, I was predisposed to be an advocate for the students and the teachers. Should those concerns play into the way I framed my research? I was aware that some researchers would encourage me to conduct my research from a stance of objective detachment, while others would urge me to cast my foreshadowed problems into a prejudgmental or critical framework. Still others would have me frame my research around deliberate advocacy for a cause or a group. I wondered: How should I convey my compelling interest in the topic? Through what sort of lens should I filter my inquiry, and how would I make that decision?

Who you are and what you bring to the process of developing a qualitative research project deserve careful and continuous thought. To recall the definition of perspective introduced in the Preface, you need to determine *how* you see and how *you* see. At issue is the fact that you have grown up in particular social, economic, and cultural circumstances, acquiring in the process many implicit assumptions about how things in the world are, how they might be, and how they should be. In turn, your academic and professional training have introduced further values and biases that lead you to regard some topics and concerns as more significant than others. How do these aspects of who you are pertain to how you develop a study? Why is this important?

As a qualitative researcher, you develop aims, pose questions, select strategies, and eventually shape relationships in the field largely according to the intellectual (rather than social) needs you bring to the setting. You may establish close connections and even friendships in the field, but you are not there with the primary intent of making friends. You are there because you want to pursue a particular inquiry and you hope to achieve something through your efforts. This does not mean that the play of social relationships and the potential for meaningful change are not central to your work; they most certainly are. But it is your *analytic intent* (your explicit desire to make sense of something) and your *intellectual orientation* (the way you are positioned to view the world) that introduce into these relationships and possibilities the trust-building, disclosure-demanding, significance-sorting, and change-inducing processes that field-based research entails. You need to come to terms with all of this in order to move forward with your efforts to conceptualize and propose a study. To help you get started, this chapter directs attention to the following interrelated tasks:

- constructing an intellectual orientation or *intellectual identity* (Lareau, 1989), an explicit articulation of basic premises that influence the stance from which and the lens through which you view the world and your particular research project
- developing a sense of what it means to be a social inquirer in a moral sense, a clarification of the basis for your decisions about how to be *with* study participants and respond to controversies and ethical dilemmas in your relationships with others involved in your inquiry

Thinking Ahead to Your Research Proposal. This aspect of your work informs nearly every component of your eventual research proposal. The concluding section of this chapter, which focuses on how and when you make your perspective known, highlights the ways in which your intellectual orientation weaves its way throughout your proposal as the essential element integrating the argument, justifications, and methodological decisions for your study. In short, you play out, rather than showcase, your perspective.

CONSTRUCTING AN INTELLECTUAL ORIENTATION

All research is informed by basic beliefs or premises about the world and how it should be understood and studied. Taken together, these beliefs contribute to one's perspective, frame of reference, or paradigm. The beliefs are basic in the sense that they can never be established in terms of their ultimate truthfulness. Rather, they must be accepted simply on faith and the persuasiveness and utility of their arguments (Guba & Lincoln, 1994; Lincoln & Guba, 2000; Schwandt, 2001).

Paradigms, sometimes called *inquiry paradigms,* are important to you as a researcher because they define how you view the world and provide a basis for deciding which of the things you see are legitimate and important to document. They give you a way to get your bearings and respond to the common query: "So, where are you coming from [in doing this research]?" Along with Rossman and Rallis (2003), however, I believe that the term *paradigm* has been "overworked, overused, and trivialized" (p. 37). It seems more practical to talk in straightforward terms about what you are actually doing: orienting yourself intellectually for your particular research project. This means building upon a stance that positions you to view the world in a certain way and deciding upon a lens through which you will be filtering your ideas and perceptions.

Whatever terms you use, you cannot avoid the bottom line: As a researcher you simply cannot gloss over the need to clarify how and why you are positioned to view ideas, issues, and relationships in a certain way. You may have your aims clearly in mind, but having purpose without perspective is like setting out on a voyage without a means to orient your ship. This chapter will help you construct your intellectual orientation.

Responding to Fundamental Questions

Patrice's decision to inquire into the experiences of families impacted by poverty turned, in large part, on the personal concerns, practical aims, and research purposes described in the previous chapter. Her decision to look at these experiences in a particular way turned ultimately on her response to some fundamental philosophical questions that all researchers must address at one point or another:

- What can I assume about "how things really are" in a setting?
- How do I learn about something?
- If someone were to ask me, "How do you know that?," what is acceptable evidence that whatever it is I claim to know is accurate?

Breaking these questions down still further, you can think of your intellectual identity-building efforts in terms of the following issues (adapted from Creswell, 1998; Guba & Lincoln, 1994; Lincoln & Guba, 2000; Rossman & Rallis, 2003).

The Ontological Issue

What is the nature of reality and what can be known about it? This refers to what Patrice might assume about "how things really are" in the setting she is investigating. For Patrice, following a premise common to qualitative studies, "how things really are" was a function of multiple perspectives, including those of the researcher, those of individuals being investigated, and those of the readers who would interpret the completed study (Creswell, 1998). As she stated:

> The "multiple nature of reality" issue points to my position that truth and reality are constructed by individuals within various social contexts; there is no universal, objective truth. In my research I expect this to be evident in perceptions of infant well-being. My notion of infant well-being has been constructed from my experiences and shaped in the context of my middle-class background. I believe that individuals who grow up in poverty, become parents, and raise children in the context of poverty will have different perspectives on infant well-being. I do not believe there can be an objective theory that states infant well-being looks like this, universally, across all settings, contexts, and cultures.

The Epistemological Issue

How do we come to "know" the world? What is the relationship between the researcher and what can be researched? This refers to the posture Patrice might assume relative to the participants in her study and is directly dependent on her belief, described previously, that "how things are" is a function of multiple perspectives. Given this understanding, it is not only appropriate but also necessary for Patrice to actively observe or engage in the lives of those whose perspectives she is seeking to understand. This is contrary to a stance of objective detachment between the researcher's influence and the people and events being studied—a stance that might follow from assuming, for example, that there is a single "true" perspective on infant well-being. Patrice's conceptions of the relationship between researcher and researched played off fundamental considerations of what could and could not be known solely from her own perspective:

I have felt comfortable in social and economic settings similar to that of my own childhood, and I find it easy to relate to families who have a similar interaction style and who share goals and priorities for their children similar to my own. It is the feeling of "disconnect," however, that intrigues me about my relationships with families who live in circumstances different from my own, and that emphasizes the need for me to engage more fully in their reality to understand their perspectives. What are the priorities of a family who is perpetually homeless when that family's goals do not seem to include housing? My need to address such questions compels me to connect directly with the lives and experiences of these families.

ASIDE: It's *Not* About Being a Detective

If some of these concepts seem a bit overwhelming at the moment, try considering them in light of a common metaphor. In a wonderfully insightful chapter entitled "How Do You Know If Your Informant Is Telling the Truth?" Atkinson and his colleagues (2003) describe the popular misconception that how you come to know what you do as a qualitative fieldworker is akin to the work of a detective. It's a handy image, they point out, but unlike a detective, the qualitative researcher is *not* bent on determining "the one single, truthful account that can reconstruct one single set of facts" (p. 139). The qualitative aim is "to understand the multiple contexts and perspectives that bring into play different accounts; different notions of truth and falsehood; competing versions of 'the same' phenomenon" (p. 139). For qualitative researchers, then, determining "how things really are" is a matter of how thoroughly they have explored the complexities of the situation rather than how conclusively they have established some study participants as truth tellers and exposed others as liars.

The Methodological Issue

How does the researcher go about inquiring into whatever he or she believes can be researched? This refers to how Patrice might conceptualize the entire research process, an issue that feeds directly from the distinctions she was making about the nature of reality and what can be known about the world. At this point she establishes the philosophical cornerstone for all her subsequent decisions about how to proceed, as she begins to figure out that not just any methodology is appropriate for her inquiry.

This is a good opportunity to clarify that I am discussing *methodology* as distinct from *method*. Methodology refers to the theory and analysis of how inquiry does or should proceed

(Metz, 2000). It entails careful examination of the issues, principles, and procedures associated with a particular approach to inquiry, say ethnography, that in turn guide the use of particular methods (Schwandt, 2000). Method commonly denotes a specific procedure, tool, or technique used by the researcher to generate and analyze data—the means supporting the theory of where you want to go with your inquiry. For example, long interviews, augmented with researcher self-reflection, are a method often associated with phenomenological studies (see Chapter 6 for further clarification of these distinctions).

In Patrice's case, a reality built upon multiple perspectives and investigated by a researcher immersed in the lives of the researched suggested a methodology characterized by:

- a letting go of control of possible confounding variables (for example, who in the setting is willing to talk to her about particular issues)
- an emphasis on describing in detail the context in which people's perspectives are being shaped and shared
- the need to work with particulars (details) before general explanations (the big picture)
- an openness to the continual refinement of questions based on knowledge gained in the field

Note once again that the way Patrice responded to the methodological issue was delimited by the manner in which she responded to the ontological and epistemological issues. The way she was making sense of, and making a case for, her developing perspective as an inquirer was consistent across all three categories of belief.

Thinking About How You View the Social World

Assumptions are also at work to influence the particular way you look at society and social phenomena. Once again, making these assumptions explicit is important for understanding and making clear to others why you attend to some things but not to others in the conduct of your inquiry. A fundamental issue is whether you tend to view the social world with greater measures of (a) satisfaction with how things are or (b) concern about how things should change. It is likely that elements of each are at play in varying amounts in whatever you do.

The predominant orientation in social science, as Rossman and Rallis (2003) note, has been to focus on the cohesiveness and functionality of the status quo. There is a comforting rationality and predictability to this perspective, an attitude that things and people make sense, work together, and function to address certain needs. Researchers with this mind-set engage in the business of sense making and generating knowledge about what makes the world go round and what might make it go round even better. In contrast, the emphasis that characterizes the work of an increasing number of researchers reflects an underlying, but presumably conscious, assumption that things are not right or good or fair as they are and require some action. Change directed at improvement defines the agenda of such inquiry.

Patrice embodied an effective and workable balance of these orientations. Her personal aim to become "a more effective help giver" was a persistent refrain in her design efforts, as was her extended practical aim of helping other service providers be more effective with the families they served. The operative assumption was that she could work with and make sense of how things were and then perhaps make them better. At the same time, she expressed her underlying sense that something was clearly wrong in the fact that privileged people, including herself, presumed to interact with and serve a particular population without giving much thought to whether they really understood its members' lives and perspectives. That was an unacceptable state of affairs that should be changed and presumably could be changed to some degree by her research.

In the process of composing your inquiry, you need to consider how your responses to the issues discussed thus far might lead you to identify with a perspective that orients your beliefs and assumptions even more specifically. This is a crucial aspect of situating your inquiry: You need to connect what you are looking at (the problem), and why (your purposes), with a particular way of knowing and looking (your perspective). The following section provides some possibilities for you to explore.

Connecting with a Lens for Your Inquiry: Some Key Examples

In this section I briefly describe four perspectives or lenses—interpretive, critical, feminist, and ecological/systems—the differences between which seem to have significant implications for the conduct of qualitative inquiry. Although relying on several categories suggested by LeCompte and Schensul (1999), my selection of these particular perspectives is a judgment call; I tend to regard them as situated (connected to other perspectives) and contested (subject to debate even among their proponents). I certainly have not tried to exhaust all possibilities regarding how you might filter your ideas (there are more out there), but I do hope to suggest through these examples how commitment to a particular frame of reference steers you in the direction of a particular kind of inquiry. Accordingly, my comments should be understood as a modest reconnaissance of the philosophical or ideological terrain in which you might locate and legitimize your research perspective rather than as a (very incomplete) shopping list from which you simply choose an appealing worldview.

The following categorizations and definitions draw heavily upon the ideas generated by Brantlinger (1999), Grant (1993), Guba and Lincoln (1994), Kincheloe and McLaren (1994, 2002), Lather (1991, 1993), LeCompte and Schensul (1999), Lincoln and Guba (2000), Olesen (2000), Reinharz (1992), Rossman and Rallis (2003), and Schwandt (1994, 2000). For further clarification of these and related perspectives, I encourage you to consult these sources.

The Interpretive Lens

Even if you are relatively new to the field of qualitative inquiry, you have likely encountered the terms *interpretivist, constructivist, naturalistic, phenomenological,* and *hermeneutical,* among other variants. Each has its proponents who argue for their term's unique meaning: sociologists, educators, and psychologists advocating for constructivism; philosophers arguing for phenomenology; and anthropologists touting interpretivism. Just as often, these terms are used interchangeably to denote similar notions or shared understandings. Following LeCompte and Schensul (1999), I will use the term *interpretive* (or *interpretivist*) as a general descriptor for what might best be regarded as "a loosely coupled family of methodological and philosophical persuasions" (Schwandt, 1994, p. 118).

Proponents of this family of persuasions share the belief that "what people know and believe to be true about the world is constructed—or made up—as people interact with one another over time in specific social settings" (LeCompte & Schensul, 1999, p. 48). A frequently cited phrase associated with this notion is the "social construction of reality" (Berger & Luckmann, 1967). As an interpretivist researcher, your aim is to understand this complex and constructed reality from the point of view of those who live in it. Necessarily, then, you are focused on particular people, in particular places, at particular times—situating people's meanings and constructs within and amid specific social, political, cultural, economic, ethnic, and other contextual factors.

Interpretivists operate from the belief that all constructs are equally important and valid. Remember, for example, Patrice's assumption regarding the need to attend to multiple perspectives. This belief presents challenging implications, especially when you consider that the task of interpretation is to construct a "reading" of these multiple meanings and voices—in effect, offering your "own construction of other people's constructions of what they . . . are up to" (Geertz, 1973, p. 9). Generating and synthesizing these multi-voiced and varied constructions requires that you engage at some level in the lives of those around whom your inquiry is focused; it is through direct interaction with their perspectives and behaviors that you focus and refine your interpretations.

Participation or interaction of this sort does not imply a change-oriented posture on the part of the inquirer. At the same time, you might be hard-pressed as a social science researcher nowadays to avoid the expectation that your inquiry serve in some way as a vehicle for reform. How you position yourself in this regard turns on the nature and explicitness of your intentions. If and when you commit to function as an advocate or to investigate possibilities for change in a situation, then you begin to connect your research to a critical lens.

The Critical Lens

A *critical* approach is consistent with the view that researchers should engage in inquiry with the expectation that their work will be instrumental in bringing about change.[1] Advocacy and activism are the key concepts, calling for the researcher to speak *for* some oppressed or exploited person or group and *from* a particular ideological or political position, rather than simply speak *to* an audience *about* a group or phenomena of interest (Appadurai, 1988). To be critical is to ask questions that probe at potentially negative effects, such as "Whose interests are being served?" and "Whose interests are likely to be ignored?" (Bushnell, 2001; Magolda, 2000). Anthropologist Michael Agar (1996) offers a helpful summary in his assessment of critical ethnography:

> Underneath all the different interpretations of the term *critical* lies a common thread—you look at local context and meaning, just like we always have, but then you ask, *why* are things this way? What power, what interests, wrap this local world so tight that it feels like the natural order of things to its inhabitants? Are those inhabitants even aware of those interests, aware that they have alternatives? And then—the critical move that blows the old scientific attitude right off the map—maybe *I*, the ethnographer, should show them choices they don't even know they have. Maybe I should shift from researcher to political activist. (p. 26)

In other words, critical inquirers add to the interpretivist's task—attending to and interpreting a perspective—the responsibility of helping others, including those in the immediate setting, attend to and act upon a perspective. This suggests an approach that may be just as participatory but is clearly more confrontational and value-mediated than that of interpretivists. It moves researchers beyond a concern for describing what is and pushes them and others toward the question of what could be.

---

[1]A number of leading scholars use *critical theory* as a blanket term to denote a set of several alternative paradigms. Guba and Lincoln (1994; Lincoln & Guba, 2000), for example, include neo-Marxism, feminism, materialism, and participatory inquiry within this set. They further suggest that the critical paradigm might productively be divided into three subcategories: poststructuralism, postmodernism, and a blending of these two. The common element of all these categories, they assert, is the *value-mediated* nature of the inquiry.

A basic premise of the critical paradigm is that the researcher, cast in the role of instigator and facilitator, understands a priori what changes are needed in a situation; the task of understanding is "cast in a prejudgmental framework" (Wolcott, 1999, p. 181; see also Lincoln & Guba, 2000). The values of the researcher inevitably influence the inquiry as he or she foregrounds the judgment call that an injustice is holding back someone from something better. This places the particular demand upon researchers to make explicit how their own class status, ethnic or gender orientation, and power relationships relative to research participants affect what is investigated and how data are interpreted. Patrice traced her own growing intrigue with a critical lens in this excerpt from an early draft of her research design:

> I began to think critically about my own position, including the position I hold with my employment—a white, female, middle-class service provider and administrator of services provided to families who often (but not exclusively) live in poverty. Why do I often feel more comfortable providing service to those who have less than I have, rather than to those who have more? Does my appreciation of class diversity really point to my relief at being middle class? In a selfish way, does it help me to be grateful for what I have—a decent house, access to medical care, and a full pantry?
>
> Is there an ideological something (more than just paying lip service to "no more taxes") about who we are as Americans—our sociopolitical constitution—that prevents us from accepting Big Government to support an equalization of opportunity, to create social justice for all? As I reflected on the nature of our sociopolitical system, I began to wonder if our social service agencies unknowingly perpetuate inequitable relationships of class and power between providers and recipients of services.

Patrice's comments, while not definitively locating her in the critical arena, suggest two levels of concern that distinguish critical inquirers. On the one hand is the thick brush stroke emphasis on investigating the ways in which gender, class, culture, ethnicity, and power intersect to shape inequities—the characteristic aim of critique and transformation (Guba & Lincoln, 1994). Patrice's comments suggest that she is seeking "not merely to understand, but to understand *what is wrong,* and to link the problem to some greater wrong operating at some grander scale" (Wolcott, 1999, p. 181).

On the other hand is the finer focus on researchers themselves taking stock of who they are and from where they come. This latter effort entails researchers' awareness of differences between themselves and research participants, including how these perceived differences may influence both the flow of communication in the field setting and the later use of research results.

An especially active tradition within the critical realm in recent years has been the research paradigm known as *critical race theory* (CRT). Rooted in the critical legal studies of scholars like Derrick Bell (1980, 1987), CRT has established itself firmly in the qualitative work of Ladson-Billings (1998, 2000), Delgado (1995), and Collins (1998), to name a few. CRT is based on the notion that racism, because it is so embedded in U.S. society, appears both normal and natural to all of us who live here. One of CRT's focal concerns is understanding how race and citizenship interact, pinpointing sustained inequities that people of color especially experience. CRT researchers frequently employ storytelling—parables, chronicles, poetry, fiction, revisionist histories—to inject the cultural viewpoints and voice of marginalized and dispossessed group members into their studies. A word of caution: This is not an approach from which you simply select out appealing elements, or that you choose simply because you are dealing with racial issues; its legitimacy and rigor rest on an informed grasp of its legal and historical foundations (Ladson-Billings, 1998).

The Interpretive/Critical Continuum: A Practical Application

What does it mean for you to balance, integrate, or choose between interpretive and critical emphases in your own research? Figure 3.1 suggests how you might locate yourself on a continuum that encompasses the interpretive aim of understanding and the critical aim of potentially unsettling the realities you are encountering. The Researcher's Aims on the top half of the figure are not the same as the precisely stated research purposes defined in Chapter 2. Instead, they are meant to suggest the broader analytic intention embedded in your purpose statements. Likewise, the Orienting Questions on the lower half of the figure are not actual research questions but are intended to suggest the underlying focus of your questioning strategy and analytic intent. As you move from left to right along the continuum, these orienting questions reveal an increasing emphasis on a critical or change-oriented researcher stance.

To provide further substance to this illustration, let's apply it to the situation faced by Carolyn in her proposed study of Cambodian immigrants. Refer back to her motivating concerns described near the beginning of Chapter 2. As noted in that brief description, her first-hand experience with the frustration and powerlessness felt by her adult ESL students fed into how she shaped a preliminary sense of problem. She envisioned her research as serving to raise awareness among those in the immediate setting of the social, economic, and other forces impacting their lives. Her emotional investment in this work stemmed not simply from a questioning of what seemed to be going on in specific situations, but a concern about what might be wrong with what's going on. We can trace hypothetically the considerations that might affect her position along the continuum in Figure 3.1, starting with an emphasis on understanding represented in the initial orienting questions and moving toward an emphasis on change:

1. *What appears to be going on here? How can I make sense of it all?* At this level of questioning, Carolyn's research stance is consistent with the way that qualitative inquiry has traditionally concerned itself with *what* and *how* questions. She is focused on matters of what is

Researcher's Aims

Understanding			**Change**
Making sense of the way things are	Questioning participants' perceptions of the way things are	Taking issue with the way things are	Unsettling and transforming the way things are

Orienting Questions

What appears to be going on here? How can I make sense of it all?	What is going on to make "the way things are" feel like the natural order of things to participants in the setting?	Do participants in the setting assume that the way things are now is the way things *must* be?	Should I assume the privilege of showing those in the setting perspectives or choices that they might not even know they have?

Figure 3.1
Positioning Yourself on an Interpretive/Critical Continuum

being accomplished by her study participants, under what conditions, and out of what resources (Gubrium & Holstein, 2000). Concerns about what is going on and how particular perspectives contribute toward the construction of a particular reality take precedent over concerns about what could or should be going on. She is not explicitly taking on a critical approach that might lead her to ask, "Why are things this way and not some other way for these local immigrants?" She is nonetheless focused on getting to the heart of the matter.

Establishing this level of understanding would be fundamental to Carolyn's inquiry, whether or not she pursued its potential to create opportunities for social action, change, advocacy, or simply raising others' awareness.

2. *What is going on to make "the way things are" feel like the natural order of things to participants in the setting?* With this type of questioning, Carolyn begins to build into her stance a more value-mediated approach to inquiry. That is, by asking this question she includes in her aim the intent to make visible how alternative possibilities and perspectives might provide a more complete understanding of what's happening with a particular individual or group in her study. For example, Carolyn might take into account competing power interests between groups within the local setting and perceive some of the Cambodian adult learners as somehow "losing out" in specific situations. Those same learners, focused perhaps on more immediate needs of simply getting by, might actually perceive matters in a favorable or neutral light.

The thinking embedded in this type of stance raises some helpful questions for discussion. Consider the hypothetical example about "losing out" I just mentioned. When Carolyn presumes to speak authoritatively on behalf of others who (she believes) do not fully understand or appreciate their own situation, is she assuming too much "analytic privilege" (Macbeth, 2003)? How does asking a question like "Whose interests are being served?" play into a researcher's efforts to be analytically and morally responsible? Should one's research aims include more than accounting for the actions of others? Does being responsible mean uncovering the knowledge and means for participants to take greater control of their own lives?

3. *Do participants in the setting assume that the way things are now is the way things must be?* Here the pendulum swings even more recognizably toward revealing the potential and desire for change. The aim implied here is conveyed by the *why* question mentioned earlier: "Why are things this way and not some other way?" This suggests that Carolyn's responsibility includes raising awareness about the forces that prevent individuals and groups within the local Cambodian community from shaping decisions that affect their lives (Kincheloe & McLaren, 2002). More to the point, it invites her to question the assumption that participants' understanding of the way things are is not the finish line where her inquiry stops, without the possibility of envisioning alternatives.

This level of questioning would signal a significant step for Carolyn, methodologically and morally, as she introduces possibilities that might not have taken shape had she not been present and active as a researcher.

4. *Should I assume the privilege of showing those in the setting perspectives or choices they might not even know they have?* That is, should Carolyn be adding to her basic research task—attending to and interpreting a perspective—the responsibility of helping those in the immediate setting attend to and act upon a perspective? Doing so means that she engage her research task with a more participatory and potentially more confrontational mind-set. She would assume responsibility for raising her own and others' critical consciousness around issues of power and justice. In framing her aims, she may attend explicitly to notions like *catalytic validity* (Lather, 1991, 1993), referring to the degree to which one's research helps participants to

understand their reality in order to transform it (see also Kincheloe & McLaren, 2002; Pilcher & Juneau, 2002).

At this level of questioning, Carolyn would push her analysis actively and deliberately toward the question of what could be. As a result, her analysis would be as much about unsettling as understanding realities.

Now consider this in light of research you may be envisioning for yourself. The constant variable in all the preceding questions is the extent to which you choose to integrate a critical perspective into your stance as a researcher. Each instance demands that you think carefully about the claims you make and the way you frame your intentions. For Carolyn to foreground a critical perspective and stipulate as the focus of her aims the "empowerment of second language learners" or the "reconfiguration of power relationships between second language learners and target language speakers" would create, as Rossman and Rallis (1998) suggest, "some tricky cognitive dissonance" (p. 79). As these authors argue, you cannot simply mandate or stipulate outcomes like empowerment, no matter how strongly you feel about the situation you are researching. You can, however, make it part of your responsibility to convey how your research creates the capacity for understanding and valuing the ways in which participants might become empowered or how relationships might be changed. In this regard, any and all questions presented in this section, even those focused merely on the whats and hows of participants' lives, have the potential to create opportunities for social action, change, or advocacy.

The Feminist Lens

Feminist thinking places gender front and center in its focus on oppressive social structures and the means to challenge and change them. The varieties of feminist perspective share both a tendency to see the world as gendered and a fundamental moral stance that assumes the inequitable treatment of men and women is unjust. Women are viewed as oppressed by men through long-standing historical structures that support and legitimate oppression (Farganis, 1994; Grant, 1993). An underlying premise of feminist work, however, is that gender oppression is not experienced in isolation from considerations of race, class, culture, ethnicity, and other identities (Maguire, 1996). In the specific context of research methods, feminists have been instrumental in both attending to and actively resisting hierarchical separation between researcher and participants.

Feminist researchers question the role that power and relationship play at both the societal level and the personal level between researcher and researched. As I noted in Chapter 1, feminist thinkers are contributing significantly to advancing the conversation on research ethics and conduct. Their efforts to establish collaborative and nonexploitative relationships through the research process are showing us much about how those relationships affect the story being told. This corresponds to an overall feminist questioning about ideas of objectivity and neutrality and a rejection of the "distancing" that traditional social science upholds as the only way to observe fairly. Feminists' emphasis upon engagement with study participants reflects a heightened awareness of *intersubjectivity*, the idea "that whatever is created through the research is different because two or more people have interacted to build new meaning" (Glesne, 1999, p. 13).

Like the broad category of critical theory, there is no single feminist perspective, but rather a number of distinct traditions (e.g., liberal, Marxist, radical, socialist, and psychoanalytic), strands (e.g., feminist standpoint theories, feminist postmodernism, feminist empiricism), and research methods (see Reinharz, 1992). Patton (2002) suggests that critical theory and feminist inquiry both fall under the category of *orientational qualitative inquiry*. By this Patton means inquiry that begins with an explicit theoretical or ideological perspective that determines the study's conceptual framework and interpretation of findings. For example, a study undertaken from a feminist perspective would presume the importance of gender in human relationships and orient the study accordingly.

The Ecological or Systems Lens

Like the critical approach, the ecological perspective builds upon the basic notion that individuals are embedded in and affected by a social context that influences their behaviors. Beyond this premise there are more points of contrast than of similarity between the two ways of looking at the world. Ecologically oriented, or what some might call *systems-oriented*, researchers do not necessarily draw upon concepts of class, power, and equity to guide their inquiry, and unlike critical theorists, they have few preconceived notions about which structures or influences are most important.

This perspective's extensive history, particularly in ethnographic research, stems from the sociological work of Emile Durkheim and the even earlier anthropological work of scholars such as Bronislaw Malinowski and A. R. Radcliffe Brown. It considers social systems in their entirety and aims to identify relationships across levels and structures (e.g., family groups, peer networks, school settings, community, the wider society) in local situations. Holistic thinking is thus central to this perspective—that is, the idea that a system as a whole cannot be understood simply by analysis of separate parts. Patton (2002) helps us understand the fundamental challenge and benefit of systems thinking through the well-known fable of the nine blind people and the elephant, which I repeat here because it illustrates so well the reasoning that underlies this perspective.

> As the story goes, nine blind people encounter an elephant. One touches the ear and proclaims that an elephant is like a fan. Another touches the trunk and says the elephant most surely resembles a snake. The third feels the elephant's massive side and insists that it is like a wall. Yet a fourth, feeling a solidly planted leg, counters that it more resembles a tree trunk. The fifth grabs hold of the tail and experiences the elephant as a rope. And so it goes, each blindly touching only a part and generalizing inappropriately to the whole. The usual moral of the story is that only by putting all the parts together in right relation to each can one get a complete and whole picture of the elephant.
>
> Yet, from a systems perspective, such a picture yields little real understanding of the elephant. To understand the elephant, it must be seen and understood in its natural ecosystem, whether in Africa or Asia, as one element in a complex system of flora and fauna. Only in viewing the movement of a herd of elephants across a real terrain, over time and across seasons, in interaction with plants, trees, and other animals will one begin to understand the evolution and nature of elephants and the system of which elephants are a part. (Patton, 2002, p. 123)

For researchers applying this perspective, knowing "how things really are" is a matter of understanding the continuous accommodations among individuals, institutions, and the human and physical environment (Poggie, DeWalt, & Dressler, 1992); the emphasis is on understanding function and adaptation rather than generating shared meanings or instigating transformation. Correspondingly, the role of the researcher in this type of research tends neither to be informed by the inquirer's personal experience in interaction with study participants (as in an interpretivist or critical approach) nor to be transformative or deliberately educative (as in a critical approach). Ecologically or systems-minded researchers instead proceed with a definitive and relatively detached (from study participants) grasp upon the tasks of description and analysis aimed at identifying those contextual factors with the greatest influence on individual or institutional behaviors. Change, if and when it comes, is something that is best considered as being introduced in all levels and structures simultaneously.

Making Connections

My use of the phrase "*connecting* with a lens" rather than claiming or adopting one is deliberate; the notion of perspective or paradigm is rarely so definitive as to expect that you can simply transfer a frame of reference unchanged from one research context to another. Most researchers do tend to emphasize their connection with one or another perspective (including possibilities not included in this text), while some situate their inquiry within a synthesis of two or more.

Patrice's approach, for example, represents something of a composite lens or *paradigmatic synthesis* (LeCompte & Schensul, 1999) through which she is likely to connect with useful elements from at least two identifiable perspectives. Her emphasis on the social construction of individual and shared meanings and her recognition of the influence of contextual factors on this process suggest that she might benefit from interpretivist guidelines. She stops short of identifying a direction of change from the start, but the explicitness with which she has begun to address her own class status and power relationships relative to study participants suggests that she also may be positioning herself, at least in part, as a critical inquirer.[2]

I cannot overemphasize the point that the terms *interpretive, critical, feminist,* and *systems-oriented* refer to perspectives, not research methods. Feminist (or interpretive or critical or systems-oriented) researchers use a range of research methods and the studies they conduct may cut across disciplinary boundaries. A feminist can engage in ethnography, grounded theory, oral history, case study, or any number of approaches. Most researchers eventually acknowledge their home within a particular academic discipline—mine is anthropology, but I make extended visits to other disciplinary homes—as well as their connections to particular forms of scholarship, theory, and even social or political movements. Your intellectual orientation grows out of and further extends these connections.

Regardless of the connections you make, the frame of reference from which you view your inquiry represents a conscious choice that informs and extends your research aims, including how, and by whom, your data are interpreted and put to use (LeCompte & Schensul, 1999; Schwandt, 1993). As such, it is important to consider which paradigmatic elements inform your inquiry and how consistent they are with the other components of your research design. Do the connections among problem, purpose, and perspective make sense? How do these connections strengthen the coherence and focus of your proposed research? Working through these questions to clarify the logic and aims of your research stance contributes directly to how you go about constructing the conceptual argument (Chapter 4) and research questions (Chapter 5) for your inquiry, as well as how you choose among methodological options (Chapter 6).

---

[2]At the time of this writing, Patrice was well into her fieldwork, having established an especially open and supportive relationship with one of the Early Head Start mothers in her study. Her growing awareness of the "silenced voice" of this woman within the context of an oppressive, male-dominated household was positioning Patrice, at least tentatively, to question the direction that a feminist stance might take her inquiry.

Exercise 3.1
Trying on Different Lenses

This exercise requires that you first obtain copies of the following two research articles:

Crepeau, E. B. (2000). Reconstructing Gloria: A narrative analysis of team meetings. *Qualitative Health Research, 10*(6), 766–787.

Rogers, R. (2002). Through the eyes of the institution: A critical discourse analysis of decision making in two special education meetings. *Anthropology and Education Quarterly, 33*(2), 213–237.

Crepeau, drawing upon narrative forms of inquiry, focuses on how stories told about a patient ("Gloria") in a hospital's psychiatric team meetings influenced the team's image of the patient. Rogers, drawing upon two years of ethnographic data, presents an analysis of a school's special education team meetings for an adolescent girl ("Vicky"). (You may want to preview the sections on ethnography and narrative in Chapter 6 before reading these articles.) In a sense, both studies involve the "reconstruction" of an individual through the stories, interactions, and/or discourses among the professionals who provide for her care and guidance. Rogers assumes an explicitly critical stance; Crepeau, a more neutral, predominantly interpretive one. Both researchers offer thoughtful, sometimes pointed analysis of the logic and assumptions that underlie decision-making processes in institutional settings.

There are various points around which you could compare and contrast these two research articles. In this case, I want to you to focus on what can be learned from an examination of the perspectives that appear to orient each researcher. Rogers made the clear choice to foreground her critical stance and reveal more about the potential influence of her own background and status on her research activities. Crepeau, while not holding a critical banner, opens several doors that could lead toward similar types and levels of critique. What does each researcher gain or lose through her respective approach? Do critical aims and outcomes demand an explicitly critical stance from the start? Read the articles carefully and then address the following questions:

- Where would you locate each researcher on the continuum represented in Figure 3.1? How are their respective research purposes, as stated in the articles, served by the extent to which they chose to emphasize a critical or interpretive perspective within their research stance?
- In her article, Rogers makes the following statement: "Further, I gained insight into how, as a female literacy researcher and teacher, I was implicated in a system of education that assumes literacy is women's work but not their right" (p. 218). How could Rogers have reshaped her research aims, focus, and/or questions to foreground an even more explicit feminist perspective?
- Would it have made sense for either researcher to filter her ideas, aims, and methods through an ecological or systems-oriented perspective? Why or why not?

THE MORAL DIMENSIONS OF BEING A RESEARCHER

Thus far we have focused your identity-building efforts on how you believe the world should be understood and studied, on the one hand, and assumptions that influence the particular way you look at society and social phenomena, on the other. Now it is time to ask: What does it mean to be a social inquirer, not only in intellectual terms but also in a moral sense? How do you integrate the analytical with the ethical?

Fieldwork requires researchers to confront controversies, encouraging (or more often compelling) them to make decisions that draw upon values, ethical codes, professional standards, intuition, and feelings, and to ask themselves:

- Is what I am doing a "right" or "good" thing to do?
- How shall I *be* toward these people (study participants)?
- Would I want others to be this way toward me?
- Do I regard my social interaction with study participants only as a means to an end? If not, how do I respond to conflicts of interest in the overlapping of my roles and relationships?

For purposes of illustration, I am leaping ahead to an excerpt from Patrice's preliminary fieldwork that highlights a moment of unanticipated vulnerability and frustration that she had to confront. Her comments refer to an interaction in the home of one of her key study participants, designated as "P." The interaction involved P's two-year-old daughter and, in particular, Patrice's observation in a moment of play that this little girl's speech development might be delayed. Patrice later reflected on the dilemma she faced:

In this situation, just what are the considerations? Because I have highly specialized knowledge in infant and toddler development, should I share my observations with others around me? The family? The Early Head Start home visitor? To what extent am I really joining the circle of care around this child? If I fully join the circle of care, what influence does this have on research matters? Should I simply observe and see how long it takes for the home visitor to make a referral? If I share my observations, will I look like a know-it-all who is interfering and undermining the credibility of the Early Head Start Program?

. . . And why did I not recognize this as an ethical issue right away?

Patrice later unpacked these questions in her fieldwork journal:

I just don't know what to do or how to help. It is frustrating for me to be in the midst of this complex social system [of Early Head Start families and home visitors] and feel like I should be helping somehow to make things better and then reminding myself that I am there to observe and learn, not in the helping role. On the other hand, I have a professional conscience that sits on my shoulder that makes me feel like I should be

> helping, but I am so confused and overwhelmed by all of the factors that I wouldn't even know where to begin. So I guess I have to be satisfied that my presence alone helps P [the mother] and the kids, at least, because I can help P by getting her places and giving her another woman to talk to. And maybe I am a positive influence on the kids, able to provide a little bit of nurturing in the midst of a chaotic home environment.

"Ethical dilemmas that admit of no comfortable outcome but must be lived are experiences that researchers need to know about," notes de Laine (2000, p. 4). Patrice's dilemma, anticipated or not, serves as a reminder that a moral choice must be made that differentiates between being a disinterested and detached researcher or one who is genuinely interested in being involved with others and their needs (Schwandt, 1995). These two perspectives may express extremes, but they do help to set parameters for determining the degree to which you want or need to be involved during fieldwork in social, ethical, and emotional terms.

Denzin (1997) discusses two such ethical models in relation to fieldwork in the social sciences. The *traditional ethical model,* of which Denzin is critical, operates from the assumption that solutions can be made for ethical problems and dilemmas on rational, objective grounds; emotions and intuition are secondary. The research norm of informed consent, according to which participants learn of the researcher's role and purpose prior to fieldwork, is illustrative of this approach (see Chapter 8 for more on this). For many researchers, and for many years, it has been sufficient to package one's ethical responsibilities within such institutionalized rules and guidelines. As illustrated in Chapters 8, however, gaining "informed" consent is problematic if, as can be the case in qualitative fieldwork, researchers encounter previously unforeseen questions that lead to new directions for inquiry and different requests of study participants. How clear is it then what participants are consenting to or where participation in the research begins and ends?

The *feminist communitarian ethical model,* in contrast, assumes personally involved, self-reflexive researchers who hold themselves personally responsible for the political and ethical consequences of their actions. Such researchers "are expected to build collaborative, reciprocal, trusting, and friendly relations with those studied and value the connectedness that forms between them and others" (de Laine, 2000, p. 28)—in a phrase, "to step into the shoes of the persons being studied" (Denzin, 1997, p. 273). Reflecting the ideas with which Julie was grappling in her memo in Chapter 2, this approach emphasizes being with and for participants. This model has attracted its own share of detractors, including some feminists, who question the possibility or desirability of forming genuinely symmetrical or reciprocal relationships between researchers and participants. They suggest instead that we accept research relationships as less symmetrical—that is, not blur power differences—and acknowledge aspects of others' positions that we do not understand but are open to questioning. The focus would be on understanding one another across differences without necessarily identifying with each other (see Birch & Miller, 2002; Young, 1997).

Keep in mind that it is not an either/or proposition, nor are these two perspectives the only options you have. Strategies for ethical decision making encompass a broad array of possibilities even within feminist perspectives on care (see Mauthner, Birch, Jessop, & Miller, 2002), or you can search outside that arena for basic guidance (Flinders, 1992). Each type of problem requires a different approach, and some problems and dilemmas defy solutions. Chapter 8's discussion of ethical considerations in anticipation of fieldwork details several practical dimensions of your role as a moral decision maker.

WHERE AND HOW DO YOU MAKE YOUR PERSPECTIVE KNOWN?

Where do you make your perspective known? Everywhere, and nowhere in particular. Despite the fact that my students rank this response right up there with the frustratingly prevalent "It depends," my words are intended to convey the pervasive but subtle play of your perspective in your inquiry. Having just worked your way through this chapter devoted to the process of clarifying your intellectual and moral positioning, you may well be questioning: "What do you mean, 'subtle play' of my perspective? What about all this effort I just put into making explicit my fundamental beliefs and values? Surely there's a place and a reason to showcase all that I've uncovered about my epistemological stance, worldview, and all that." Actually, no, at least not in the sense of exposing your intellectual and moral self for its own sake or simply to show others what you are made of. But neither does this mean that you should conceal your perspective and political views.

You give voice to your perspective in discussing how you engage with a preliminary sense of problem and purpose (Chapter 2) and how you portray your involvement with study participants (Chapter 7). You reveal it in the way you choose to define key concepts supporting the logic and coherence of your inquiry (Chapter 4) and in the degree and types of information you share with study participants (Chapter 8). Your perspective finds expression in terms of how you address assumptions within your research questions (Chapter 5) and in your decision to pursue a more or less participatory approach to research (Chapter 6). In short, your intellectual and moral stance should inform all aspects of your conceptualization in the sense of being essential to your argument and justifications. It should speak *to* your developing inquiry rather than speak about itself in the form of "political polemic or irrelevant self-display" (Maxwell, 2005, p. 137) or simply a "decorative flourish" (Behar, 1996, p. 14).

Chapter 9 will include consideration of how your intellectual and moral perspectives find expression as you shift from the largely discovery-focused process of conceptualization to the largely presentation-focused documentation of this process in the form of a proposal. Exercise 3.2 will help you position some of your ideas for that shift.

Exercise 3.2
Developing Sensitivity to Your Perspective

Included in Chapter 9's suggested outline of how to write your research proposal is the suggestion that your proposal's introductory section include contextual background on the personal perspective you are bringing to your inquiry. Now is the time to start thinking, however tentatively, about how this might take shape. Think of this exercise as an opportunity to begin sensitizing yourself to your perspective by sorting through subtle differences among feelings of bias, advocacy, emotional investment, and intellectual interest in your topic.

Write a brief analytic memo on why you find the topic or problem that you are pursuing so compelling. Bear in mind that this memo is not about purpose (Exercise 2.1) or focus (Exercise 2.2), but about your intellectual and/or moral relationship to issues that surround your research topic. Specifically, reflect on some or all of the following:

- the beliefs, values, and feelings you bring to your study
- prior personal, professional, and/or political connections you have to the topic, people, or context you envision researching
- expectations and assumptions you think might be at work in these connections
- why you might be giving greater significance to some research aims over others
- how you would respond to someone who asks, "So, what's your agenda in doing this research?" or "Why are you so fired up about this research?"

Keep revisiting this memo as a source of reflection that informs your developing sense of who you are as a researcher and what you bring to your particular inquiry. This memo can be especially helpful as you check for assumptions that may be embedded in your eventual research question(s) (for more on this, see Chapter 5).

SUMMARY OF KEY POINTS

- Researchers cannot meaningfully engage a study without some idea of how, and from what perspective, they are focusing on the topic of their inquiry.
- The process of developing an intellectual identity for yourself as a researcher entails building upon a stance that positions you to view the world in a certain way and deciding upon a lens through which you will be filtering your ideas and perceptions.
- The frame of reference from which you view your inquiry represents a conscious choice that informs and extends your research aims, including how and by whom your data are interpreted and put to use.
- Fieldwork requires that you confront controversies and, in doing so, make decisions that draw upon values, ethical codes, professional standards, intuition, and feelings.
- The intellectual and moral perspective you bring to your research is not a banner you wave overhead or a badge you wear conspicuously on your sleeve. Its influence is pervasive but subtle.

RECOMMENDED READING

If you want additional help regarding how to define terms (e.g., ontology, epistemology) and distinguish perspectives (e.g., interpretive, critical,), refer to Denzin & Lincoln (2000) and Schwandt (2000). Even if you are feeling pretty confident with the basics, you should still have Schwandt's (2001) invaluable dictionary of qualitative terms as part of your personal library. Chapter 2 in Rossman and Rallis (2003) offers an alternative way of thinking about paradigm or perspective that focuses on assumptions about objectivity, subjectivity, radical change, and the status quo. Ladson-Billing's (1998) informative cautionary article is an accessible entry point for critical race theory. DeCuir and Dixson (2004) provide an excellent illustration of how CRT can be applied to an educational study. Tong (1989) provides a comprehensive introduction to the varieties of feminist thinking, while Reinharz (1992) covers a range of feminist research methods. Mauthner et al.'s (2002) edited volume includes a range of issue-focused chapters that offer practical guidelines on ethical decision making rooted in feminist ethics of care.

Chapter 4

CONSTRUCTING A CONCEPTUAL ARGUMENT

How do I build a sound argument for my inquiry? How do I make a case for how and why my ideas matter relative to other people's ideas about what's important? What is the role of theory in shaping my inquiry?

Time now to address an assumption that has underlain your sense of problem and purpose since your initial efforts to shape your inquiry. That assumption is one of coherence. *Coherence,* following Agar (1996), does not refer to a rigid framework of ideas, nor does it mean the absence of speculation or uncertainty. What it does mean is this: You are assuming a point of view, a way of thinking and seeing, a context for your inquiry in terms of which your problem, and your reasons and strategies for pursuing it, make sense. You need to be able to convey that way of thinking to others.

We all know what it feels like to have an idea we're passionate about, just as we know the challenge of communicating that idea to others in a way that persuades them of its importance and viability. Think of the times you have discussed your ideas with a group of students or professors just *knowing* you were on to something and wishing you could simply transfer the connections you were making in your own mind right into their heads. These connections seem clear enough to you, so why do your friends and advisors still have those puzzled (or perhaps sympathetic) expressions on their faces? Ideas need a context, a sense of how they fit within a bigger picture, to attain significance. In constructing an argument for your inquiry, you need to give explicit form and substance to that context so that others can grasp the connections among your ideas. The task is one of establishing the *conceptual integrity* of your inquiry, making a case for how and why your ideas matter relative to some larger body of ideas embodied in the research, writings, and experiences of others.

Thinking Ahead to Your Research Proposal. This aspect of your work takes shape in your eventual research proposal as the section variously referred to as the Conceptual Context, Theoretical Orientation, Theoretical Framework, or some combination of these headings. What you label it is not as important as being clear about what you are trying to accomplish. For reasons discussed in this chapter and again in Chapter 9, my emphasis here is on how you construct a persuasive conceptual argument for your research, a task that is arguably more focused and formative than simply presenting a traditional review of the literature. It is formative especially in terms of laying the groundwork for your research question(s) and channeling your ideas toward a specific line of inquiry.

SEEKING THEORETICAL LEGITIMACY

The confidence with which Patrice, Jayson, Carolyn, Julie, and others identified a research problem of personal and scholarly importance was matched by their desire that others regard their studies as theoretically legitimate. They expressed the common concern, often shared after a frustrating "hunting and gathering" session in the library stacks or online, that their proposed research might be judged as conceptually or theoretically "thin." Establishing themselves theoretically—a pivotal part of constructing an argument for their proposed research—highlighted a twofold challenge:

> . . . on the one hand to come up with an original problem and a theoretically adequate approach to it, on the other hand to be able to demonstrate how a unique case is embedded in some larger concern related to a significant body of theory. (Wolcott, 2005, p. 175)

We can break this down still further into key considerations and guiding questions that you might use in constructing an argument for your inquiry:

- **significance:** How is my inquiry, and the manner in which I am approaching it, important?
- **situatedness:** How does my inquiry fit within a broader array of significant ideas?
- **transferability:** How might my inquiry contribute to an understanding of similar issues in other settings?

Making a case for your inquiry demands a proactive mind-set bent on persuasion and powered by your ability to make clear connections among ideas. Among the more daunting aspects of this task is coming to terms with the role of theory in your efforts, to which I turn next.

Thinking Theoretically

In his classic work, *The Conduct of Inquiry* (1964), Abraham Kaplan tells the story of a drunkard searching under a street lamp for his house key, which he had dropped some distance away. Asked why he did not look where he had dropped it, he replied, "The light is better here!" Like the drunkard's search, in which the light determined what was looked for and why, your early efforts to lend coherence to your proposed research can have you tacking between neatly packaged theories and intellectually appealing explanations, looking for "right" answers before you really know the questions and context for your inquiry. On the one hand, you are understandably cautious as a novice researcher, letting the hot topics and compelling theories of the day suggest the way to frame your inquiry. On the other hand, your intellectual appetite might get the better of you as you eagerly devour what the literature has to offer, only realizing during your struggle to digest it all that your drive lacks direction. It is a delicate balancing act: how to think theoretically without being overly driven by theory.

Theory does not have to start with a capital T and have someone's name attached to it. Conversely, you have to wonder at the practicality of the expansive view that theory means any kind of structured reflection. Your best avenue is to consider theory's role in terms of its relative and shifting emphasis between these extremes. That is, you can identify theory along a continuum that extends from formal explanatory axiom (Bowlby's Infant Attachment Theory), to tentative hunch ("Something about that interaction between mother and infant doesn't seem right"), to any general set of ideas that guide action ("It's more appropriate to ask the mother about it first"). You can expect to "work" your inquiry by attending to varying amounts of Theory and theory at the same time and over a period of time.

What you are doing at any of these theoretical levels along the continuum is attempting to make coherent what might otherwise appear as disconnected or idiosyncratic. This is the work of theory, whether little t or big T. The underlying assumption is that you never start generating a research project empty-handed (or empty-headed). You may feel like a blank slate because you do not have one of those big-name Theories at the forefront of your thinking, but you are never without some conceptual leverage to guide your early decisions. By *conceptual leverage*, I am referring to how certain concepts or bits of theory have already sensitized you, in a general sense, to the ways that things are alike and the ways that they are different in the situations you encounter. Rightly or wrongly, these concepts help you see a pattern in an event or happening that makes you feel that you can explain what you see (Glaser, 2002). If you are a former teacher planning to conduct research in a classroom, for example, you are already sensitized to anticipate the play of concepts such as turn taking, peer pressure, and gender bias. This does not mean you have to predict the occurrence or prove the significance of these notions; they merely provide you with a provisional sense of reference—a general lay of the land—when deciding what is significant to focus on in your research.

The common assumption is that we need theory at some level to lend legitimacy and purpose to what we do as researchers. It may be affirming to be able to assert one's status as a researcher by claiming, "My theory is . . . " but that assertion means little if you fail to understand the practical ways in which theory can contribute to your work. These ways include:

- **Connectedness:** Theory offers a way to join your work to some larger issue or body of knowledge, in part by inviting you to consider classes of events rather than only single instances.
- **Critique:** Theory offers a critical (in its broadest sense) perspective by directing attention to prior work "in which certain aspects of a problem may have been singled out because they have been inadequately attended to or have raised new doubts or concerns" (Wolcott, 2005, p. 181).
- **Purposefulness:** Theory helps you avoid opportunistic study of "everything" by linking broader principles and perspectives with your decisions to attend to some things but not others in the course of your inquiry (Sanjek, 1991).

Conversely, and as suggested in Kaplan's parable of the drunkard's search, what you should avoid is the tight embrace of theory as a singular preoccupation in your work. Imposing a well-established theory on your developing inquiry may set you up with a neat and satisfying framework for your study, but it may also prematurely shut down avenues of meaningful questioning or prevent you from seeing events and relationships that don't fit the theory. As one experienced researcher suggested, "Theory does not determine the fieldwork experience, but it may provide the dictionary with which it is read" (Van Maanen, 1988, pp. 97–98). Stated another way, theory can provide perspective and suggest pattern, but it need not define what you can see.

When working through ideas for his study of adventure-based education, Jayson spoke on several occasions of having to pry himself free from the "heavy theoretical grasp of the literature." Experience suggests that this is not an uncommon challenge for the novice researcher. A sense of security—but also an intimidating weight of responsibility—accompanies one's decision to embrace ideas that have already received validation in published scholarship.

As soon as you start waving the banner of this or that theory, or simply admit to linking up to it, you proclaim your willingness to take on responsibility for defining and defending it. This is why, in practical terms, you need to distinguish between *having* a grip and *being in* the grip of existing theories; your decision to frame your inquiry in a certain way should reflect your aims, not someone else's agenda. Jayson felt some sense of the latter in the months leading up to his research proposal, and made a deliberate effort at one point to step away from his readings and revisit instances from his own personal experience that initially prompted his exploration of the literature. Regaining these personal footholds through analytic memos helped him to distinguish between ideas that were moving his inquiry forward and those that, however intellectually compelling, were causing him to spin his wheels.

Theory as a Way of Asking

In addressing the question of precisely when and how theory should play a role in your work, you might even regard the entirety of your conceptual framework as a theory of sorts. Maxwell (1996), for example, characterizes the construction of your study's conceptual context as a "formulation of what you think is going on with the phenomena you are studying" (p. 25). However anxiety-producing this notion of conceptual context as theory might be to you as a novice researcher, consider its practical expression in this definition proposed by Wolcott (2005): "Theory is a way of asking that is accompanied by a reasonable answer" (p. 178). He explains:

> If the research problem you intend to pursue is accompanied by a reasonable answer, you can proceed more-or-less theoretically, more if your "answer" is linked to some larger body of thought and prior work, less if the answer is your own modest hunch or hypothesis. Recognize, however, that you can proceed with fieldwork without a reasonable answer to the question(s) you are asking, as long as you have a reasonable sense of how to proceed, how to focus your attention. (pp. 178–179)

Jayson fueled his preliminary ideas for research by foregrounding existing applications and perceived shortcomings of well-established theories. For Patrice, an intuitive sense that "something is not right" in a social situation was sufficient to set off purposeful inquiry. Each entered the cycle of inquiry at a different point and with different handholds. The difference in their approaches lay in when and how theory became *more* or *less* a matter of explicit concern, a contrast that highlights the useful distinction between *significant theories* and *theories of significance* (Sanjek, 1991).

Significant Theories and Theories of Significance

Thinking theoretically may or may not entail making a theory explicit and formal, as, for example, when you enlist a set of principles that is well established in the literature and perhaps even associated with an individual's name (e.g., Kohlberg's Theory of Moral Development). Theories at this "big T" level—Sanjek's (1991) *significant theories*—relate what you intend to do in the field to the larger constellation of ideas and issues brought into focus by your inquiry. Theory in this sense provides something of a legitimizing and narrowing influence upon the wide-ranging trajectories of hunches, tentative musings, and other forms of entry-level theorizing in which you have engaged. As illustrated in a later section of this chapter, Patrice filtered her definition of problem and purpose, with all the accompanying entry-level hunches and tentative musings, through the concept-rich categories of infant mental health, early intervention, and culture theory.

In addition to significant theories, field-oriented researchers develop *terrain-specific theories of significance* (Sanjek, 1991) to help them accomplish what they want to accomplish relative to the people, processes, and places that comprise their fieldwork. *Terrain-specific* refers to the idea that you are making judgments of significance on a local or immediate level—that is, you are generating modest "little t" theories that enable you to take a particular slice of experience and make sense of it by putting it into context. By context, I am referring both to how your "little t" theory relates to other events in the immediate setting and to how it relates to any larger significant theories you have enlisted. Recall, for example, Patrice's entry-level theorizing about the infant in the restaurant and how that interaction played off established understandings of healthy and age-appropriate behavior.

Whether or not you are all that explicit about the theoretical dimensions of your inquiry, a basic rule of thumb is that, as a researcher, you must know what you are up to and be able to explain to others what this is. To this end, you should embrace theory to the extent that it is useful in serving your purposes, not the other way around and not simply for show. Thinking in terms of how concepts (rather than theories) inform your inquiry allows you to be relatively modest when making claims about the ideas you are weaving into your work, while also inviting (but not demanding) consideration of how these ideas may fit into some broader theoretical scheme. As a matter of practice, you might pose the question:

> What do I need by way of theory—or more modestly, by way of concepts—to help me to make sense of, and develop a sound argument for, what I am doing, how I am going about it, and what I am choosing to attend to in my fieldwork?

FORMULATING AN ARGUMENT

At a fundamental level—that is, at a modest level relative to claims about theory—your aim in constructing what will eventually become the Conceptual Context or Theoretical Framework section of your proposal is to develop a working argument that says,

- "Here's how I am positioning my problem within an established arena of ideas," and
- "Here's why that matters."

Constructing this argument is a generative process that calls for something more than a neatly packaged description of ideas that have influenced your thinking. You need to make a contestable case for how your inquiry matters relative to a larger landscape of ideas. Constructing an argument is also a selective process, in which the central issue is how effectively you make use of existing research, concepts, and theories, including your own experiential knowledge, to launch the research question(s) that will set you on a particular trajectory of inquiry.

The biggest risk lies in equating this formative task with the customary summative effort associated with a traditional review of the literature. With an eye toward the former, consider how you might respond to the following issues and questions in the course of developing your argument:

- **Authority:** Am I treating the literature as "a useful but fallible source of *ideas* about what's going on" or as "an *authority* to be deferred to" (Maxwell, 2005, p. 35)?
- **Focus:** Am I engaging directly and meaningfully with my problem by drawing on the relevant work of others on a "when-and-as-needed" basis (Wolcott, 2001, p. 74), or am I simply plowing through and then parading everything I can find on this topic?
- **Ownership:** Are the concepts and theories in the literature serving my purposes or the other way around?

- **Purposefulness:** Is my argument leading toward a meaningful research question or toward some neat and tidy, self-fulfilling explanation and solution?
- **Comprehensiveness:** Is my argument helping me to see alternative ways of framing the issues?
- **Credibility:** How is my argument helping to establish my credibility as a researcher who should be considering these ideas and pursuing this inquiry?

The crucial point, following Maxwell (2005) in particular, is that a conceptual context is something you construct, not something that is waiting passively out there in the literature, intact and ready-made as a framework for your particular inquiry. Developing your conceptual context does not mean trying to cover everything that has been written about a topic; nor does it mean relying entirely on an existing theory as a conceptual container in which you try to fit all your insights and arguments. Rather, the task is one of uncovering what is relevant and what is problematic among the ideas circling around your problem, making new connections, and then formulating an argument that positions you to address that problem in a particular way. Let's explore how this might look in practice.

DIRECTING THE FLOW OF IDEAS

Your ultimate goal in constructing a conceptual or theoretical context for your inquiry is to produce a coherent, focused, integrative, and contestable argument that is comprehensible to readers who are not directly acquainted with your topic. The prospect of making such a case from the mass of prior research and existing perspectives that you have encountered in the literature and elsewhere can be overwhelming. In this section I offer several practical strategies aimed at moving you through this process in a manner consistent with your stated purpose and perspective.

Early on, as we have already seen, you start to develop memos on a number of discrete topics, notions, or phenomena. As initially characterized in Chapter 2, these memos reflect your thinking in progress and are accordingly open to and inclusive of a range of ideas and potential linkages. This phase of generating preliminary theoretical memos is referred to in the following pages as *identifying currents of thought*. The example of Julie's memo shared in Chapter 2 illustrates precisely the type of generative role a memo can play in determining the potential of an idea or concept.

Eventually, as you develop a clearer and more confident sense of those ideas you want to pursue, your memos take on a more focused and integrative character. You try to relate what were previously distinct analytic points or currents of thought and link them together. I refer to this phase as *integrating currents of thought*. When you get to this point, you may find it helpful to begin writing with future audiences other than yourself explicitly in mind. This is because you are now starting in earnest to frame the contextual argument that a reader unfamiliar with your topic or sense of problem would need to know in order to follow your ideas and claims.

Identifying Currents of Thought

In developing her conceptual context, Patrice suggested a simple but elegant notion, "currents of thought," to describe the categories of knowledge that informed her eventual argument. *Current* is an apt term that encompasses both the distinct flow of a category of ideas and the capacity for those ideas to join, or flow into, related categories. In Patrice's case, the three currents of infant mental health, early intervention, and culture theory each presented a means for her to uncover and connect with issues relevant to the problem she had defined.

Her search of the literature and her prior research in these three areas extended no further than she needed to establish meaningful conceptual linkages between a particular category of knowledge and the problem she was proposing to study. My use of the term *meaningful* refers directly to the issues of authority, focus, ownership, and purposefulness, as described earlier. It especially refers to one's ability to engage, rather than simply fall in line with, ideas in the literature. *Conceptual linkages* refer to:

- insights from prior research or theory that support or extend an idea with which you are working
- perceived problems with prior research or theory
- contradictions, paradoxes, or gaps in existing perspectives
- ways in which one's concerns might extend current thinking about what's going on with an issue or topic

To illustrate, some of the meaningful conceptual linkages that emerged for Patrice as she developed the currents of her conceptual work follow. Bear in mind that each of these assertions is an encapsulation of a series of memos and papers for research seminars in which Patrice played her thought-about positions off her selective analyses of the literature. I share them here to illustrate the sort of clear, concise statements you should aim to produce in identifying the currents of thought that feed into your conceptual framework.

- The literature on infant development does not reflect a notion of infant well-being that takes into account the social and economic diversity of U.S. society. (*"infant mental health" current*)
- Professionals in the fields of infant development and early intervention apply concepts of emotional health and development created outside the social and economic contexts of the families to which they are often applied, particularly in the determination of eligibility for human service programs like Early Head Start. (*"early intervention" current*)
- Current diversity paradigms place an emphasis on ethnicity at the expense of social and economic considerations. Notions of what it means to work in families' "natural environments" tend not to encompass ways of being that are related to the values and beliefs of those who are different from the mainstream. (*"culture theory" current*)

For comparative purposes, consider the linkages developed by Carolyn in her proposed study of adult Cambodian students in rural New England. She identified her primary currents of thought as language learners and the social world, transnationalistic behaviors and forces, and the play of self and identity. The fact that both Patrice and Carolyn ended up focusing on three currents of thought is coincidental; there is no magic number, although it is common to have three or four. The following currents of thought convey the pages of conceptual work and theoretical framing that Carolyn generated in making the case for her inquiry:

- Current theory about the relationship between language learners and the social world is problematic. Second language acquisition theorists have not adequately explored the significance of how unequal power relations in the schooling context affect some learners, particularly with respect to their social experiences outside the classroom. (*"language learners and the social world" current*)

- Recent scholarship challenges the notion that most emigrants now move to America, sever old nationalistic ties, assimilate, and live the American dream. We need to complicate how we view nationalism and what it means to "belong to" or "identify with" one cultural context or another. (*"transnationalistic behaviors and forces" current*)
- Self is not the same as identity, but the two are related. Researchers need to redirect attention to the interplay between the two as a means of understanding behavioral and attitudinal change among second language learners. (*"self and identity" current*)

Working Through Titles: A Practical Strategy for Identifying Meaningful Concepts

As you work toward identifying the most promising conceptual emphases (currents of thought) to guide your inquiry, consider the practical strategy of generating working titles for your proposed research as a means to focus and monitor your efforts. It is never too early to start thinking about titles for your inquiry, bearing in mind that they are provisional and intended in these early stages to keep your ideas moving forward. If systematically monitored and reflected upon as the focus and direction of your study evolves, your changing titles can become a means to track the evolution of your conceptual focus and settle on your primary currents of thought. Alan Peshkin (1985a) first championed this idea, noting that as researchers become increasingly immersed in what they are doing and discovering, they necessarily contend with different issues that compete for center stage in their thinking. As suggested in the following examples from Patrice, these issues can be effectively and efficiently conveyed through one's title.

Patrice began developing a title for her study long before her proposal was in place, in order to track changes in her thinking during the initial phases of conceptualizing her study. As suggested by Peshkin (1985a), she continued to track her titles throughout her ensuing fieldwork. The following three titles, with comments, are selected for illustrative purposes from roughly a dozen titles drafted by Patrice over a two-year period from her initial conceptualizing work to her proposal.

May 1999 (When Patrice First Began Framing Her Ideas in Terms of a Potential Research Project):

"Mother Knows Best: Shared Understandings Among Early Head Start Families and Staff"

Patrice's Reflection: The first part of this title reflects my speculation that parents *are* the ones who hold the "best" cultural knowledge to be transmitted to their children, and it is not anybody's job to judge whose cultural knowledge is better. The second part of the title is intended to reflect my working hypothesis that Early Head Start staff share common understandings about infant well-being with the families they serve, but those understandings may be transmitted differently. I suspect that a significant influence on the developing home visitor/family relationship is the manner in which these differences get negotiated. I am thinking of a situation, for example, when a mother might choose to give her 10-month-old baby whole milk when doing so is contrary to program policy.

Author's Commentary: This preliminary draft is noteworthy for several reasons. It does suggest the locus of Patrice's inquiry, namely, interactions between families and the program staff. However, it stops short of explicitly identifying what is at issue in her inquiry. This tentativeness reflects that she is still in the early stages of conceptualizing her focus. (*Strategy note:* Her focus may become clearer if she grapples with what she is trying to get at with "shared understandings." Unpacking what she thinks she means by these two words could be the basis for an analytic memo.) What takes center stage in this initial title is the way that it reflects

Patrice's conscious effort to deal with assumptions that may be at play around her topic of inquiry. This is a healthy emphasis in her early title-building efforts, as she works through perspectives that either help or hinder her ability to focus in on key conceptual concerns.

December 1999 (During Patrice's Early Attempts to Situate Her Problem):
"Mary, Mary, Quite Contrary, How *Does* Your Garden Grow?: Infant Well-Being from the Perspectives of Families Impacted by Poverty"

Patrice's Reflection: Although I intend to critique the role of Early Head Start in the lives of family participants as part of my research, the overriding question for me is how families who live in poverty view infant well-being. My hunch is that families who live in poverty have different contexts, that theirs is not one of "silver bells and cockle shells and pretty maids all in a row" [the line that follows "Mary, Mary, quite contrary . . . " in the old nursery rhyme]. I recognize the power of context and maintain that the contexts of infants being reared in poverty are misunderstood by home visitors enlisted to help their families.

Author's Commentary: Note that, in contrast to her earlier draft, this title contains a potentially key conceptual concern of Patrice's study, namely, *infant well-being.* "Families impacted by poverty" suggests, albeit rather vaguely, the context in which her inquiry was starting to take shape. "Mary, Mary, Quite Contrary . . . ", aside from being an attempt at a catchy title, reflects some preliminary positioning around a critical perspective and, specifically, Patrice's stance that federal programs like Early Head Start, despite their stated intentions, actually serve to perpetuate class and power relationships in U.S. society. The subtitle starts to hint at Patrice's methodological inclination to engage these families directly and understand matters from their perspectives, angling her toward the potential of an ethnographic approach.

March 2001 (The Title of Patrice's Research Proposal):
"Infant Well-Being and the Participation of Families in Early Head Start"

Author's Commentary: Patrice did not write a reflection on this title, as she did with her others, focused as she was at the time on writing up and presenting her research proposal. Several features are worth nothing, either for their presence or absence in this draft. First, and perhaps foremost, this title contains the two key conceptual concerns that orient Patrice's study and find expression in her central research questions: infant well-being and the experience of families in Early Head Start. With this title Patrice clearly identifies what is at issue in her study. "Participation of Families in Early Head Start" also serves to alert us to the specific context in which her inquiry is embedded. Overall, it is a clearly focused but somewhat neutral title—a good strategy at the proposal stage, when you are understandably cautious about making claims.

Exercise 4.1
Generating Working Titles as a Means to Focus Your Ideas

Apply the practical strategy just described in Patrice's case to monitor the evolving focus of your own inquiry. Start now to generate working titles you feel convey the conceptual essence, or at least conceptual points of reference for your proposed study. Then, as Patrice did, reflect in writing on how each successive title conveys your emerging insights and currents of thought. Make this an ongoing effort. Date and file each title and reflection. When you reach the point of writing your actual proposal, revisit these memos as a means to reconstruct the evolution of your thinking and assess how effectively your current title captures the focus of your inquiry. If you want to realize the full potential of this strategy, continue documenting and systematically reflecting on the evolution of your inquiry from title to title as you engage in fieldwork, analysis, and final write-up of your research. For the original reference on this strategy, see Peshkin (1985a).

Integrating Currents of Thought

Integrating currents of thought refers to the capacity for your ideas—your currents of thought—to flow into each other in the form of more elaborate and encompassing lines of inquiry. This is when you effectively begin to see conceptual context as theory building, a way of asking accompanied by a reasonable and arguable answer. More than at any other point in the design process, this is where you see how the play of your ideas feeds directly into the formation of your research questions. *Play* is the operative term here, in the sense of encouraging creative, exploratory thinking—what Maxwell (2005) calls "thought experiments"—with the aim of generating speculative "if . . . then . . . " types of questions or propositions focused on the implications of approaching your problem in a certain way.

You should not expect the discrete currents of thought you generate through reading, reflection, and writing memos to emerge intact in your eventual research questions. You are not working toward separating variables and simplifying matters. You are working toward linking a variety of distinct ideas and exploring relationships among them. You certainly should not view the strategy of constructing if-then propositions or questions as the only way to proceed. I present them here as an option that my own students have found both workable and generative, particularly in terms of forming linkages between big T theories they encountered in the literature and their own little t notions about what might be going on in a specific situation. If-then propositions provide you with a concrete way of addressing the previously discussed issues of authority (treating the literature as a fallible source of ideas) and ownership (making sure concepts and theories serve your purposes). That is to say, you are engaging these concepts and theories on your own terms. And because of their speculative tenor, your propositions do not position you in a way to suggest you are deferring to this theory or that theory. They allow you to be purposeful without being predictive.

As you consider the following examples of if-then propositions generated by Patrice in her conceptual work, keep in mind that these are not her research questions. Rather, these are lines of speculation and inquiry that direct attention to the pivotal concerns of her proposed study. Think of them as the conceptual underpinnings of her still-to-be-formulated research questions(s). If you want to look ahead to Example 5.2 in Chapter 5, you can see how the following propositions plant the seeds for her central research questions.

- If parents and social groups have differing goals for their children based on the socially determined competencies necessary for survival in a group, then what are the values and behaviors of families who live in chronic poverty that adults reward and pass on to their children?
- If infants' and toddlers' day-to-day environmental experiences most strongly predict later well-being and competence, then maybe "we" (mainstream Americans) don't like

the implications for expanding our conceptualization of who we are because it may weaken our perceived competence as a whole.

- If cultural models provide individuals with understandings of what is "right" and "natural," then what does that imply about the perceived value of those who cannot achieve what is right or natural?
- If the children who are raised in socially and economically different contexts are perceived as less competent than those in the American mainstream, then they are likely never to be included in the aggregate; they will continue to be "outsiders" and may not succeed in school.
- If, however, we can understand children's experiences in terms of their contexts and see their competencies as revealed in these experiences, then I wonder if school success might follow.

Again, for comparative purposes, let's look at the lines of inquiry generated by Carolyn as she integrated the currents of thought for her proposed study:

- If a significant part of the local Cambodians' lives is their experience as language learners within a formal educational context, then how do power relationships and social structures inherent in that context impact how they are able to construct a sense of who they are in the local community setting?
- If Cambodians in rural northern New England can be described as "living their lives across borders," then what does it mean to experience a sense of community in the local setting?
- If contemporary immigrants' understandings of family obligation, national identity, and gender role expectations are being shaped within a context of transnationalistic behaviors and forces, then what does that imply about how they perceive the value of community and their place within it?
- If cultural constructions of the self provide a way to address the interplay between forces of continuity and adaptation, then how might attention to the concept of self inform an understanding of study participants' ability to develop and sustain a sense of group identity and community?

Carolyn eventually channeled these lines of speculation—emphasizing some more than others—into her central research questions:

1. How do these Cambodian families perceive learning English as impacting their lives?
2. How do these Cambodian families sustain a sense of who they are in the local setting?

To the extent that you can be effective in delineating pivotal concerns in the form of if-then types of questions or propositions, you are that much closer to closing out your conceptual or theoretical argument and asking the "right" research questions. In the preceding example with Carolyn, the immediate juxtaposition of her lines of speculation and her research questions may have inadvertently conveyed a rather easy and automatic transition from one to the other. That's not quite the case. I like to encourage students with the claim that their research questions naturally and logically flow from their conceptual work— and they do, but not without significant input on their part. As detailed in Chapter 5, you still need to work through a number of issues to come up with meaningful, workable research questions. I jumped ahead to Carolyn's questions here just so you might see how they related to her earlier speculative propositions. After working through this next chapter, you will have a firmer basis on which to judge the adequacy and appropriateness of Carolyn's (and your own) research questions relative to the conceptual work that led up to them.

Exercise 4.2
Using If-Then Propositions and Questions to Move Your Inquiry Forward

If-then propositions or questions can be an effective way, but are not the only way, to move your ideas toward a clear articulation of your key conceptual concerns and research questions. My students have found them to be especially helpful at those times when they feel at a loss about how to integrate the ideas they've encountered in the literature and give shape and direction to the speculative notions whirling around in their heads. The primary characteristic and benefit of such propositions is that they are provisional; they can move you forward without locking you into a position. This should also be the basis on which you judge their efficacy: Are they inviting consideration of a pathway to take and planting the seeds of an actual research question, or are they putting up barriers to your progress?

Try generating your own if-then propositions and questions. You have several possible points of entry to this process:

- If you have worked your thought-about positions into the sort of clear, concise statements illustrated in the previous examples from Patrice and Carolyn, start there. Ask yourself how some or all of these statements are related and then generate if-then propositions or questions that highlight the connections among them.

- If you are not at the point of having generated such preliminary concise statements, revisit some of your analytic memos in their entirety. Especially if your memos conclude with questions that reposition you relative to your research topic (like Julie's memo in Example 2.1, Chapter 2), then try to identify connections and contradictions among these questions that point you toward one or more speculative propositions.

- Consider the possibility that you may have an easier time expressing your ideas orally than in writing. Talk through your ideas with a friend, colleague, or mentor. Ask them to restate what they are hearing you say, even (or especially) if you are simply pouring out a stream of consciousness jumble of ideas. Record the conversation and use this information as "data" to explore patterns, consistencies, and contradictions in your statements and questions. Pay attention to key words and phrases you use in talking about your proposed problem or topic; these likely point toward concepts that might be orienting your inquiry. Build these into your if-then propositions and questions.

ASIDE: Coherence Is About Connections, Not Completeness

The assumption of coherence, as introduced at the start of this chapter, may imply a sense of completeness, but what it really calls for is an understanding of the linkages between and among ideas. In building conceptual and theoretical connections, you are making the assertion that, however modest in scope your particular inquiry may be, it does relate in meaningful ways to broader perspectives and issues. You build the case for your proposed study by inviting consideration of your problem and your research question as something that is more, rather than less, complex. This construction of a conceptual context for your inquiry is an essential part of your claim to a qualitative stance.

Thinking Ahead to Your Research Proposal

As you anticipate the ways in which you will actually integrate your conceptual and/or theoretical context into your written proposal, you need not limit yourself to the conventional format of lumping it all together in one section or chapter. This can be an effective approach and is familiar to, and expected by, most faculty committees. Patrice, for example, presents her conceptual underpinnings in this way (see Chapter 9). It is also how you typically see a traditional review of the literature. The underlying assumption is that your linkages with the ideas of others serve as precursors to, rather than integral, ongoing, and evolving parts of, your inquiry. (Piantanida & Garman, 1999, suggest some useful ways to think about this distinction.) As an alternative, you might consider the strategy used by Jayson, in which he integrates many of his conceptual and theoretical arguments into the Research Questions section of his proposal (see Chapter 9). Specifically, he clarified how particular currents of thought fed into his central research questions and, in so doing, offered a more focused alternative to the general framework for formulating a working argument discussed earlier in this chapter:

- "Here's how I am positioning and justifying each of my research questions within an established arena of ideas," and
- "Here's why that matters."

The basis of his decision to format his proposal in this way had its roots in the way he formed his research questions (see Example 5.3 and the accompanying discussion in Chapter 5). More broadly speaking, it reflected a deliberate move away from thinking in terms of a monolithic review of literature that you assume readers of your proposal can apply to the relevant parts of your proposed research. As one student remarked in response to Jayson's decision to integrate his conceptual work into the Research Questions section of his proposal: "I can really see purpose in his [Jayson's] use of the literature . . . he is literally making a case for how and why his research questions matter."

Jayson's approach is no more or less effective than Patrice's, just different. Both pursued formats they felt were most responsive to the nature of their respective approach and questions, just as you will need to do. Chapter 9 will revisit some of the options you face as you decide how to present the conceptual underpinnings of your research in your proposal document.

Exercise 4.3
Tuning Your Inquiry

The premise of this exercise is simple: seeking and processing feedback from others in the early phases of conceptualizing your inquiry, especially if you are having problems, is often the most effective way to focus your ideas and move them forward. The key to success in the form of collective inquiry embodied in this exercise is the group's commitment to abiding by its structure. What you want to avoid is simply an evaluative, offense-defense discussion that can limit the depth and focus of feedback you seek. You need a framework for discussion that emphasizes purposefulness, clarification, well-defined opportunities for listening, and the ability to be critical without criticizing.

To this end, I have adapted a process initially developed by the Coalition of Essential Schools (Allen, 1995) through which educators hone their skills by examining student work in a supportive, problem-solving small group format. Termed a *tuning protocol*, the process has proven to be an effective way to structure a group's close examination of a colleague's efforts while fostering productive dialogue. As adapted for use in the context of a research seminar, I have found it especially appropriate early on when students are struggling to come to terms with such issues as focus, locus, research aims, or the impact of various theories or Theories on the shape or direction of their inquiry. A group comprised of five individuals seems especially effective—large enough to encourage a range of perspectives yet small enough to allow everyone to contribute. Here is how it works for the purpose of tuning one's inquiry, using one of my students, JoAnne, as an example:

Preparation. Prior to class JoAnne generated a brief memo that outlined a proposed focus and locus of her inquiry, as well as a preliminary rationale for a possible research question based on several influential concepts circling around her topic. Her preparation included some key questions she wanted the group to address. These were fairly straightforward: Do the focus and locus make sense? Are they what *you* would perceive the focus and locus to be? Does my question appear to get at what I am saying I want to understand?

Opening (3–4 minutes). One of the group's participants, serving as the facilitator, reviewed the steps of the tuning protocol. Throughout the session, the facilitator makes sure that the group keeps to the schedule and does not skip steps. This role does not exempt him or her from actively participating as a group member.

Presentation (15 minutes). JoAnne shared copies of her memo with the group, expanding on key points and concerns. For example, in clarifying the evolution of her ideas, she shared earlier drafts of her focus statement or key passages from articles she had read. While she spoke, everyone else remained silent and took notes. Near the end of the 15 minutes, she reiterated the questions she wanted the group to address and gave them time to read or reread her materials.

Clarifying Questions (5 minutes). When 15 minutes had passed, the facilitator asked group members if they had any clarifying questions before proceeding. Clarifying questions simply seek more information and should not be evaluative statements cast as questions. For example, instead of asking, "Why didn't you consider X?" group members should ask, "Did you consider X?" or "Can you clarify what you meant by Y?"

Participant Discussion (15–20 minutes). JoAnne physically backed out of the circle. (*Note:* This is not a minor point. The process works best if the presenter literally puts herself out of eye contact—for example, at a side table with back turned to the group—so that she can listen to the group. In turn, group members can grapple with the questions on their own without directly addressing her. This even means referring to her in the third person as they talk.) JoAnne remained silent during this discussion but took copious notes on what was being said. Participants' comments focused on how JoAnne's comments made sense to them, affirmed promising directions, and suggested "what ifs" or aspects that might be improved or redirected. They also brainstormed ways for JoAnne to proceed. (One student once remarked about this phase of the process: "It felt like I was listening to conversation in my own head, except in this case I had the luxury of being able to attend to every point in an objective manner!")

Presenter Playback and Reflection (10 minutes). JoAnne returned to the circle and used her notes to reflect aloud on what she had heard. The group listened, without interruption, while she reviewed her interpretation of the discussion and her assessment of suggested directions in which she might proceed. The facilitator then wrapped things up with an opportunity for group members to informally debrief the process and add any concluding comments or observations.

If this seems like a rather structured format through which to receive feedback, you're right—but that structure is the key to its effectiveness. The protocol builds in a space for listening and creates a structure that makes it safe to ask challenging questions of each other. The existence of this structure, which everyone understands and has agreed to, permits a certain kind of conversation to occur.

Care should be taken not to overuse this strategy. Over the course of a semester, each of my students has derived benefit from engaging in a tuning protocol no more than just a couple of times.

SUMMARY OF KEY POINTS

- Making a case for how and why your ideas matter relative to some larger body of ideas embodied in the research, writings, and experiences of others is the essence of what will become the conceptual context or theoretical framework in your research proposal.
- This is a generative and selective process that can be distinguished from the customary summative effort associated with a traditional review of the literature. Fundamentally, the task is one of uncovering what is relevant and what is problematic among the ideas circling around your problem, making new connections, and then formulating an argument that positions you to address that problem in a particular way.
- Determining when and how theory plays a role in your thinking is a key aspect of establishing the conceptual integrity of your work. The distinction between *significant theories* and *theories of significance* can be helpful in this regard.

- You should avoid the tight embrace of theory as a singular preoccupation in your work.
- Systematically generating and reflecting upon working titles for your proposed research can be an effective means to identify the conceptual focus of your inquiry.
- The delineation of pivotal concerns in the form of if-then types of questions or propositions provides an effective way of closing out your conceptual context and positioning you to ask the "right" research questions.
- You can present your conceptual and theoretical context in a variety of ways in your written proposal, ranging from a discrete section or chapter to selective integration of relevant portions of your conceptual argument throughout your document.

RECOMMENDED READING

Flinders and Mills's (1993) edited volume includes engaging personal accounts by qualitative researchers about their efforts to come to terms with the role of theory in their work. This helpful supplemental text affirms that struggling with theory is the healthy norm rather than the exception among researchers. In his detailed explanation of what it means to generate grounded theory, Glaser (2002) offers some specific ways to think about concepts, patterns, and theory bits. In general, you may find that grounded theorists like Glaser have a lot to say about the roles and relationships of concepts and theories in qualitative research. Take care, however, that you do not simply equate your understanding of theory in qualitative inquiry with the tenets of grounded theory. Flinders and Mills's incorporation of a wide array of qualitative approaches helps to counter this tendency.

Thomas (1997) presents a lengthy but readable critique focused on the use of theory in educational research. He defines four broad uses of theory, while questioning what it means to "locate" one's work in theory. Creswell (2003) includes a chapter focused on the use of theory, presented in a format that compares and contrasts qualitative, quantitative, and mixed methods applications.

Chapter 5

FORMING RESEARCH QUESTIONS

How do I take the ideas I have filtered through my problem, purpose, perspective, and conceptual context and transform them into a meaningful research question? And once I form a question, how do I determine whether it is the right question to pursue?

Moving your inquiry toward a point of clear definition in the form of a research question is the focus of this chapter. As you have likely determined from the preceding chapters, getting at a research question is not like driving down a clearly marked road to a scenic destination according to a travel club's map. Rather it is something closer in kind to the preliminary give-and-take discussion you have with yourself and others about whether, where, why, and how you might want to go somewhere—interactive, spiraling, but not without points of reference.

To help you identify your points of reference and move toward an appropriate and workable research question, I have organized this chapter around the following issues and key concerns:

Moving Toward Your Question

Tacking Between Breadth and Precision

Key Concern: How do you negotiate the many different questions and issues swirling around your topic to "get at" a worthwhile research question?

Attending to What Matters

Key Concern: Does it matter whether your inquiry is driven by a single, central research question or by several questions?

Justifying Your Question

Assessing Goodness of Fit

Key Concern: How do you determine whether your research question is a "good fit" for what you want to understand?

Orienting and Rationalizing Your Approach

Key Concern: How do you determine whether your research question is the right question to be asking as a qualitative researcher?

Going Somewhere with Your Question

Defining the Evolution of Your Inquiry

Key Concern: What does it mean for the question that you bring to the research setting to "evolve" during the course of your inquiry?

Thinking Ahead to Your Research Proposal. This aspect of your work takes shape in your eventual research proposal most directly and prominently in the section that addresses the focus and purpose of your research questions—what I later describe as the heart of your proposal. In less obvious but no less important fashion, the work of forming research questions contributes to your Research Procedures section, providing the focus that enables you to establish the appropriateness of a particular research approach.

MOVING TOWARD YOUR RESEARCH QUESTION

Tacking Between Breadth and Precision

Key Concern: How do you negotiate the many different questions and issues swirling around your topic to "get at" a worthwhile research question?

In the introduction to Part One I described the research question as one of a number of mutually responsive components—engaging with a sense of problem, clarifying purposes, establishing an intellectual orientation and moral stance, and developing a conceptual argument—in a dynamic process of conceptualizing and generating your study. Following Maxwell (2005) and my own experience, I argued that research questions are in most cases the result of an interactive design process rather than being the starting point for that process. This discussion helped to establish how your research questions give specific shape to your stated purposes and make explicit that which you want to learn.

With this basic understanding in mind, consider the situation of Deb, a student at the point of defining the question that would guide her study. Deb's introduction to graduate work in qualitative research coincided with her responsibilities as Director of the Academic Support Center at a private, two-year, post-secondary institution. The support center was a place where students could receive additional academic assistance in the form of peer tutoring and faculty support. Deb's proposed research was rooted in her perception that the center's programs failed to provide adequate support for some students; for others, the center provided too much support, effectively taking away students' ownership of their work. She was concerned that the "equal educational opportunity" promised for these students by the college was, as she stated, "merely the illusion of an opportunity."

Where and how does she proceed to identify her central research question? Does she start at the conceptual or theoretical level and try a "big picture" approach to her problem (e.g., sorting through conflicting perspectives on "equal educational opportunity," as explored in her conceptual context)? Or, does she focus first on small, discrete pieces—detailed slices of life—that could give more definite shape to her question but might just as easily turn out to be irrelevant (e.g., asking why some students are expressing frustration about their classroom experience or why some faculty are expressing frustration about their students' performance)?

Both of these seemingly contrary ways of perceiving and proceeding through inquiry inform the qualitative perspective. For researchers like Deb, the dual ability to "peer broadly" while attending to the nitty-gritty of the particular (Peacock, 1986) provides a way of homing in on a well-formulated research question. In practical terms, this means tacking continuously between questions that address "What's the big picture here?" and those that address "What, in particular, is going on here?" until these complementary lines of inquiry converge as a single image around which the researcher can wrap his or her research question. This is the familiar rhythm of qualitative inquiry, a sort of "intellectual perpetual motion" (Geertz, 1984, p. 134) between breadth of vision and precision of focus.

Figure 5.1 offers a glimpse into how this dialectical tacking between breadth and precision played out in Deb's case. I have developed this example from working questions and if = then formulations Deb addressed as she worked through the conceptual argument for her inquiry (see Chapter 4). These questions and others like them served as her key reference points as she sought to give specificity and direction to her research purpose in the form of a central research question.

The stated purpose of Deb's study at this point in the process was "to better understand the notion of real educational opportunity in higher education." If we examine the questions

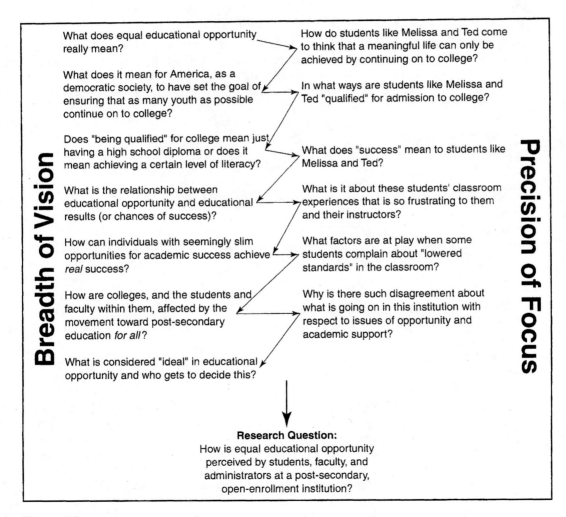

Figure 5.1
Moving Toward a Research Question: A Study of Equal Educational Opportunity in Higher Education

emphasizing breadth of vision in Figure 5.1, we see Deb trying to make conceptual or theoretical connections between educational opportunity and assumptions people have made about its value, its ties with individual achievement, the nature of success, and so on. If we examine the same issue emphasizing precision of focus, we see "reality check" types of questions that highlight the particularity of lived or observed experiences. Keep in mind that this is not a linear process, but rather a dialectical one in which questions from both sides play off and inform each other.

Attending to What Matters

Key Concern: Does it matter whether your inquiry is driven by a single, central research question or by several questions?

For qualitatively oriented research, in which one is never quite sure where to set the boundaries of relevant context, there can be a different twist to the challenge described in the previous section. In many cases, especially early on, your "tacking" may lead you to the decision that your inquiry is best served not by one but by several research questions.

While researchers tend to agree that trying to work from more than a few major research questions is looking for trouble—what Miles and Huberman (1994) discuss as "research question proliferation"—there is no solid consensus on whether it is best to proceed from one or several research questions. Nor is there agreement, if the decision is made to use a number of questions, on whether each question holds the same status or function in one's inquiry (Are some actually subquestions? Do they build on each other in a linear or logical fashion? If not, how do they complement each other?).

Creswell (2003), for example, recommends that researchers ask one or two central questions followed by no more than five to seven subquestions. Stake (1995), specifically addressing case study research, offers a model that distinguishes between *issue* questions and *topical* questions. The former provide the conceptual structure for organizing one's inquiry by addressing major problematic concerns. The latter address anticipated needs for information as, for example, questions that relate to a description of the context. Miles and Huberman (1994) suggest drafting and iterating a set of six or seven general research questions and, over time, honing a smaller number of major questions, each with specific subquestions. They leave open the possibility of drawing out a "key question" from this process.

Consider the experience of another student, Linda, who began by drafting the following set of five (or more, depending on how you distinguish them) general research questions. The purpose of the study, in her words, was "to describe the experiences of Asian American students as they pertain to racial and ethnic identity development in a predominantly white, small college setting." She settled herself into her inquiry with the intent of generating an explanation of identity formation, with a dual focus on individual self-identification and the sociologic processes involved in group membership. The following questions, including the manner in which they are grouped, emerged from an early draft of her research design:

1. How do Asian American students construe their identities in a rural, elite college environment? How do they self-identify and what meaning do they attach to these identities?
2. What have been the experiences of Asian Americans in this community (primarily students but also including faculty and administrators)? What roles have race and ethnicity played in the lives of these individuals?

3. What types of communities do the students come from? What factors within their home communities played important roles in the development of racial and ethnic identity prior to college?
4. In which communities do the students participate in college? What factors within the students' college-based communities play an important role in the development of racial and ethnic identity during college?
5. What is the role of the institution, and how does it affect the experiences of Asian American students?

At first glance, Linda's listing of what are actually nine distinct questions might seem to put her at risk of losing the forest for the trees, overly fragmenting the way she approaches data collection. But laying out her questions in this preliminary manner proved to be an eminently productive strategy for her as she sought to articulate more precisely the nature and focus of her inquiry. In particular, it placed in stark relief the crucial distinction noted by Maxwell (2005), Stake (1995), and others between questions that formulate what you want to understand and questions you ask to gain that understanding.

In Linda's case, all the questions listed under numbers 2 to 5 (and to some degree the second question in number 1) are closer in kind to the topical questions that cover anticipated needs for information and, in practical terms, feed directly into the specific questions she would ask as an interviewer and observer in the field. Reconsidered as a "topical outline" (Stake, 1995), for example, these questions (or subquestions, if you prefer) served to foreshadow and actually set into motion procedures of data collection and analysis (Creswell, 1998, 2003). Sorting through her questions in this fashion, Linda eventually identified her key research question as it rose to the surface—a version of the first question in number 1. This question could not be directly operationalized or translated into a question she might ask to guide an interview or observation, but it did serve the broader purpose of directing attention to the issue she really wanted to understand.

The winnowing aspect of this process serves well to remind us that the critical and ongoing task for qualitative inquirers is not, as might be expected, to try to account for everything (as suits our inclination to set few limits on what we can uncover through our investigations). Rather, as Wolcott (1988) pointedly reminds us, it is to "try to get rid of almost everything, of honing the topic and sharpening the focus, so that increasingly there is less to be concerned with, and thus what is of concern can be observed with greater attention" (p. 27).

Figures 5.2 and 5.3 illustrate the working relationship between central research questions and their topical subquestions. The example in Figure 5.2 draws from Patrice's study of infant well-being from the perspectives of families participating in Early Head Start. Note how her topical questions establish a sequence of inquiry that builds incrementally and logically toward her central concerns, as expressed in her two research questions. Her topical questions also served the aim of setting in motion what she might actually do and say in the field setting.

Figure 5.3 draws from Jayson's study of how participants construct meaning in facilitated, small group adventure experiences. Here, too, you can see how topical questions provide shape and substance to the overriding research question. Each of Jayson's questions also includes what he called "working hypotheses." *Hypothesis* in this context does not refer to the conventional definition of hypothesis as a prediction about behavior that is logically deduced and tested. Instead, Jayson's working hypotheses refer to tentative theories that he constructed

Central Question #1
What is the meaning of infant well-being from the perspective of families who participate in Early Head Start services?

Topical Questions
How do parents understand infant development—do they see themselves as having the ability to influence development, or do they attribute development to factors outside their locus of control?

How do parents understand the context of infant development—the relationship between themselves and their infants, and the influence of environmental factors on the development of their infants?

Do parents have goals and priorities for their infants? If they do, are they able to identify and articulate them? Which goals do they hold most dear?

What values and beliefs do parents pass on to their children? To what extent are these imbued in the experiences that infants have with their families?

Central Question #2
What is the experience of families who participate in Early Head Start?

Topical Questions
Are there implicit goals that home visitors bring to the relationship? If so, what are they? How do these goals influence the relationship, if they do?

What is the process of relationship building that unfolds between home visitors and their partner families? What helps or hinders this process of relationship building? How do families perceive the "help giving" that is intended by their home visitor?

What meaning do families ascribe to having a home visitor? What do the families perceive to be the implications of participating in the home visiting component of Early Head Start?

Figure 5.2
Central Research Questions and Their Topical Subquestions: A Study of Infant Well-Being from the Perspective of Families Impacted by Poverty

about what he thought might be going on and why. Some people might refer to these variously as *propositions, foreshadowed problems,* or simply *informed hunches.* Stated as propositions, they incorporate concepts, assumptions, and expectations that help him to develop questions that are realistic and relevant to his aims.

Jayson's use of working hypotheses illustrates how researchers can effectively meet the challenge of distinguishing between what they want (or need) to know and what they think is going on. In other words, behind every question asked, there ought to be a working notion of how and why the answer to that question matters (Wolcott, 2005). This is different than embedding in your question a claim, however tentative, about what you think the answer might be. This distinction is crucial: asking how and why an answer matters encourages you to keep tabs on what you don't know; claiming what you think the answer might be may prevent you from seeing what's actually happening. Jayson's work provides a solid example of how to manage this distinction. (This is especially apparent when you examine more of the text from which his questions and working hypotheses are drawn. See a fuller explanation of Jayson's strategy in the Research Question section in Chapter 9.)

Central Question
How is participant experience constructed in a facilitated, small group adventure experience?

Working Hypothesis: Participant experience in the adventure workshop is constructed by the interaction of social agents using language, actions, and physical objects to mediate activity in certain ways that reflect the values of the cultures, institutions, and participants represented but open to culturally expansive forms of participation. The "adventure" is not inherent to any part of the workshop event, but is based in this constructive process.

Topical Questions
➤ How is the construction of the adventure experience related to the institutional and social context in which it occurs?

Working Hypothesis: First, participant experience is situated in a specific institutional context that is influenced by the values and meanings provided by Project Adventure (which itself exists in a broader historical context), interpreted by a trainer, and enacted differentially based on specific forms of participation. Second, Project Adventure workshops involve socially and culturally situated actors. Actions and their meanings will be interpreted through broader cultural influences such as beliefs about the application of adventure techniques, gendered experience, and conflicts between a relational and individualist ontology. It is believed that the identity-conferring meaning enabled through the process of constructing "adventure" in Project Adventure workshops will interact with these cultural influences.

➤ How is the construction of the adventure experience related to the intentions and orchestrations of the trainer?

Working Hypothesis: The construction of the experience is influenced by the intentions, tacit and explicit theories, language use, and prop (physical artifact) choices of the trainer, who must make determinations about how to structure the workshop.

Figure 5.3
A Central Research Question, Topical Subquestions, and Working Hypotheses: A Study of the Social Construction of Meaning in Facilitated, Small Group Adventure Experiences

ASIDE: Practical Advice About Language and Focus

It is worth noting several practical but easily overlooked aspects of research questions illustrated in the work of Patrice and Jayson (Figures 5.2 and 5.3). Each of their central questions incorporates the following guidelines, drawn from Creswell (2003), that are commonly applied to the construction of qualitative research questions:

- Begin qualitative research questions with the words *what* or *how* to convey openness to emerging concerns and unanticipated possibilities. *Why* questions, in contrast, suggest cause and effect, a concern more consistent with a quantitative approach. (I revisit this guideline in more detail later in the chapter.)

- Use nondirectional language. Verbs with a directional orientation like *determine, cause,* or *influence* infer an approach not well suited to qualitative inquiry (see Table 5.1).
- Try to focus on a single concept or phenomenon. Patrice, for example, focuses in her first question on infant well-being. Jayson focuses on participants' construction of an experience in his question.
- If you can do so without being too wordy or unnecessarily repeating information contained within your purpose statement, specify study participants and/or the research context in your research question. Patrice's two central research questions do this quite effectively. Jayson's question is less precise but does sufficiently alert us to the context of his inquiry.

JUSTIFYING YOUR QUESTION

Assessing Goodness of Fit

Key Concern: How do you determine whether your research question is a "good fit" for what you want to understand?

Assessing the goodness of fit between your research question and what you want to understand by doing the study is a necessary step in establishing a coherent inquiry. It also gets at the heart of what you can and should expect a qualitative research question to do for you. The issue here is what we might call the *responsiveness* of your research question: how well it addresses your problem, purpose, focus, and assumptions and what implicit claim it makes of being an answerable question in the first place.

In a manner that reflects the more comprehensive process of constructing a conceptual argument for a study (see Chapter 4), you might find it useful to delineate what you think is going on with your research question. Specifically, consider in systematic fashion how you might respond to a set of queries that address how your research question works for you and why it makes sense. The following questions and issues can help you think through your research question and assess its goodness of fit. Exercise 5.1 then encourages you to apply these questions to your own developing inquiry.

Is my research question working to address my problem?

The underlying issue: Convincing readers that your study is worthwhile plays off your ability to situate your research as addressing a particular, important problem (Marshall & Rossman, 1999). Defining the problem, of course, is a first step in shaping your study's significance, but it is in demonstrating a problem that your study's significance is affirmed. Your research question provides the crucial link between these two aims.

For illustration, consider again the trajectory of questions posed by Deb in her study of educational opportunity (Figure 5.1). We can see embedded in her line of inquiry the growing sense that things are not quite right as they are or, at the least, are not as good as they might be. Also underlying her questions is an increasing awareness of circumstances under which educational opportunity might be considered problematic. Eventually, more in character with a raised eyebrow than a pointing finger, her central research question emerges, inviting consideration of the situation as something other than the way things appear to be or are expected to be.

Purposeful, but avoiding prediction, Deb's central research question helps to address her problem by appropriately anticipating the possibility that a problem exists, in this case, around how different people in the setting understand educational opportunity. In basic terms, then, we can view the "work" of the research question as *creating the capacity for problem finding* in the setting.

How am I deciding whether my question is too focused or too broad?

The underlying issue: What is at stake here is the role of your research question in indicating what, and how much, you are likely to attend to in your study. Practicality is a major consideration when determining one's scope of inquiry, of course, but even this can be a fuzzy standard in an approach so uniquely suited to uncovering the unexpected and exploring leads as they emerge. Herein lies a tension. Your research question should be flexible enough to permit exploration but focused enough to delimit the study (Marshall & Rossman, 1999).

Take care when attempting to heed the general advice to keep your focus as broad as possible for as long as possible when entering into a qualitative field study. While such openness is the hallmark of qualitative methods, it does not obligate you to formulate a research question that remains at the preliminary "What's going on here?" level.

Conversely, caution should be also used when considering the advice commonly directed at the novice to "think small." Thinking small, Bogdan and Biklen (2003) remind us, means thinking about practical limitations as you formulate your question; it does *not* mean making your research question overly specific. Among other considerations, they argue, a question that is too specific may cause difficulty for the qualitative researcher because the issues posed may not arise in the time available for studying them. An example of such a question would be, "How do teachers incorporate models of peer coaching into their first year of teaching?" Questions that are too focused may also lead you to not pay attention early on to a wide enough range of data, thereby leading you to overlook important but unanticipated findings (Maxwell, 2005).

Marshall and Rossman (1999) address the issue of focus by presenting a useful categorization of types of initial research questions. While not exhaustive or accounting for the overlapping of categories, their examples provide one way of thinking about how one's initial research question can serve to bound a study without unduly constraining it.

- **Theoretical questions** can be researched in a number of different sites or with different samples. Examples include:
  - How does play affect reading readiness?
  - How does the mentoring process function in the socialization of professionals?
- Questions focused on **particular populations** can also be studied in various places but direct attention to a particular person, group, or class of individuals. Examples include:
  - What happens to women who enter elite MBA programs?
  - How do first-year teachers perceive their relations with their more experienced colleagues?
- **Site-specific** questions seek to highlight the uniqueness of a particular program or organization. Examples include:
  - How do grassroots environmentalist groups in coastal New Hampshire influence practices among local commercial fisherman?
  - How do home-school relations of an elite private school differ from those in the neighboring public school?

A basic consideration when determining whether your question is too diffuse or too focused is to assess its effectiveness in serving as a guide for decisions you need to make as you prepare to enter the field and conduct your study. An appropriately focused question should foreshadow and set into motion procedures of participant selection, data collection, and analysis (see section on Using Questions to Anticipate Procedures in Chapter 6).

How have I checked for assumptions that may be embedded in my question?

The underlying issue: Assumptions are inevitably and insistently present throughout the process of inquiry. They represent an invariable component of research that is not inherently good or bad but does impact how you pose questions and conduct fieldwork. Left unexamined, assumptions may lead you to focus on what you think is going on in a setting and prevent you from seeing what is actually happening. Giving your assumptions the meaningful attention they deserve can make you aware of how they may be shaping your inquiry and its outcomes (Glesne, 1999; Peshkin, 1988).

Tim, a graduate student in mathematics education, undertook a case study of how a mathematician who had just completed a Ph.D. was socialized into his first university faculty position. His research focused on the question of how being a mathematician and "doing mathematics" influenced the ways in which the newcomer learned about and adapted to the values and practices of his new departmental work setting.

In early drafts of his write-up, Tim revisited a key assumption that influenced the way he presented his problem and posed his research questions. He wrote:

> Questions posed in preparation for this study were all predicated on the belief that department members would be "doing mathematics." If I asked, "How do these people measure success?" I was really asking, "How do these people, who have a professional life built around doing mathematics, measure success?"

As Tim conceptualized it, "doing mathematics" meant engaging in mathematical activity for rewards that were intrinsically related to mathematics: either enjoyment of the process itself or recognition as a mathematician. The assumption that underlay his central research question was that this type of engagement was necessarily a part of any new faculty member's socialization into a mathematics department. Not until he was several months into his fieldwork did Tim realize the assumed significance of doing mathematics was both irrelevant and potentially misleading for describing what was actually going on in the setting (namely, a lot of talk about how to teach and deal with students).

Clyde Kluckhohn is reputed to have once stated, "If a fish were an anthropologist, the last thing it would discover would be water." Assumptions often work this way—that is, their impact can be felt as a consequence of the familiar being all too familiar. Tim was a mathematician "fish" in his own element. His research question, built around the notion of doing mathematics, served to reinforce what he thought must or should be going on in a community of mathematicians. His assumption kept him focused on an aspect of mathematicians' lives that was true in some cases (including, no doubt, his own experience) but was not valid for the case on which he was focused for his study. Consequently, he spent a great deal of time looking for something that wasn't there and, as he describes, had to revisit the emphasis in his original research question:

> For a good deal of the time on site I struggled with the question of how to pursue my original research questions in a setting in which, based on my definition, mathematics was not being done. To get at how mathematics is important in shaping the social interactions of department members, and how it influenced [my key informant's] enculturation process required a different focus. Rather than looking at what mathematics people are doing, it became necessary to consider people's mathematical biographies, attitudes toward mathematics, and a variety of issues related to teaching mathematics.

For Tim, giving his assumptions the meaningful attention they deserved meant adopting a particular stance toward his inquiry—*making the familiar strange* (Eliot, 1950; Erickson, 1984; Salvio & Schram, 1995; Spindler & Spindler, 1982). The basic strategy entailed in making the familiar strange is to ask questions aimed at unearthing the taken-for-granted aspects of a situation, including assumptions that may be embedded in your research question itself (adapted from Erickson, 1984; Salvio & Schram, 1995):

- Why is this _____ (act, person, situation, concept, question) the way it is and not different?
- What am I leaving out (of my question) and what am I leaving in?
- What is the rationale for my selection of what's left out and what's left in?
- How might someone less familiar with this situation or problem interpret my research question?

These types of considerations are embedded within broader questions about your proper analytic stance as a qualitative researcher—whether it is better to emphasize familiarity or detachment, social engagement or marginality. These issues have been cast and recast over the years as researchers have become better at questioning assumptions about who they are relative to those with whom they interact in the field. Chapter 7's discussion of familiarity will offer some practical guidance about how to position yourself in relation to others as you create and manage your researcher role.

On what basis can I claim that my research question is answerable?

The underlying issue here is straightforward: The data that could provide an answer for your question need to be obtainable through the means you have available. This, of course, raises practical concerns that pertain to available resources, time, access to a site or population, and the like—what Marshall and Rossman (1999) refer to as the "do-ability" of a study.

Underlying this level of practicality, the pivotal concern in addressing answerability is whether your question helps to establish a sense of *boundedness* for your study, a sense that your answers are not *out* there but rather are *somewhere*. To illustrate, consider the following question posed early on by Deb as she "tacked" toward a central research question for her study of educational opportunity (Figure 5.1):

> What does it mean for America, as a democratic society, to have set the goal of ensuring that as many youth as possible continue on to college?

This question functioned well in the developmental role it played, namely, offering a view of the larger conceptual context and then angling Deb toward fresh grounding in a question tied to everyday realities. Had she tried to settle on this question to drive her study, however, it is difficult to envision how she would know where to start and how to proceed (beyond the general indicators of youth, college, and America). Now compare this earlier question with the one she settled upon to orient her study:

> How is equal educational opportunity perceived by students, faculty, and administrators at a post-secondary, open-enrollment institution?

This comparison illustrates a fundamental consideration in assessing the claim of whether a research question is answerable: The question reserves enough flexibility to permit consideration of a range of answers, including unanticipated ones, but also sets, at least provisionally, the boundaries for fieldwork and analysis.

Exercise 5.1
Assessing Your Question's Goodness of Fit

A useful step in confirming the "rightness" of your research question is to respond critically to questions about the logic and reasoning that helped to shape it. Framing your argument with reference to some or all of the questions just described, write a memo that addresses how your tentative research question works for you and why it makes sense. Overall, your memo should focus on the key concern of whether your research question is a good fit for what you want to understand. Specifically, you should ask:

- Is my research question working to address my problem?
- How am I deciding whether my question is too focused or too broad?
- How have I checked for assumptions that may be embedded in my question?
- On what basis can I claim that my research question is answerable?

If you are still trying to sort through alternative versions of a research question, then use this memo to assess the relative strengths and challenges of each choice. Keep in mind that the difference between possible questions might be at the level of a single term or phrase.

To illustrate, look back at Jayson's central question in Figure 5.3. It took quite a bit of critical reflection for Jayson to settle on the word *facilitated* in this question, primarily due to the assumptions and potential misperceptions he believed might be embedded in the term. In a prior memo he had wondered whether *facilitate* was the best term to use if the group trainer was structuring the experience that he or she *wanted* participants to have rather than helping them respond to an experience they were having by chance. In other words, would *facilitated*—rather than *structured* or *designed*—convey enough about how a group trainer's intentions and position of leadership played into the experience? In contrast, would *structured* imply more than he wanted? Consider the point made in a previous section about viewing the work of the research question as creating the capacity for problem finding. In Jayson's case, use of the term *facilitated* did just that: It left room for the play of a leader's intentions but also created space for his or her response to unanticipated experiences.

Purposeful but avoiding prediction. Focused enough to guide decisions in the field. Attentive to assumptions. Flexible within manageable bounds. Your question's goodness of fit works through all of these considerations. One memo won't settle the matter, but starting to address these issues now will make it easier to argue for the focus and logic of your inquiry when it comes time to do so in your research proposal.

Orienting and Rationalizing Your Approach

Key Concern: How do you determine whether your research question is the right question to be asking as a qualitative researcher?

The caution that Wolcott (1999) offers regarding the nature of an ethnographic question holds as well, and in only slightly varied form, for the art of posing questions in the broader context of qualitative inquiry. That is, you should not ask a qualitative question without some idea of what a qualitative answer looks like, some idea of the circumstances under which it does and does not make sense to pursue a qualitative approach beyond a commitment to fieldwork. The prerequisite condition is that you have formed a research question prior to the decision that your inquiry is best pursued by qualitative means. Remember, you choose a qualitative (or any type of) approach because of the nature of the research question, not vice versa. Following this basic premise, your research question plays a dual role. It orients your movement down a qualitative path and helps to rationalize it. That is, it embodies basic considerations that make a particular qualitative approach the more appealing and appropriate way to proceed with an inquiry.

The appeal of qualitative approaches is commonly attributed to the acknowledgment of multiple or partial truths, the need for contextual and holistic description and analysis, concern for the particular nature of occurrences rather than their general character and overall distribution, and the need to consider the meanings that happenings have for the people involved in them. In practical terms, these attributes suggest that qualitative fieldwork is well suited to answering the following types of questions (adapted from Erickson, 1986; Marshall & Rossman, 1999):

- What specific social actions and events are happening within this particular setting?
- What do actions, events, and ideas mean to the people engaged in and with them, and how do these understandings influence their behavior?
- How are events, actions, and meanings influenced by the particular context or unique circumstances in which they occur?
- How do happenings in the setting reflect patterns of behavior, meaning, or interaction? (Or, what plausible relationships are shaping what is happening?)
- How is what is happening in this setting as a whole (e.g., a classroom) related to happenings at other system levels within and beyond the setting (e.g., the school building, a child's family, the local community, federal immigration policies)?

Determining whether a qualitative approach is appropriate to your inquiry requires that you consider the nature of your research question and, in particular, the kind of understanding your study can generate. Maxwell (1992, 1996) offers a useful categorization of kinds of understanding in qualitative inquiry, emphasizing three that pertain most directly to the types of questions qualitative researchers ask:

- descriptive questions that ask what is going on in terms of actual, observable (or potentially observable) events and behavior

  Example: What is the experience of families who participate in Early Head Start? (Patrice)

- **interpretive** questions that seek to explore the meaning of these things for the people involved

  Example: What is the meaning of infant well-being from the perspective of families who participate in Early Head Start? (Patrice)

- **theoretical** questions aimed at examining how these happenings can be explained

  Example: How do participants construct meaning in a facilitated, small group adventure experience? (Jayson)

Qualitative research questions typically start with a *how* or a *what*. This should not be construed as part of some formulaic approach to the construction of research questions, but rather as a useful point of contrast to the *why, to what extent,* or *how much* questions for which qualitative studies are normally not appropriate. Regarding the latter choice of terms, qualitative studies rarely entail the sampling procedures or sample size required to generalize systematically to some wider population or context. So, too, are explicitly evaluative questions a risky and problematic way to orient an approach for which you are the primary research instrument. This does not mean, as Maxwell (1996) points out, "that you can never generalize or evaluate on the basis of a qualitative study, only that such concerns are usually best not incorporated directly into your research questions" (p. 60). Table 5.1 distinguishes among various aims of research questions according to how well they are suited to a qualitative approach.

Table 5.1

The Fit Between Your Question and a Qualitative Approach

Well Suited to Qualitative Inquiry	Not Well Suited to Qualitative Inquiry
Questions aimed at:	*Questions aimed at:*
• documenting real events or cases bounded in time and circumstance	• testing relationships or establishing cause and effect
• understanding how participants in a setting make sense of and give meaning to their lives and experiences	• addressing the generality or wider prevalence of the phenomena being studied
• understanding contextual influences on actions and behaviors	• providing a comparison of groups or a relationship between variables, with the intent of establishing an association or cause and effect
• identifying unanticipated or taken-for-granted influences and phenomena	• predicting outcomes
• understanding processes by which events and actions take place	
• understanding the relationship between a particular scene and its wider social environments	

GOING SOMEWHERE WITH YOUR QUESTION

Defining the Evolution of Your Inquiry

Key Concern: What does it mean for the question you bring to the research setting to "evolve" during the course of your inquiry?

Take a moment to consider what underlies your formulation of a research question. You create the question so that it communicates—in the way good questions do—the heart of what you want to understand. This is one of its essential functions, to serve as an initial indicator that identifies what is primary among your conceptual concerns and that channels your energy in the direction of what you want to know most or need to know first. A carefully formulated research question never loses its significance in this generative and orienting sense.

Now consider the fact that you are carrying this question forward, not toward a bounded experiment with a clearly defined set of variables, but toward a profusion of fieldwork experiences that are going to clamor and compete for center stage in your thinking. "Given their complexity," writes Peshkin (1985a), "field settings seldom contain a single point or story" (p. 214). How you sort out what is central from what is peripheral to your inquiry is likely to change over time, demanding, in turn, that the form and function of your research question also change. Let's see how this might look in Patrice's case.

Patrice decided in the process of designing her study to orient her inquiry around two major research questions, as noted in Figure 5.2. Her central questions reflected the twofold emphasis of her research, addressing, first, the concept of infant mental health and, second, the experience of participation in a program that provided services for families with infants:

1. What is the meaning of infant well-being from the perspective of families who participate in Early Head Start?
2. What is the experience of families who participate in Early Head Start?

The first question, Patrice reasoned, was intended to help her develop a "construct" of infant mental health derived from the meaning given to this notion by families impacted by poverty. It was important for her to understand the perspective of these families, she reasoned, because she was working from the assumption that these families value the well-being of their babies but in ways she did not understand. Her second question was posed to provide information leading to an appraisal of Early Head Start for families who access the services. If families have different goals for their children based on culturally different ways of raising a baby, she reasoned, then understanding their experience in the program could illuminate barriers to their relationships with home visitors and increase the program's effectiveness. Although each question served in this early phase as a candidate for being the ultimate focusing issue of her inquiry, the potential also existed for a central question to evolve, as something of a hybrid, at the intersection of the two. Consider, for example, the following hypothetical outcomes:

- Patrice's first question leads to findings that suggest families impacted by poverty view infant well-being differently than middle-class service providers in Early Head Start.
- Her second question leads to findings that suggest families who participate in Early Head Start experience persistent frustration when trying to convey their needs and questions about their infants' development to the service providers.

- After considering these findings, Patrice asks the question: "How are differing notions of infant well-being negotiated by families and service providers who participate in Early Head Start?"

The fitness and viability of this last question as a freshly honed focus for her research stem from when and how the question evolved. For Patrice, in this hypothetical scenario, the "differing notions" question was generated out of the dialectical process of linking ideas in her mind with what she observed and documented. This might be thought of as the *orienting phase* of field inquiry, a phase defined in large part by the deferral of judgment on what may be most significant to study in greater depth. In formulating her original two questions, Patrice had some notion of what was out there to be found, but the phrasing of these questions reflected a movement toward (not from) judgment; she did not merely set forth a prior, unsubstantiated hunch to be "tested" against data still to be gathered. In her emergent question, Patrice could ground—in solid data—her claim that differing views existed.

Does this mean that Patrice should substitute this last question for the first two as the central question in her research? Certainly not. The emergence of this question does not alter the fact that her research was driven initially by the first two questions; their original qualities and contributions are unimpaired by this reformulation. In particular, their significance in defining the evolution of her inquiry—and particularly, in reconstructing changes in her thinking about what was primary in her research conception—remains as vital as ever. The underlying point of this example is that your research questions serve a number of different functions, which vary in importance at different phases of the research.[1]

Exercise 5.2
Ensuring That Your Purpose and Question Work Together

The aim of this exercise is to help ensure that your research question and your statement of purpose complement rather than compete with each other. Bear in mind that your research question is not simply a restatement of your purpose in the form of a question. Both serve to highlight the issues you want to understand, but your question should do more to point you toward specific research action. For example, here is the statement of purpose from Patrice's study:

> The purpose of this study is to explore the social context of infants born into poverty and to understand the home visiting relationship when families receive intervention services from home visitors who are socially and economically different from them.

[1] I am grateful to Joseph Maxwell who, in his review of an earlier draft of this chapter, helped me to make this point more explicit.

Here are her central research questions:

> What is the meaning of infant well-being from the perspective of families who participate in Early Head Start?
>
> What is the experience of families who participate in Early Head Start?

Note how her research questions give specific shape to her stated purpose by putting into play particular concepts and issues, positioning them as potentially significant in relation to particular people and contexts. This effectively sets in motion procedures for what she might actually do and ask in the research setting. A good statement of purpose, in other words, serves to orient one's *interests,* while a good research question serves to orient one's *actions.*

For this exercise, revisit the memos you wrote on research purpose and focus in Chapter 2 (Exercises 2.1 and 2.2). With your own proposed research question in hand, write a new memo that clarifies how your research question and your statement of purpose complement and strengthen each other. You might address some or all of the following concerns:

- How does your research question connect with your purpose(s) for conducting the study? Or, alternatively, how will answering this research question help you achieve your research purpose(s)?
- Is your research question consistent with what you claim to be the focus and locus of your inquiry?
- How is your research question orienting you toward decisions about the selection of study participants and methods in a general sense (that is, interviewing, observing, participating, or some combination of these) that you might use?

SUMMARY OF KEY POINTS

- Moving toward a viable research question is a dialectical process in which you shift creatively between questions that emphasize breadth of vision and precision of focus. This process is built in part on the distinction between questions that formulate what you want to understand and questions you actually ask to gain that understanding.
- Justifying your question refers to how you assess the goodness of fit between your research question and what you want to understand by doing the study. Assessment of this fit includes consideration of the following: how your research question works to address your problem, how you decide whether your question is too focused or too broad, how you check for assumptions embedded in your question, and how you determine whether your question is answerable.

- Formation of your research question should *precede* the decision that your inquiry is best pursued by qualitative means.
- As a qualitative researcher, you should expect your perspective and your question to evolve in the course of sorting out what is central from what is peripheral to your inquiry.
- Your research question should keep you focused on what is actually going on in a setting. It should reflect what you want to know rather than what you think is going on or what you think the answer might be.
- Research questions are in most cases the result of an interactive design process rather than the starting point for that process. They give specific shape to your stated purposes and make explicit what you want to learn.

RECOMMENDED READING

Processes of formulating and judging the adequacy of research questions have not received the attention they deserve in the qualitative research literature. One notable exception is Maxwell (2005), who describes a number of helpful distinctions between types of research questions not included here. Creswell (2003) offers a brief but practical chapter on qualitative research questions within a framework that contrasts them to questions developed for quantitative and mixed methods studies.

Chapter 6

CHOOSING A RESEARCH APPROACH

When and how do I lay claim to a particular research approach? How do I decide which is the most appropriate approach with which to align myself? Must I adopt a research approach in its entirety, or can I draw upon selected aspects of it to guide my inquiry? How does the process of deciding how to identify my research approach help to clarify and strengthen my inquiry?

A central message of this chapter is conveyed by Kenneth Burke's oft-quoted statement, "A way of seeing is always a way of not seeing" (1935, p. 70). Your decision to commit yourself to or associate yourself with a particular research approach reflects the potential you believe to be gained from that perspective. An informed decision also takes into account the limitations or blind spots that commitment to a particular approach might entail.

The allure of affixing an impressive-sounding methodological label to the research you are doing is undeniable, drawn as we all are to the sense of comfort and validation that comes with being able to say "I'm doing an ethnography" or "I'm using a constructivist grounded theory approach." Timing in this regard does matter, as does a discriminating eye. As noted in previous chapters, claiming a particular methodological label as a first step is inadvisable. Doing so suggests that your chosen research approach can serve as an all-purpose vehicle suitable for any problem, without apparent regard for what that problem or the accompanying research question might be. Your decision about how to proceed should always follow decisions about why, where, around what concerns, and from what perspective you are proceeding.

The assumption underlying this chapter is that you are bringing to your methodological considerations the definition of problem, the clarity of purpose and perspective, and the focus of questions that enable you to establish the appropriateness of a particular research approach. The following sections proceed from this assumption and explore what it means to be an informed and discriminating decision maker when it comes time to affix a label to your research efforts.

Thinking Ahead to Your Research Proposal. This aspect of your work takes shape in your eventual research proposal directly and almost wholly in the section on Research Procedures. Thinking of your procedures as a *course of action*—a point I reiterate in Chapter 9—means that you should have a clear sense of the decisions leading up to your choice of a particular research approach. This chapter will help you work through these decisions about the strategies and methods you will eventually employ during fieldwork.

DEFINING RESEARCH APPROACHES

My decision to attend to certain research traditions and frameworks but not others in this chapter filters down to considerations of practicality, perception, and purpose. Qualitative researchers have never agreed among themselves about what to make of the differences and commonalities among their approaches, except to concur that there exists an almost baffling number of classifications or typologies from which to choose (see Chapter 1). My aim is not to try to resolve or account for these differing views, but to clarify how commitment to a particular approach to research predisposes you to a characteristic way of seeing and sets you up to achieve your purposes in certain ways.

Tradition, Method, and Analytic Framework

It is important to maintain a clear distinction between research tradition and research method, as well as the further distinction between these two terms and analytic framework. When I speak of ethnography, grounded theory, and phenomenology as qualitative research *traditions*, I am defining them as rigorous, discipline-based, carefully specified ways to conceptualize, describe, and analyze human social behavior and processes (building on Wolcott, 1992, p. 37). Wolcott's (1999) useful distinction between a *way of seeing* (directing attention to perspective and intent) and a *way of looking* (directing attention to methods and procedures), although applied specifically to ethnography in his case, conveys the twofold nature of the definition I am using here.

To illustrate, phenomenology is not a method in and of itself, although it does incorporate specific methods. A study can be labeled phenomenological if it borrows techniques or methods associated with phenomenology. But a researcher should not claim to be doing phenomenology (or ethnography or grounded theory) solely on the basis of technique. Such claims rest more substantially on one's commitment to a research perspective that includes standards for what is worth knowing and how it is to be applied. Similarly, Charmaz's (2000) statement that "grounded theory methods specify analytic strategies, not data collection methods" (p. 514) seems to bolster the idea that taking on a research approach entails more than simply using particular fieldwork tools.

In accordance with this view I do not label narrative inquiry a tradition, but include it as a viable and valuable approach to consider. It does not fall within the sole grasp of any specific disciplinary field but touches quite a number of them, a point on which there are illuminating differences of opinion. Clandinin and Connelly (2000), for example, trace its origins in the social sciences, but note particular influences from history, literary theory, anthropology, and certain forms of psychology. Riessman (2002b) lists no less than seven possible disciplinary homes for narrative. Rossman and Rallis (1998) associate it with phenomenology, but not exclusively. Following Seale and his colleagues (2004), I choose to label narrative as an *analytic framework*, highlighting its strategic value in terms of conceptualizing and interrogating data in a particular way. (It is instructive to note the proportionally greater number of texts entitled narrative *analysis* rather than narrative *research*.) In this sense, it is perhaps more a way of looking than of seeing, although I think we should be mindful of those, most notably Bruner (1990) and Rosaldo (1989), who regard narrative as a fundamental organizing principle for how people make sense of the world. For our purposes here, I encourage a practical embrace of narrative's interdisciplinary nature and, mindful of the qualitative conversations introduced in Chapter 1, see tremendous value in highlighting the research options and opportunities that narrative can provide.

The seemingly omnipresent case study does not implicate any particular tradition, but is the approach of choice for many researchers. Its popularity tends to mask debate over the way in which it seems to be at home almost everywhere in the qualitative arena, but grounded nowhere in particular. For that matter, a case study need not even be qualitative (Stake, 2000; Yin, 1994). Two of the leading texts on case study research (Merriam, 1998; Stake 1995) locate their operating assumptions in a relatively generic vision of qualitative research and naturalistic inquiry; they suggest that case studies can be ethnographic, historical, psychological, biographical, or sociological, among many other options. These authors join other researchers (e.g., Yin, 1994) in regarding the case study as an identifiable method or strategy, in contrast to those who treat it simply as an end product or format for reporting a range of qualitative work (Wolcott, 2001). Creswell (1998), citing the broad interdisciplinary evolution of case study in political science, sociology, and other social sciences, chooses to label it a research tradition.

Where does that leave us? Is case study a distinct strategy or method? Is it, by itself, a way of conceptualizing human social behavior and processes? Or does it need to be linked to discipline-based approaches like ethnography or history to be considered in such a comprehensive manner? Wherever you stand, case study is insistently present in considerations about qualitative research, and you should at least be aware of what it does and does not offer you as a researcher. I will address definitions, issues, and disagreements surrounding its use immediately following the sections on ethnography, phenomenology, grounded theory, and narrative.

I acknowledge that the distinctions I make regarding any of these approaches place me on contested terrain, but my aim is to be illustrative rather than exhaustive. Through a closer look at these influential and frequently used qualitative approaches—ethnography, grounded theory, phenomenology, narrative, and case study—I hope to suggest how commitment to a particular methodological frame of reference influences and informs an inquiry in distinct ways.

The bulk of this chapter is devoted to helping you establish a preliminary level of identification and comfort with a research approach. To this end, I have organized the discussion around two methodological concerns: how to distinguish among research options and how to assess the appropriateness of your decision to use a particular approach.

DISTINGUISHING AMONG OPTIONS

**What are some key distinguishing features of selected approaches
to field-based qualitative research?**

As suggested in the previous pages, distinctions among research approaches turn more on ways of seeing than ways of looking. Ways of looking—observing, asking, and examining what others have done—are notably similar across many qualitative research traditions. Ways of seeing—encompassing underlying intent, guiding concerns, focus, and perspective—are not so similar. To be an ethnographer, a phenomenologist, a grounded theorist, or a narrativist, you must develop a sense of what constitutes, respectively, an ethnographic, phenomenological, grounded theory, or narrative problem and question. Then you must come to terms with what concepts and assumptions guide an inquiry so that it results in that type of study. The considerations contained within these last two statements frame the following examination of research approaches.

Ethnography

The following summary draws upon the work of Agar (1996), Atkinson, Coffey, and Delamont (2003), Atkinson and Hammersley (1994), Brumann (1999), Delamont (2004), Emerson, Fretz, and Shaw (1995), Geertz (1984), Kuper (1999), LeCompte and Schensul (1999), Peacock (1986), Wolcott (1999), and Zou and Trueba (2002). For in-depth exploration of the following ideas, I encourage you to consult these sources.

The Focus and Purpose of Ethnography
Unlike other forms of qualitative research, the defining characteristic of ethnography is that it is oriented toward the description and interpretation of cultural behaviors, as reflected in the following definition:

> The underlying purpose of ethnographic research . . . is to describe what the people in some particular place or status ordinarily do, and the meanings they ascribe to what they do, under ordinary or particular circumstances, presenting that description in a manner that draws attention to regularities that implicate cultural process. (Wolcott, 1999, p. 68)

The term *ethnography* represents both a process and a product. Ethnographic fieldwork, rooted in cultural anthropology and undertaken most commonly as participant observation, is the process by which a researcher comes to discern patterns and regularities of behavior in human social activity. The process embraces multiple techniques, demands prolonged time in the field, and requires deep appreciation for the characteristic ethnographic tension of holding together corroborative, contrasting, and even incompatible perspectives as a necessary condition for documenting what is actually going on (Schram, 2000).

The ethnographic text, or product, is the means through which these cultural patterns, processes, and behaviors are interpreted and portrayed. Scholars generally agree that culture itself is not visible or tangible but is constructed by the act of ethnographic interpretation and writing (Kuper, 1999; Schwandt, 2001).

Basic Assumptions of the Ethnographer

- Human behavior and the ways in which people construct and make sense of their lives are highly variable and locally specific.
- Social behavior and interaction reflect varying patterns of what *should* occur (ideal behavior), what *does* occur (actual behavior), and what *might* occur (projective behavior).
- It is possible to discern these patterns of socially acquired and shared behavior through *experiencing* (observing and participating in people's lives and activities) and *inquiring* (asking people about their experiences and the meanings they ascribe to them).
- Before you can offer interpretations of people's actions and behaviors, you must uncover what they actually do and the reasons they give for doing it.
- The representation or interpretation you construct of people's lives and behavior is neither "theirs" nor "yours." Instead, it is built upon the points of understanding and misunderstanding that occur between you and them.
- Ethnography cannot provide an exhaustive, absolute description of anything. Rather, ethnographic descriptions are necessarily partial, bound by what can be handled within a certain time, under specific circumstances, and from a particular perspective.

Orienting Concepts of Ethnography

Culture. Culture is the knowledge that ethnographers construct "to show how acts in the context of one world can be understood as coherent from the point of view of another world" (Agar, 1996, p. 33). In other words, culture is an abstraction, an analytic framework that ethnographers apply to provide an underlying cohesiveness to their description of the common behaviors, concepts, and practices that arise when people interact regularly. This also means that culture is not something that groups of people "have," particularly in the obsolete use of the term to convey an exhaustive description of isolated, traditional communities in which each member always and only participates. That's how culture grew up as a concept in the "old days" when anthropologists needed to invent an idea of what they studied when they conducted fieldwork in some far-flung corner of the world. Times have changed, as have understandings of how we make sense of differences, similarities, and points of misunderstanding among people.

Ethnographers describe evidence of certain *cultural patterns*—people sharing or withholding information as clues to their assumptions about power, for example—but culture itself remains an abstraction that they make based on such evidence. The fallacy lies in treating the abstraction *culture* as a concrete thing that can be observed firsthand or that can do this or that. When you see the term *culture* used as a convenient label to name a problem—"That school's culture is really dysfunctional!"—you should take some time to consider what particular issues and questions are left hidden or unexamined behind that characterization.

To describe culture as an abstraction is not to say that the attitudes, beliefs, and other acquired social behaviors that people manifest, which we categorize under the concept *culture*, are not real; all of these human dispositions have reality and power in everyday experience. Nor does ethnography's overarching concern with cultural interpretation mean that an explicit cultural framework must be imposed on every study. But for a study to be ethnographic, it "must provide the kind of account of human social activity out of which cultural patterning can be discerned" (Wolcott, 1999, p. 68).

Holism or Contextualization. In describing what it means to "perceive holistically," anthropologist James Peacock (1986) tells the story of a Russian factory worker who habitually pushed his wheelbarrow through the factory gate at quitting time. Every evening the guards inspected the wheelbarrow and, after determining it was empty, let the worker pass. Months went by before it was discovered that the worker was stealing wheelbarrows. The guards' mistake, as Peacock explains, was to inspect the contents but not the carrier and his circumstances, to focus narrowly on the parts and not the whole, to fail to see holistically.

The concept of holism orients ethnographers toward an examination of things in their entirety rather than only in parts. Some ethnographers prefer the term *contextual* rather than holistic, although the two are not synonymous. The distinction is subtle but instructive. Holism seems to point to completeness or to the idea of something being greater than the sum of its parts. Contextualization suggests a more dynamic and dialectic process of making connections between parts and between parts and the whole (Agar, 1996; cf. Wolcott, 1999). Accordingly, instances of observed behavior make sense as part of a larger picture; in turn, that larger picture is continually brought into view through examination of its parts (Geertz, 1984).

This movement between parts and whole as a way of understanding both, which is central to ethnographic interpretation, can also refer to the trajectory of what is called the *hermeneutic circle.* Simply stated, and as originally applied to a text, the interpretation of each part depends on the interpretation of the whole, and vice versa. The notion of a circle, explains

Schwandt (2001), highlights the idea that "every interpretation relies on other interpretations" (p. 112).

Holism is not an invitation to "fill up" a study. Rather, a holistic and/or contextual perspective invites consideration of how parts and whole fit together so that ethnographers can "present human social behavior as *more*, rather than *less*, complex, to keep explanations from becoming simplistic or reductionist" (Wolcott, 1999, p. 79).

The Nature of Ethnographic Questions

Given the strong descriptive aspect of ethnography, ethnographic questions focus on what ethnographers are looking at and looking for in a particular context of human behavior and activity. By tradition and by design, ethnographic questions also position researchers to be especially attentive to the broad social context in which human behavior and activity occur.

Considered together, these seemingly opposing ways of posing questions—bringing into focus the encompassing milieu of an experience as well as the specific experience itself—inform ethnography's holistic perspective. Or, as framed in simple terms by Wolcott (1999), "A question such as 'What is going on here?' can only be addressed when fleshed out with enough detail to answer the related question, 'In terms of what?'" (p. 69). With this in mind, consider once again the research questions posed by Patrice in her study of families served by Early Head Start:

1. What is the meaning of infant well-being from the perspective of families who participate in Early Head Start?
2. What is the experience of families who participate in Early Head Start?

The first question addresses the need for her inquiry to reflect the focus and details of her description (the meaning of well-being, the experience of participation) as well as how she is choosing to render this description (from the perspective of families). The second question suggests a softening of her focus, broadening her depth of field so that she does not miss the place of these behaviors and meanings in context.

Such dual emphases illustrate the complementary themes contained within an ethnographic perspective: a sharp focus on the circumstances of observed behavior and a holistic breadth of vision that embraces, and works toward making explicit, the shared understandings of culture.

A Word on Critical Ethnography

In Chapter 3 I introduced several research perspectives, including those consistent with a critical approach. What is commonly termed the *critical* ethnographic tradition deserves more attention than I am able to provide here, especially given the range and diversity of perspectives among critical ethnographers. Even so, it is important that you are at least aware of its significance and the ways it might influence your own approach to ethnography.

Most commentaries on the changing trajectories of ethnography generally agree that a new orientation took root in the early 1970s. Works such as *Learning to Labor* by Paul Willis (1977) redefined the nature of ethnographic research in a critical manner and inspired a wealth of critical studies. Now, nearly three decades later, we can look to an increasingly rich store of studies and theoretical frameworks that have firmly established critical ethnography's presence and influence. Methodologically, most critical ethnographers, regardless of their specific critical orientation, still employ the traditional ethnographic techniques embodied in prolonged, systematic fieldwork with key participants. Unlike traditional ethnographers, however, they bring to their empirical work a more collaborative stance framed by a "serious political intent to change people's consciousness, if not their daily lives" (Foley, 2002, p. 140). Studies of this kind are often, though not necessarily, informed by Marxist and post-Marxist theory and tend to produce focused ethnographies of societal institutions or subgroups with intent to change the status quo.

Critical ethnography is not something that you simply decide to take on as an approach. Nor does it mean simply "biasing" your work in the direction of social justice. To paraphrase Fine and her colleagues (2000, p. 123), it demands an acknowledgment of responsibility to talk about your identity as a researcher, why you question what you do, what you choose not to report, how you frame your data, on whom you focus attention, and who is protected and not protected as you conduct your research. It requires an understanding of the historical and theoretical roots of critical research. It means engaging in a kind of scholarship/action that places you in a participatory framework of researching with and for individuals and groups in the interest of social justice. Your reflections on, and responses to, such responsibilities as a researcher need to inform any decision you make to proceed as a critical ethnographer.

For further insight into these ideas and the emergence of critical ethnography, I encourage you to consult Carspecken (1996, 2002), Fine, Weis, Weseen, and Wong (2000), Foley (2002), and Kincheloe and McLaren (2002), to list just a few of many helpful references. If you want to delve right into some exemplary book-length critical ethnographies, a good starting point might be *The Unknown City* (Fine & Weis, 1998), *Practice Makes Practice* (Britzman, 1991), or *The Heartland Chronicles* (Foley, 1995).

Phenomenology

The following summary draws upon the work of Benner (1994), Cohen and Omery (1994), Giorgi (1994, 1997), Holstein and Gubrium (1994), Laverty (2003), Moustakas (1994), Polkinghorne (1989), Ray (1994), Schutz (1967, 1970), Seidman (1998), Stewart and Mickunas (1990), and Van Manen (1997). For further exploration and clarification of these ideas and concepts, I encourage you to consult these sources.

The Focus and Purpose of Phenomenology

Phenomenological studies investigate the meaning of the lived experience of a small group of people from the standpoint of a concept or phenomenon. Rooted in the philosophical perspectives of Edmund Husserl (1859–1938) and subsequent philosophical discussions by Heidegger, Merleau-Ponty, and Schutz, phenomenology in its varied forms has figured prominently to influence research approaches in sociology, psychology, nursing and the health sciences, and education.[1]

Phenomenological researchers, particularly those of a descriptive bent, focus on what an experience means for persons who have had the experience and are able to provide a comprehensive description of it. The underlying assumption is that dialogue and reflection can reveal the essence—the essential, invariant structure or central underlying meaning—of some aspect of shared experience (e.g., the essential structure of a respectful interaction between

---

[1]It is beyond the scope of this text to explore in depth the range of philosophical camps under the phenomenological banner. Potential users of this approach should have some knowledge of the philosophical underpinnings of what it means to study how people experience a phenomenon, looking to references such as Stewart and Mickunas (1990) as a good place to start. Researchers in education and the social sciences might be especially attentive to distinctions between social phenomenology (see Holstein & Gubrium, 1994; Schutz, 1967, 1970) and psychological phenomenology (see Giorgi, 1994, 1997; Moustakas, 1994; Polkinghorne, 1989; Tesch, 1990).

parent and teacher, or the essence of being a participant in a particular program). A phenomenological description is not just an idiosyncratic perspective of an experience or subjective opinion of a meaning. The researcher seeks to convey a meaning that is fundamental to the experience no matter which specific individual has had that experience.

As Polkinghorne (1989) suggests, the reader of a phenomenological study should come away with the feeling, "I understand better what it is like to experience that" (p. 46). Typically, phenomenologists generate information through long, in-depth interviews (see Seidman, 1998), augmented by critical self-reflection by the researcher. It does not offer theory but rather plausible insights that bring you in more direct contact with the world of your study participants (van Manen, 1997).

Basic Assumptions of the Phenomenologist

- Human behavior occurs and is understandable only in the context of relationships to things, people, events, and situations.
- *Perceptions* present us with evidence of the world, not as the world is thought to be but as it is lived. Thus, understanding the everyday life of a group of people is a matter of understanding how those people perceive and act upon objects of experience.
- The reality of anything is not "out there" in an objective or detached sense but is inextricably tied to one's consciousness of it. Phenomenologists discuss this idea in terms of the *intentionality of consciousness.* Accordingly, you cannot develop an understanding of a phenomenon apart from understanding people's experience of or with that phenomenon.
- Language is the central medium through which meaning is constructed and conveyed. Thus, the meaning of a particular aspect of experience can be revealed through dialogue and reflection.
- It is possible to understand and convey the *essence,* or central underlying meaning, of a particular concept or phenomenon as experienced by a number of individuals. This premise is associated primarily with descriptive phenomenology, an approach that rests on the thesis that essential structures constitute any human experience.

Orienting Concepts of Phenomenology

Epoché. This refers to the ability to suspend, distance ourselves from, or "bracket" our judgments and preconceptions about the nature and essence of experiences and events in the everyday world. This is an integral part of the phenomenologist's approach: to suspend judgments about what is real until they are founded on a more certain description of how everyday life (or some aspect of it) is produced and experienced by its members. Such bracketing lies at the heart of the "phenomenological attitude" and sets that posture apart from what Schutz (1970) labeled the "natural attitude," which assumes that the world is "out there," separate and distinct from our perceptions or interpretations of it (Holstein & Gubrium, 1994). Thus, phenomenological descriptions focus not on things (what is) but on their meaning (the nature of what is).

Life-world. The *life-world* refers to one's ordinary conscious experience of everyday life and social action. It encompasses the practical reasoning and commonsense knowledge that people take for granted. In these terms, the aim of phenomenology is to describe what the life-world consists of or, more specifically, what are the concepts and essential structures of experience that give form and meaning to the life-world (Schwandt, 2001). As you explore various qualitative conversations, you may encounter the term *life-world* used in similar ways by different types of researchers. For example, in building his explanation of discourse analysis, Gee (1999) describes "the lifeworld" as "all those contexts in which we humans think, act, and communicate as 'everyday' people and not as 'specialists' (e.g., physicists, doctors or lawyers, etc.)" (p. 45). People's ways of knowing in this life-world are thus locally situated and grounded in actual practices and experiences.

The Nature of Phenomenological Questions

Phenomenological questions are targeted toward understanding the meaning of lived experience and the essence of a particular concept or phenomenon. For example, had Patrice proceeded with her study in the manner of a phenomenologist, she might have attempted to substantiate the essential structure of a caring service provider–family interaction during a home visit. (We would have to assume, as well, that her definition of problem, purposes, conceptual context, and so on had helped to establish her problem and question as best suited to a phenomenological approach.) She might then have stated her research question as follows:

> From the perspective of a parent whose family participates in Early Head Start, what is the essential structure of a caring service provider–family interaction?

or

> What is essential for the home visit experience to be described by the parent as a caring interaction?

These types of questions translate into a type of inquiry that encompasses basic tenets of a phenomenological approach:

- The researcher enters the field of perception of participants.
- The researcher sees how participants experience, live, and describe the phenomenon.
- The researcher looks for the meaning of the participants' experiences (Creswell, 1998).

Not explicitly conveyed by either of these questions but just as integral to a phenomenological approach would be Patrice's commitment to set aside, or bracket, her preconceptions about the nature of the home visit experience. The only explicit assumption she might carry into this inquiry, one that she would likely address and substantiate in her conceptual context, would be to suggest that there is an essential structure of a caring interaction in the home visit situation. The nature and substance of that interaction would be the focus of her study.

Grounded Theory

The following summary draws upon the work of Annells (1996), Charmaz (1990, 2000, 2002), Charmaz and Mitchell (2002), Clarke (2003), Glaser (1978, 1992), Glaser and Strauss (1967), Melia (1996), Piantanida, Tananis, and Grubs (2004), Stern (1994), Strauss (1987), and Strauss and Corbin (1994, 1998). For further exploration and clarification of the following ideas, I encourage you to consult these sources.

The Focus and Purpose of Grounded Theory

The explicit aim of grounded theory is to develop a substantive theory that is derived from and grounded in data. Or, if an existing theory seems appropriate but somehow inadequate relative to a topic of inquiry, then this theory may be elaborated and modified as the researcher plays additional and ongoing instances of data against it. Conventional grounded theory has focused on generating the *basic social process* occurring in the data—that is, the basic form of human action in the situation of concern (Clarke, 2003; Glaser, 2002). For example, grounded theorists have studied *surviving* and *coping with* sexual abuse (Morrow & Smith, 1995), *living with* chronic illness (Charmaz, 1991), *crafting* scientific work (Fujimura, 1996).

Grounded theory proposes a methodological stance and set of tools designed to lead to theory, based on the study of social situations, rather than being an actual theory itself. In this regard, specific analytic strategies, not data collection methods, are what distinguish it as a form of qualitative research (Charmaz, 2000). Grounded theorists generally begin analysis as soon as there are data. As researchers code (give temporary labels) to particular phenomena (data), they also begin theorizing, however provisionally, based on that data. They determine whether codes and categories generated through one data source also appear elsewhere and, if so, continue to build on the properties of those codes and categories. Continued sampling of data is not necessarily based on researchers' efforts to be representative of some population, but is focused on finding new data sources (persons or things) that can help them elaborate upon the provisional theory that they are developing through ongoing analysis. Since its formal beginnings in the late 1960s, most grounded theory research has relied on fieldwork to generate (primarily interview) data through which to analyze human action and social processes (see Glaser, 1993, for an edited volume of examples).

A Common Misunderstanding About Grounded Theory. The term *grounded theory* is often used in a nonspecific way to refer to any approach to developing theories or concepts that somehow begins with data. This unfortunate and misleading characterization relates to a fundamental misunderstanding regarding practice. The fallacy pertains to the notion that the researcher enters a setting as a "blank slate" who gathers data and then watches theory emerge inductively from the data. In fact, the task is far from purely inferential. This complex process incorporates varying emphases of induction, deduction, verification, and/or conceptualization (depending on which grounded theory scholars you base your approach), bringing together prior theoretical commitments with emergent and evolving analytical schemes.

Forms of Grounded Theory Research. Grounded theory is rooted in the sociological work of Barney G. Glaser and the late Anselm L. Strauss in the 1960s. As originally conceived and reflected in their pioneering book, *The Discovery of Grounded Theory* (1967), the approach reflected basic tenets of symbolic interactionism and highlighted the authors' respective expertise in the inductive development of theory (Glaser) and qualitative field research (Strauss). To some researchers, most notably Glaser, grounded theory represents the one "homegrown" methodology true to symbolic interactionism.

In subsequent decades, differing perspectives about conducting grounded theory research, including separate tracks developed by Glaser and by Strauss, led to several dominant designs: the systematic approach associated with Strauss and Corbin (1994, 1998), the emerging approach associated with Glaser (1992), and the constructivist approach associated with Charmaz (1990, 2000, 2002). To supplement the following brief summary of distinctions, see the thorough discussions by Creswell (2002), Babchuk (1997), and Melia (1996).

Arguably the most widely known and applied grounded theory approach, the *systematic* design of Strauss and Corbin is also the design most associated with detailed, rigorous techniques for data analysis. Prescribed procedures in the form of coding categories and subcategories, and the development of a visual diagram to present the theory thus generated, are characteristic components of this approach. A grounded theory study of this type might conclude with propositions that explain the relationships among categories contributing to the developed theory.

In a break from his earlier work with Strauss, Glaser (1992) proposed an *emerging* design that counters what he believed was Strauss and Corbin's overemphasis on a preconceived framework for categories and for theory verification rather than theory generation. Glaser's more flexible and less prescribed approach does not force theory into categories but instead focuses on connecting categories and emerging theory according to a set of criteria that includes fit, work, relevance, and modifiability (see Glaser, 1992).

Charmaz's *constructivist* approach counters what she sees as a descriptive emphasis on facts and acts in the other two designs with a more subjective emphasis on the feelings, assumptions, and meaning making of study participants. It does not assume, as in the other more objectivist approaches, that some external reality is waiting to be discovered by an unbiased observer who records facts about that reality. Rather, this approach grants greater significance to the mutual construction of data by researcher and participant in the process—framing interview materials more as "views" than as hard facts, for example—and also avoids predetermined categories as might be found, for example, in Strauss and Corbin's coding scheme.

A continuum encompassing these various approaches might reflect, at one end, an objectivist pull to "let the data speak for themselves" (e.g., Glaser, 2002) and, at the other end, a constructivist stance that requires concepts to "earn their way into the analysis" (Charmaz, 2003, p. 320). All variants of grounded theory, however, include the following strategies, as summarized by Charmaz (2002, p. 313):

- simultaneous data collection and analysis
- pursuit of emergent themes through early data analysis
- discovery of basic social processes within the data
- inductive construction of abstract categories that explain and synthesize these processes
- sampling to refine the categories through comparative processes
- integration of categories into a theoretical framework that specifies causes, conditions, and consequences of the studied processes.

In sum, each approach demands accountability to the data while at the same time helping researchers to avoid forcing their explanations on the data or making an early appeal to existing concepts in the literature.

Basic Assumptions of the Grounded Theorist

- Human beings are purposive agents who take an active role in interpreting and responding to problematic situations rather than simply reacting to experiences and stimuli.
- People act on the basis of meaning, and this meaning is defined and redefined through interaction.
- Reality is negotiated between people (that is, socially constructed) and is constantly changing and evolving.
- Central to understanding the evolving nature of events is an awareness of the interrelationships among causes, conditions, and consequences.
- A theory is not the formulation of some discovered aspect of a reality that already exists "out there." Rather, theories are provisional and fallible interpretations, limited in time (historically embedded) and constantly in need of qualification.
- Generating theory and doing social research are part of the same process.

Orienting Concepts

Theory. As described by grounded theorists Strauss and Corbin (1994), theory consists of plausible and provisional relationships the researcher proposes among concepts and sets of concepts. The assumption is that the plausibility of a theory can be strengthened through continued research; that is, tentative theories or theoretical propositions are further explored and refined through application to additional instances of data. Researchers can aim at various levels of theory, but most grounded theorists direct their efforts toward developing *substantive* theory that stays close to the data to explain the case at hand rather than higher-level "general" or "grand" theory (see Schwandt, 1997, for further explanation of these distinctions).

In sum, two features of grounded theory are especially notable: (1) grounded theories are always traceable to the data that gave rise to them, and (2) grounded theories are fluid and provisional, demanding a reexploration of their relevance and goodness of fit with each new situation that emerges.

Conceptual Density. Grounded theorists seek to construct theory that is *conceptually dense*—that is, a theory that contains many relationships among concepts. In contrast to the phenomenological concern for the essence or essential structure of a concept or phenomenon, for example, grounded theorists are interested in evolving patterns of action and interaction among events and happenings, and hence with capturing process analytically (Strauss & Corbin, 1998). The constructivist grounded theory approach (see Charmaz, 1990, 2000) would vary this emphasis on relationships among facts and acts to incorporate the feelings and perspectives of participants, including the researcher, as they experience and give meaning to a process. For example, whereas objectivist grounded theorists like Strauss and Corbin might assume that a particular term in the data (e.g., "independence") holds the same meaning for participants as for the researcher, constructivists would tend not to make such an assumption.

Constant Comparison. In the process of analysis, grounded theorists employ the method of *constant comparison*. This method reflects the characteristic stance of refusal to accept a report at face value. The researcher is constantly asking not only "What is going on here?" but also "How is it different?" In this sense, it is a self-corrective process in which the researcher draws upon analysis of one set of data to guide analysis of the next set (Charmaz, 2000, 2002).

As summarized by Schwandt (2001), constant comparison means that the researcher looks at indicators or incidents from the data (actions, events, perspectives) for similarities and differences. From this the analyst identifies underlying uniformities in the indicators and constructs a preliminary category or concept. These categories are compared with each other and with additional indicators from the data to further define the concept. The researcher develops theories by proposing plausible relationships among concepts, and these theories are reexplored through additional instances of data. The process goes on until additional analysis no longer contributes anything new about a concept—that is, until *theoretical saturation* is reached.

The Nature of Grounded Theory Questions

Research questions in grounded theory tend to reflect an interest in understanding a process or change over time. For example, had Patrice proceeded with her study as a grounded theorist, she might have focused on how some dimension of the home visitation process in Early Head Start (e.g., the nature of the family/home visitor relationship or social class differences) influenced family experiences or interactions. She might then have proposed a research question like the following:

> How does the home visitation process in Early Head Start affect participants' perceptions and priorities regarding the parent-infant relationship?

Or, working with a different aim and another core concept:

> What is the influence of social class on the nature of interactions and the development of relationships between families and home visitors in the Early Head Start program?

Both questions reflect the grounded theorist's commitment to understanding the ways reality is socially constructed. And each, in its own way, sets Patrice up to remain close to her data and build categories systematically from incident to incident (e.g., home visit to home visit) and from incident to category. A category for the process addressed in the first question might turn out to be the parents' understanding of infant well-being or definition of help-seeking behavior. The second question, in particular, would orient Patrice toward tracing the influences of class differences as precisely as possible. She would also study influences flowing in the reverse direction (i.e., the impact of developing relationships on perceptions of class differences). In both cases, she would proceed with a single story line, offering a core concept and its attendant theory as a way of making sense of the data.

Narrative Inquiry

The following summary draws upon the work of Andrews, Sclater, Squire, and Tamboukou (2004), Clandinin and Connelly (2000), Coffey and Atkinson (1996, Chapter 3), Cortazzi (1993, 2002), Czarniawska (1998, 2002), Daiute and Lightfoot (2004), Gee (1996), Labov and Waletzky (1997), Mishler (1986), Polkinghorne (1988, 1995), and Riessman (1993, 2002a, 2002b). For in-depth exploration of the following ideas, I encourage you to consult these sources.

The Focus and Purpose of Narrative Inquiry

Narrative researchers focus on the ways in which people "produce, represent, and contextualize experience and personal knowledge through narratives" (Coffey & Atkinson, 1996, p. 54). The aim is to understand how people structure the flow of experience to make sense of events and actions in their lives. This form of inquiry builds upon people's natural impulse to tell stories about past events and personal experiences. Not surprisingly, some researchers have conveyed the gist of narrative inquiry through stories of their own work. Both Czarniawska (2002) and Riessman (2002b) recount early fieldwork encounters in which study participants responded to their seemingly straightforward interview questions with "long stories" which the researchers at first interpreted as digressions. "I must admit that this used to bring me to the verge of panic—How to bring them back to the point?—but now I have learned that this *is* the point," writes Czarniawska (2002, p. 735). In other words, narrative researchers take as the object of investigation the story itself, rather than treating interviews or documentation of naturally occurring conversations solely as a means to obtain information.

Narrative inquiry is viewed by many as counteracting the fragmentation and reassembly of data that is characteristic, for example, of the coding and categorizing in systematic grounded theory approaches. Narrative researchers' *storied* data refers in a general sense to data that are embodied and wholly represented in first-person accounts of personal experience. This storied quality of data—preserving, not fracturing, its essential structure—enable narrative inquirers to consider "both *how* social actors order and tell their experiences and *why* they remember and retell what they do" (Coffey & Atkinson, 1996, p. 57; emphasis added). This is a key contribution of narrative; it lets the researcher analyze not only meanings and motives but also how those meanings and motives connect to the ways people structure their experience. In other words, narrative researchers extend their focus beyond content to include how people "package" that content and how they recount events with an audience in mind.

Narrative is clearly not appropriate for studies of large numbers of anonymous participants. Its demonstrated value is in the systematic study of personal experience and meaning, emphasizing the need for researchers and participants to construct their texts in particular contexts. Narrative inquiry encompasses a number of activities used to generate and analyze stories of life experiences (e.g., narrative interviews, life histories, journals, memoirs, biographies, and autobiographies) and is often combined with other forms of qualitative analysis, such as ethnography (e.g., Cortazzi, 2002; Mattingly, 1998).

Basic Assumptions of the Narrative Inquirer

- People do not deal with the world event by event or sentence by sentence. Instead, they frame these events and sentences in larger structures—narrative or stories—that provide a context for interpreting the meaning of these parts.
- The story, precisely because it is a primary form of discourse used in everyday interaction, is a natural, obvious, and authentic window into how people structure experience and construct meaning in their lives.
- Narrative is inherently sequential: Each narrative is composed of a unique sequence of events and processes involving human characters.
- The way people tell stories influences how they perceive current events, remember past events, and prepare for future events.
- Narrative can be real or imaginary without losing its power as a story.
- Narrative needs to have a "voice"—that is, it requires a narrator's perspective. This is another way of saying that stories are rooted in human agency: A story is always told *by* someone, even though that person may not know everything about the story he or she is telling.

Orienting Concepts of Narrative Inquiry

Temporality.   Temporality is a central feature of narrative thinking. Simply stated, it refers to the assumption that locating things (people, events, ideas) in time is a natural way to think about them. Any event is an expression of something happening over time: it has a past, a present, and an implied future. Narrative inquirers are concerned not only with events and ideas in the here and now but also with how those events and ideas are given meaning on a continuum of experiences. Meaning will change as time passes.

Analysis of Narrative and Narrative Analysis.   These two terms reflect distinct ways to analyze the storied qualities of qualitative data. *Analysis of narrative* means that the researcher deliberately elicits complete stories, or narratives, which are then analyzed in terms of concepts from preexisting (often literary) theory or inductively in the manner of grounded theory. These might be called "tales *from* the field" (Van Maanen, 1988). In contrast, *narrative analysis* means that the researcher pulls together events (for example, from interview responses) and transforms them into narratives or stories by means of a plot or other narrative qualities (including poetic structure; see for example, Crepeau, 2000; Gee, 1996). The basic idea is that the researcher can construct a coherent narrative out of the diverse thoughts and commentaries contained throughout interview material (Czarniawska, 2002). These might be termed "tales *of* the field" (Van Maanen, 1988). Both forms of analysis can stem from either the "natural" collection of stories (for example, by recording them as they occur during participant observation in a research setting) or from research-driven activities like interviews.

The Nature of Narrative Questions

Narrative researchers tend to question how events become meaningful, or meaningful in a particular way, through their placement in a narrative or story. Questions are geared toward understanding not simply the "stuff" of experience but also what can be learned through opening up the *forms of telling* about experience. Broadly speaking, narrative researchers might ask, "Why was the story told that way?" or "What does a narrative representation of these events and interactions reveal?" For example, had Patrice sought to structure her analysis in terms of narrative, she might have been more self-consciously attentive to why her study participants remembered and retold what they did. She might wonder how they might be trying to make a point through the way that they recount an experience. She might want to explore their reactions to narrated events. With these concerns in mind, she might then have posed the following types of research questions:

> How do the stories told by home visitors about Early Head Start families shape their perceptions of the families' behaviors and activities? (Or, conversely, how do the families' stories about home visitors shape their perceptions of and interaction with the home visitors?)

or

> How do accounts by home visitors reveal their changing attitudes toward Early Head Start families? How do these accounts reveal or facilitate particular types of reasoning in their work with these families?

Any of these questions would highlight a concern on Patrice's part about how events become meaningful, or meaningful in a particular way, because of their placement in a narrative or story. This emphasis on storied data presumably would help her maintain a stronger sense of how participants construct events in their original context than were she to break down and reassemble bits of data so that they are seen in a different fashion. In sum, narrative researchers ask questions aimed at connecting people's meanings and motives to how they structure their experience.

Case Study

> Case studies have become one of the most common ways to do qualitative inquiry, but they are neither new nor essentially qualitative. (Stake, 2000, p. 435)

Precisely what constitutes the strategy of case study is a matter of considerable debate, so I have chosen to address it through a less structured format than the previous four research options. For a more thorough examination of issues and distinctions addressed in the following discussion, I encourage you to consult Creswell (1998), Flyvbjerg (2004), Hamel (1993), Merriam (1988), Stake (1995, 2000), and Yin (1994).

I begin with the assertion by a leading proponent of the approach that case study is "not a methodological choice but a choice of *what* is to be studied" (Stake, 2000, p. 435; emphasis added). In other words, case study is defined by an analytic focus on an individual event, activity, episode, or other specific phenomenon, not necessarily by the methods used for investigation.

This may account for its ability to adapt to such a wide range of disciplinary associations, such as ethnographic, historical, sociological, biographical, psychological, and legal. Stake's assertion is also consistent with the key defining characteristic on which researchers do tend to agree, namely, that case study involves the exploration of a "bounded system," something identifiably set within time and circumstance. Creswell (2002), for example, uses research on a specific incident—a university's response to a student gunman (Asmussen & Creswell, 1995)—to exemplify a case study approach.

Let's consider our own familiar case within this book. If Patrice were to consider a case study strategy for her research, she might define her bounded system as one family's experience in responding to the program requirements of Early Head Start. Using a conventional definition of case study structure (Creswell, 2002; Lincoln & Guba, 1985), she might then organize her research in terms of a problem (e.g., how program requirements are communicated and received), the context (the social, economic, political, and/or community mechanisms at play in the local setting), the issues (e.g., power imbalances, diverse socioeconomic perspectives), and the "lessons learned" (e.g., service providers and beneficiaries may unknowingly hold conflicting aims and motivations). It could be argued that Patrice's completed ethnographic study did in fact contain a number of such case studies that detailed the experiences of particular families. Given the broader ethnographic concepts and the larger, overlapping units of analysis that shaped Patrice's research, however, it would be inaccurate to argue that her study as a whole was *a* case study or that it was simply the joint investigation of a number of cases.

Whether you consider case study as a way of conceptualizing human social behavior or merely as a way of encapsulating it, its strategic value lies in its ability to draw attention to what can be learned from the single case. (Flyvbjerg, 2004, and Stake, 2000, provide especially useful explanations regarding this point.) Further distinctions among intrinsic, instrumental, and collective case studies (Stake, 1995, 2000) add to the practical value of case study as a research strategy.

Intrinsic case study refers to the idea that the case itself is of interest; the researcher is focused on teasing out what can be learned about that particular case. For Patrice, an intrinsic interest might prompt a question such as, "What can I learn from an investigation of this one family's experience with home visitors?"

Instrumental case study refers to the idea that a case can facilitate our understanding of something else; the researcher is focused on developing insight into an issue or external interest through the case. For Patrice, an instrumental interest might prompt a question such as, "What does this family's experience tell me about how program intentions are communicated to participants in Early Head Start?"

Collective case study is an instrumental case study extended to a number of cases; the researcher is focused on moving toward a better understanding, perhaps better theorizing, about a more general phenomenon or condition. For Patrice, a collective focus might prompt a question such as, "What do these four families' efforts to qualify for Early Head Start reveal about the program's operating assumptions?"

In sum, the value of case study lies in facilitating appreciation of the uniqueness, complexity, and contextual embeddedness of individual events and phenomena. As a practical decision, you need to determine whether your research aims and questions can be addressed by remaining within the bounds of a particular case or set of cases. Conceptually speaking, you need to determine where you place yourself on the continuum defined at one end by case study as a methodological choice, as some claim, and at the other end by case study as a choice of what is to be studied, as others claim. Between these choices lie a range of possibilities, including the use of case studies as one of several strategies for how you present and delimit data in a larger ethnographic, grounded theory, or other type of study.

A Cautionary Summary

Ethnography, phenomenology, grounded theory, and narrative, if not viewed holistically as discipline-related approaches to inquiry, all run the risk of being co-opted as fashionable stores of methods and techniques in qualitative research. So, too, does a definition of case study focused exclusively on method rather than analytic focus contribute little to understanding what researchers actually do. The caution in this summary relates to the ease of appropriating selected procedures associated with an approach—that is, selected ways of looking—but failing to realize the full meaning and potential of these procedures as part of a systematic and well-defined way of conceptualizing human behavior and social processes. As Wolcott (1999) warns in the case of ethnography, people who claim they are doing ethnography based solely on their use of participant observation as a strategy or on their repeated but unexamined use of the term *culture* fall short of realizing their claim. So, too, with those who might claim to be doing grounded theory based solely on a characterization of their approach as inductive, or phenomenology based solely on an expressed concern for participants' perspectives, or narrative based solely on the inclusion of participants' stories in their work.

If your conceptual components are aligned, at least provisionally, reflecting thoughtful consideration of how *problem* relates to *intent* relates to *theoretical context* relates to *question* and so on in dialectical fashion, your methodological approach should present itself as an inevitable option. This was the case with Patrice, whose eventual commitment to an ethnographic label flowed naturally and logically from her extensive conceptual groundwork and the nature of her research questions. The remaining sections in this chapter address how you might reach a similar level of commitment in your own work.

ASSESSING GOODNESS OF FIT

When and how does it matter to distinguish and declare that I am using a particular research approach?

Affixing a label to your research approach means that you can situate your work within a specific set of assumptions, intentions, conceptual emphases, and disciplinary roots like those described in the previous section. It also indicates that you are confident enough to identify yourself with others engaged in similar work. This is a significant commitment: When you engage a particular research approach, you also assume responsibility to participate in the ongoing dialogue to define it (Wolcott, 1990).

This suggests that a dose of discretion may be warranted when laying claim to a research approach. Discretion does not mean that you avoid a solid commitment but rather that you make sure your decision is informed by thoughtful consideration of the following types of issues:

- how you link question and approach
- where you focus your attention
- whether you claim the whole or borrow pieces

Linking Question and Approach

Key Consideration: Understanding the fit between research question and approach helps you to establish your claim to a particular mode of inquiry.

A strong argument can be made for claiming your research approach at the point when you have a well-thought-out research question in hand. The link between research question and approach builds upon a set of fundamental propositions:

- Particular types of questions position you to look at certain aspects of reality more (or more effectively) than others do.
- Particular research approaches serve to illuminate certain aspects of reality more (or more effectively) than others do.
- Some types of questions are thus better suited to certain approaches; that is, they position you more effectively to see what is illuminated.

Some researchers claim in rather direct terms that the nature of the research question "determines" the research approach (Morse, 1994) or that the research question can be "encoded" with the language of a research tradition (Creswell, 1998). To illustrate, Morse suggests the following linkages:

- A research question focused on describing values, beliefs, and behaviors that come into play as people interact regularly suggests an ethnographic approach.
- A research question focused on the meaning of a phenomenon, particularly one that elicits the essence of experiences, directs one to a phenomenological approach.
- A research question focused on process, in the sense of understanding change or experience over time (which may entail phases or stages), feeds into a grounded theory approach.

Even if you are hesitant to reason in such direct terms, consider the underlying logic and necessity of a good fit between question and approach. Whether or not this means your question has determined your approach, your explicit examination of the linkage between the two is a key step in affirming your decision to claim a particular research approach.

Using Questions to Anticipate Procedures: A Practical Step Toward Defining Your Approach

At times it is helpful to think about the link between questions and approach in more modest and practical terms. If laying claim to a "formal" research methodology or label seems beyond your comfort level at this point, cut your Research Approach down to size by taking a practical look at what fieldwork procedures would actually be set in motion by the particular questions orienting your research. Think in concrete terms: If I want to understand this, I need to look at this particular thing, I need to talk to these people, I need to put myself in these situations, I need to experience this type of interaction. In other words, take the intermediate step of anticipating and identifying procedures and strategies before making the bolder methodological claim, "To understand this, I'm going to use an ethnographic approach" or "I'm going to use a grounded theory approach." You are still moving toward that "named" approach, but rather than leaping into it, you are seeing how the application of key questions to fieldwork strategies can help you establish a case for that approach. Let's see how this might look in practice, drawing upon the experience of one student.

JoAnne, whose work was among those used to illustrate focus and locus in Chapter 2, was developing a research project on the experiences of students with emotional and behavioral disorders in a high school. Months prior to her actual research proposal, she was working with this tentative research question: How do students with emotional and behavioral disorders construct and experience a sense of agency in the high school setting? In one memo, she documented how this question, her research aims, and her conceptual work were prompting her to weigh the relative appropriateness of ethnographic, grounded theory, and phenomenological approaches to her inquiry. She was not ready (in her mind) to make a broad methodological claim but was prepared, as she stated, to "shift my thinking to a practical gear" and consider in more specific terms the strategies she might employ during fieldwork to get at what she was after. She turned to the topical questions that underlay her central research question (see Chapter 5) in order to assess what procedures of participant selection and data collection those questions might actually set in motion. Here are some excerpts selected from JoAnne's memo:

> *Topical Questions:* How do the students with emotional and behavioral disorders perceive academic tasks and their own abilities to "measure up" with other students? How do the teachers perceive the academic capabilities of their students with emotional and behavioral disorders?
>
> *Procedural Considerations:* A LOT of participant observation will be necessary to generate these data. Additionally, I will need to develop questions to ask of key participants in the setting, both formally (interviews) and informally. These questions may prompt me to look for disparities between "what is" and "what should be," and between what "people say about what is going on" and "what people say ought to be going on." I must also collect documents that relate to academic and behavioral activities, including exams, quizzes, and essays, as well as teachers' written feedback on this work.
>
> *Topical Questions:* What types of relationships do students with emotional and behavioral disorders have with other students? How do these students perceive their peer relationships?
>
> *Procedural Considerations:* Again, participant observation seems a key strategy for gaining insight into how these relationships play out in the setting. I need to consider that adolescents engage in behavior that is quite different when adults are not around. If I want to have opportunities to see how they interact as peers in as genuine a sense as possible, I am going to have to be patient and take considerable time to establish open, trusting relationships with them. Again, I think I need to be attentive to disparities between what is and what participants think ought to be, so I will be interviewing students and their peers to see what is going on in that respect. I will also look for and collect written documents (including informal notes or graffiti). Many peer interactions occur outside of school. I will have to put myself in a position to observe and participate at dances, athletic events, and informal social gatherings that include or exclude the students with EBD.
>
> *Topical Questions:* Which school policies seem to relate to or are directed at students with emotional or behavioral disorders? How does the implementation of these policies affect the success or failure of these students?
>
> *Procedural Considerations:* It seems to me that I must collect and analyze past and current school documents, including any documentation of the processes that produced those documents and their revisions. I must also collect information that is not in written form about how individuals in the school and the school community implement, interpret, and perceive the discipline policies. The methods I see for gathering these data are participant observation and semi-structured interviews of school staff, students, parents, and community members.
>
> Through participant observation in the setting, I will be looking for interactions between students and school staff around issues of discipline. I may seek to 'tell a story' of how these interactions lead to other events or interactions over a period of time. I'll need to observe informal and formal disciplinary meetings. I may want to focus some on the 'discourses' of these interactions because, again, my experiences with these youth tell me that

an articulation of these discourses (ways of interacting, representing, and being) may high-light pivotal points of tension defining perceptions and interactions in the setting.

As these excerpts suggest, JoAnne moved through a relatively straightforward process of brainstorming prompted by her topical questions. She was not taking any great leaps in terms of methodological claims, but was laying claim to a territory of fieldwork procedures that could situate her within certain methodological boundaries—in effect, inviting consideration of how the procedures might fit under some broader methodological label. Framing this process in ref-erence to the set of propositions I presented earlier, her topical questions served the aim of po-sitioning her to see what was likely to be illuminated through a number of actual fieldwork procedures. Further consideration of these procedures, ongoing reading and training in meth-ods, and increasingly integrative memos eventually positioned her to choose an ethnographic approach, with the capacity to include some form of (possibly critical) discourse analysis.

With reference to this last possibility, I cannot understate the importance of familiarizing yourself with prior, related research. In JoAnne's case, school-based studies such as Rogers (2002), which embedded critical discourse analysis within a broader ethnographic approach, served to affirm the viability and appropriateness of her eventual choice.

Exercise 6.1
Using Your Questions to Anticipate Research Procedures

Like JoAnne in the preceding example, you may find yourself working to build the case for a particular research approach but not feel ready to move beyond relatively modest methodological claims. If so, try drafting a memo that, like hers, takes a practical look at what fieldwork procedures might actually be set in motion by the questions currently orienting your research. Topical questions, because they address anticipated needs for information, provide the most logical and focused starting points for this exercise. As il-lustrated in JoAnne's case, think in practical, concrete terms. Organize your memo as if you are interrogating each of your topical questions. Ask yourself: If I want to pursue this question, I need to look at _____, I need to talk to _____, I need to put myself in situations that allow me to _____, and I need to experience inter-actions between _____.

Further reflection on your memo, combined with opportunities to expand your knowledge of and experience with different research approaches, can then prompt you to locate identifiable parameters for your fieldwork. For example, JoAnne identified par-ticipant observation, informal interviewing, and document analysis—including how each plays off the others—as likely components of her research task. When combined with her emphasis on context and her persistent interest in playing *what is* against what people say *should be*, these procedures and strategies pointed her toward an ethno-graphic orientation.

With respect to your own efforts, do not expect this exercise to lead to a clear, con-clusive decision about a research approach, though it can certainly move you along in that direction. Rather, think of your questions and considerations as another source of "data" to inform your growing understanding of which research approach might be ap-propriate to your inquiry.

Focusing Your Attention

Key Consideration: Distinguishing what you are doing as associated with a particular approach matters in the sense of helping you attend to certain types of things and not others.

Research purposes and questions enable you to approach fieldwork with a sense of what you are looking for and why that might matter. But they provide limited guidance when it comes to determining to what or whom you actually attend as you pursue your questions in the field. For additional help you can look to the orienting concerns and focus of the research approach with which you choose to align yourself. For instance, identification with a research approach as you enter the field enables you to shape and orient the initial query "What's going on here . . . ?" with qualifiers like the following:

> ". . . in terms of what I can learn from talking to individuals who have directly experienced and can describe this particular phenomenon" (phenomenology)

> ". . . in terms of what I can learn from attending to what some people say they are doing, what these people say they should be doing, and what I actually see them doing relative to what they have said" (ethnography)

> ". . . in terms of what I can learn by attempting to trace some aspect of experience over time, attending especially to how this process is made apparent through interactions between people and between actions and their consequences" (grounded theory)

> ". . . in terms of what is revealed through a narrative or storied representation of events and interactions" (narrative)

> ". . . in terms of what I can learn by bounding the focus of my inquiry within a particular time and set of circumstances" (case study)

Note that such qualifiers do not direct you to attend to specific people or things (e.g., "If I'm proceeding ethnographically, I need to speak with this person in that place at this time"). Instead they provide guidance as to the types of people or things toward which you should direct attention (e.g., "If I'm proceeding ethnographically, I need to speak to these types of people in these types of circumstances"). As such, they reflect your intent as an ethnographer, phenomenologist, grounded theorist, narrative inquirer, or case study researcher while contributing at a practical level to decisions about where to direct your attention in the field.

Claiming the Whole or Borrowing Pieces

Key Consideration: You should be clear about whether you are laying claim to a research approach in its entirety or drawing upon selected aspects of it.

Any research approach, even if embraced in its entirety, is only a broad prescription for research, and you should not count on your selection of one to put your entire set of research procedures neatly into place. So, too, you should not claim to be doing phenomenology (or ethnography or grounded theory or narrative) if all you are doing is employing specific and selected techniques from the phenomenological (or ethnographic or grounded theory or narrative) storehouse of procedures.

At times it can appear difficult to identify studies that are the exclusive or "pure" expression of a particular research tradition or approach. It is often easier (and more accurate) to claim that studies are only relatively more oriented toward this or that approach.

In the case of my own doctoral research, which I labeled an "anthropological life history," I claimed to be using life history as an approach within an ethnographically oriented study of an experienced teacher's adjustment to a new school and community context. The complementary features of ethnography's detailed observation of behavior in a naturalistic setting and life history's retrospective reconstruction of an individual's life resulted in something less than "pure" anything, but significantly more than a convenient or attractive pairing of perspectives. There is certainly nothing wrong, and potentially everything right, with this type of blending, as long as you are clear about how and when each research approach is informing your decisions about what is worth knowing and how you are applying that knowledge.

To that end, you need to be attentive to the types of distinctions and assumptions discussed earlier (see "Distinguishing Among Options"). You also need to keep in mind that (a) being well versed in a research approach and (b) feeling the need to follow its every tenet to the letter are different matters. My contribution as an ethnographer to my dissertation study did not demand the level of immersion, contextualization, cultural interpretation, and so on that would enable me to claim that I was doing an ethnography. That I was sufficiently oriented along ethnographic lines to situate my life history work within a cultural frame of reference did support my claim to be doing a "good" study, appropriate to the research aims and questions I had posed. That more than satisfied my (and my committee's) claims-making needs.

ASIDE: On Methodological Commitment

As you gain experience in the qualitative arena, do not let my cautions about how research questions precede and inform choice of method prevent you from discovering your natural attachment to a particular approach. You will likely discover that it pleases you to pursue a certain type of inquiry, that you get satisfaction from the experiences it provides you. You may eventually decide—and in so deciding, be in the company of countless experienced researchers—that you have developed a methodological commitment that goes in search of something to study. Alan Peshkin (1992) wrote of this in addressing how the research methods we use are associated with our subjectivity:

> I realized that I was probably never in my whole life ever going to study anything that didn't fit being done ethnographically. What this says to me is that notwithstanding the fact that you may be just as skilled doing nonquantitative research as quantitative research, there is something about a particular way of doing research that suits you, is good for you, that you feel you like to do. (p. 4)

Methodological commitment requires more than familiarity, and developing attachment to an approach takes time, trial, and error. The fact is, comprehensive in-depth knowledge of even the relatively limited range of qualitative approaches addressed in this chapter goes beyond what any one person might ever know or need to know. If you think of these approaches as conversations, like those presented in Chapter 1, bear in mind that claiming the ability to engage authentically in any one of them demands much more than a single encounter.

SUMMARY OF KEY POINTS

- You need to have more practical and compelling reasons for deciding upon a particular type of qualitative research than the appeal of a label.
- Just as there is no one way to see the world, there is no such thing as *the* approach to a problem identified for inquiry.
- Ethnography, phenomenology, grounded theory, and narrative illustrate four distinct ways, among many other options, for *seeing* (reflecting perspective and intent) and *looking at* (reflecting methods and procedures) a problem or topic as a qualitatively oriented researcher.
- Researchers are cautioned against appropriating selected procedures associated with an approach—that is, selected ways of looking—without grasping the full meaning of these procedures as part of a systematic, well-defined, and discipline-based way of approaching inquiry.
- Questions of when and how it matters to declare that you are working within a particular research approach encompass issues of the fit between question and approach, the way you focus your attention, and your decision to claim the whole or only parts of your selected approach.

RECOMMENDED READING

If you want to take further steps toward ethnography, start off with the eminently practical and informative book by Emerson, Fretz, and Shaw (1995), and then follow that up with Wolcott (1999). If you want to trace ethnographic research from its cultural foundations through new approaches influenced by critical theory, discourse, and ethnicity, take a look at the edited volume by Zou and Trueba (2002). For an engaging and jargon-free exploration of the culture concept, read Agar's (1994) seventh chapter.

It is hard to know where to start with phenomenology, but Van Manen (1997) can serve as a practical entry point. The short articles by Laverty (2003) and Cohen and Omery (1994) help to clarify distinctions among phenomenological approaches. Seidman (1998) provides a practical application of phenomenological principles to interviewing strategies.

The chapter by Charmaz (2000) provides a helpful summary and can orient you toward additional sources on grounded theory. Strauss and Corbin's (1998) text is probably the most widely used one on systematic grounded theory, but it can be an overwhelming place to start as a novice. The short article by Melia (1996) is quite useful for understanding distinctions among the different forms of grounded theory.

My students have found either of Riessman's (2002a, 2002b) chapters to be especially helpful jumping-off points for understanding narrative, but at some point you will probably want to go back to a comprehensive text like Mishler (1986), Polkinghorne (1988), or Riessman (1993) for a more substantial foundation. Daiute and Lightfoot's edited book (2004) is useful for those interested in detailed examples of how narrative research has been applied to study a wide range of contexts (e.g., school-based violence, Holocaust survivors, undocumented immigrant families, and other challenging social situations).

For case study, start with Stake (1995 or 2000) and Flyvbjerg (2004) for some of the fundamentals and clarification of key issues, but then spread out from there.

Finally, take a look at any of the fine journals focused on qualitative methods and methodologies. The following journals, also noted in Chapter 1, are especially helpful in terms of staying current with qualitative issues and debates: *Qualitative Inquiry, Qualitative Research,* and the online *International Journal of Qualitative Methods* (www.ualberta.ca/~ijqm).

When Patrice sat down with faculty members on her dissertation committee to discuss and initially defend her proposed research on the participation of families in Early Head Start, questions arose around the role she envisioned for herself "in the field." Given her experience as an early childhood educator and home visitor for early intervention programs for more than two decades, concerns naturally turned toward how the substantial professional knowledge she would be bringing to her interactions might affect her research aims. The following dialogue is an excerpt from that meeting.

"So, Patrice, if you happen to be conducting fieldwork in a household when the mother puts the baby to bed with a bottle of Kool-Aid or sugar water, are you going to say anything? Or what if one of the parents is a smoker, and the baby is constantly inhaling secondary smoke? Are you going to offer any comments?"

Patrice considered her response carefully. "Initially, I expect, I will name such episodes in my fieldnotes and explore their implications in my field journal. The families, of course, will know that I have worked as a home visitor, but I will be a researcher from the get-go, and my goal will be to learn from them."

"Yes, but you will be changing over time, as will your relationships with these families, so you may eventually do more than simply name these instances," suggested Bruce, a committee member.

"Absolutely," interjected John. "You cannot avoid the fact that, with your presence and your expressed interest, you are in a very genuine sense joining the circle of care around these infants and these families. And you will be bringing more than 14 years' worth of professional experience and knowledge to the setting, not to mention your own insights as a parent."

"I'm not going to pretend to know 'nothing,'" offered Patrice. She paused to consider her next response. "But I also realize that, up to this point, I have given more attention to my role as participant observer than I have to my role as interventionist, and it is critical that I pay attention to the experience of interventionist as participant observer. As John said, I am joining the circle of care around the participant families, and I do want to align with them."

"What does that mean—'align with them'—in terms of your dual role as researcher and practitioner?" asked Mary Jane, also an early childhood educator.

"Well, I'm not sure yet if I actually envision myself as having that dual role in this case," responded Patrice. "However, I do know that to enhance my understanding of the influence I exert on the family context in which I am present, I will have to be sensitive to and track instances where I am aware of my own interventions, intentional or not . . . I will have to monitor my interventionist self."

GETTING INTO PLACE

In raising hypothetical scenarios about Kool-Aid and parental smoking, Patrice's committee members foreshadowed moments in her fieldwork when she might have to play out her research aims against possibilities for professional or personal intervention. How would Patrice balance what she knows, what she needs to know, and what she wants to know when interacting with others as a fieldworker? How might her concerns about what could be or what should be affect her decision to share something openly with her study participants or keep it to herself? Patrice's response and the ensuing discussion direct attention to a key challenge associated with getting into place as a fieldworker—namely, how to portray oneself and one's purposes to participants in the setting (Rossman & Rallis, 2003).

Portrayal of involvement is just one of many practical and ethical concerns that researchers must address before and during their engagement in a field setting (see Chapter 8). Generally speaking, positioning yourself as a fieldworker entails not only how you get to, get around, and conduct yourself in a particular setting—the physical, procedural, and mechanical aspects of being in the field—but also what your intentions and questions are as you go about it. "Being there" is a prerequisite for conducting field-based inquiry, but ultimately, it is your intent, not your presence, that makes fieldwork what it is (Wolcott, 2005).

The chapters in Part One considered this matter of intent, addressing what it is that brings you to the point of fieldwork in the first place. Time now, in Part Two, to consider how you situate yourself to learn whatever it is you want to learn.

MAKING GOOD USE OF OPPORTUNITIES

Fieldwork is largely a matter of recognizing what might be learned as situations present themselves. As a theory of how your inquiry should proceed, this statement no doubt lacks the specifics you are seeking as you anticipate your own efforts in the field. It does, however, suggest an eminently practical way to direct your thinking as a fieldworker concerned with strategy. In *The Art of Fieldwork* (2005), Harry Wolcott states,

> The element of strategy turns on two complementary questions to be reviewed over and over:
>
> - Am I making good use of the opportunity before me to learn what I set out to learn?
> - Does what I have set out to learn, or to learn about, make good use of the opportunity presenting itself? (p. 83)

Chapters 7 and 8 maintain a steady focus on both questions, mirroring Wolcott's advice to keep concerns of strategy in mind as you attempt to observe and experience what you are interested in observing and experiencing. These two chapters also advance Part One's central theme of orchestrating connections, highlighting in particular the intrinsic link between *substance* (what the fieldworker finds out) and *method* (how the fieldworker finds it out) (Emerson, Fretz, & Shaw, 1995). Together, the chapters move through considerations of approaching and anticipating fieldwork decisions and strategies.

Strategic Considerations for Fieldwork (Chapter 7)

This chapter suggests strategies for selecting and justifying how you as a fieldworker will collect and generate data, highlighting strategic considerations prior to fieldwork.

Establishing Your Inquiry's Integrity (Chapter 8)

This chapter addresses practical and ethical considerations involved in establishing the credibility and integrity of your study.

Writing Your Proposal (Chapter 9)

This chapter addresses the ways in which discrete aspects of the conceptualization process find expression as you shift from efforts to establish the logic and coherence of your inquiry (Chapters 2–8) to the presentation and justification of your study in the form of a written proposal.

Chapter 7

STRATEGIC CONSIDERATIONS
FOR FIELDWORK

How does fieldwork serve the aims of my inquiry? What are the key strategic and relational issues I need to consider as I approach fieldwork? What judgments underlie my decision to go about fieldwork in a particular way?

The overarching theme for this chapter and Chapter 8 might best be conveyed by the cautionary phrase, "Look carefully before you leap into fieldwork." Taking a cue from Wolcott's complementary questions in the introduction to Part Two, are you in place—conceptually, methodologically, and ethically—to make good use of fieldwork to serve your inquiry? And does "the field" that lies before you make sense as the place where your inquiry can and should play out?

As you address these questions (over and over), take a second helpful cue from Clifford Geertz's time-honored observation that it is "not necessary to know everything in order to understand something" (1973, p. 20). Even if that seems self-evident, it is crucial to keep in mind the ease with which being in the field invites you to consider everything going on about you, while also suggesting that the something you are after is to be found wholly through the methods and techniques of fieldwork. It can feel wonderfully affirming to finally be out there in the field, but it is deceptively so if you neglect to precede fieldwork with a thorough questioning of why and how it serves the aims of your inquiry.

This chapter addresses a number of critical issues that can help you determine whether what you want to accomplish is most effectively accomplished through fieldwork. And if fieldwork is the way to go, what should factor into your decision to go about it in a particular way? These strategic considerations will help you find that something in the everything of the field.

The following strategic considerations come together under six conceptual headings, a set of fundamental issues that address whether you are in place as well as in the right place to pursue field-based inquiry: intent, focus, involvement, familiarity, positioning, and role awareness. Each of these, respectively, feeds into secondary considerations of need, purposefulness, role portrayal, sense making, context, and topic sensitivity (Figure 7.1).

Thinking Ahead to Your Research Proposal. This aspect of your work takes shape in your eventual research proposal in the Research Procedures section, particularly as you address the relationship you hope to establish with research participants and the manner in which you will gather and generate data. Much of the strategic emphasis within this chapter centers on coming to terms with your researcher self. This means positioning yourself in a manner that reflects your aims and the way you want to relate to people as you pursue those aims.

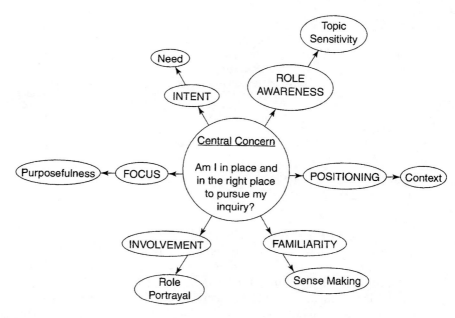

Figure 7.1
Strategic Considerations for Fieldwork

INTENT

With intent we revisit a basic premise emphasized in the introduction to Part Two: Simply being in the field is not enough to make what you are doing fieldwork; your intent makes it so. Doing fieldwork, or simply borrowing a fieldwork technique or two, must serve your research aims, and a fundamental criterion for evaluating your decision to pursue fieldwork is whether, as you proceed, you are moving closer to accomplishing those aims.

This criterion may seem obvious, but it is important to consider that fieldwork can be a remarkably inefficient way simply to gather factual data that, for example, a skilled survey researcher could generate in a more timely and less labor-intensive manner. Intent thus feeds into the secondary consideration of *need*, as you determine whether and how efficiently fieldwork will give you what you need, all the while keeping in mind that it may be more than you need to pursue your research question (Figure 7.2).

To illustrate, a number of years ago I was involved in a cross-disciplinary research project that teamed qualitative researchers like myself with mathematics educators in developing descriptive case studies of 12 school sites throughout the United States. The project was designed to portray the complexity of changing mathematics teaching and learning by describing the efforts of schools as they implemented their particular visions of what school mathematics should be (Ferrini-Mundy & Schram, 1997).

During an early planning session involving all the project documenters, one memorable exchange between two team members over the nature and extent of fieldwork that

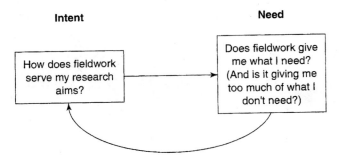

Figure 7.2
Fieldwork and Intent

was required for the study revealed significant differences in their interpretation of the project's aims. One researcher clearly tended to look intensively, but seldom more than once, at a phenomenon, embodying in her stance the structure and economy of research aimed at limiting or reducing the variables of study. The other favored a contextual and holistic emphasis that meant looking again and again at a site to capture both its ordinariness and its variety. Research aims for the first tended to be derived, whether explicitly or implicitly, from the question, "How can mathematics instruction be improved?" For the second, the central aim was embedded in the question, "Why is mathematics teaching occurring this way in this setting?" The first sought consistency across contexts; the second expected variety within and across settings. Each reflected a distinct intent and a different level of need for fieldwork.

Intent is what makes the difference between simply putting yourself out there in the field and using fieldwork to take you somewhere consistent with your research aims. The worth of fieldwork as fieldwork is assessed by the basic question: Is this experience giving me what I need (or, conversely, is it giving me too much of what I don't need) to pursue my research question? As Wolcott (2005) cautions, if you feel that fieldwork is getting in your way rather than helping you make your way, reconsider your decision to pursue it, or at least to pursue it in the manner in which you have initially approached it.

FOCUS

Attention to research aims in the context of fieldwork also demands renewed consideration of the important distinction between the *focus* and *locus* of your inquiry. Chapter 2 discussed the significance of this distinction in terms of helping to clarify the purposes of your inquiry. My intent here is not to repeat that line of reasoning but to underscore the need to put your study's focus—its driving, conceptual concerns—back on the front burner now that you are actually going to have contact with your research phenomenon. It is at this juncture when the temptation to confuse where you are looking with what you are looking for returns as an immediate, tangible concern.

Attending to the focus/locus distinction in a meaningful way means that you continually return to the question "What's at issue here?" and systematically revisit your research aims. If you find yourself continually falling back on the feeling that "there must be something

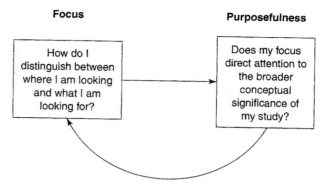

Figure 7.3
Fieldwork and Focus

intrinsically valuable about this place," then your fieldwork may already have become a data-driven activity in which you have traded resolution, or focus, for scope (Seidel, 1992).

Focus thus feeds into the secondary consideration of *purposefulness,* as you monitor the ongoing relevance and emerging significance of your original aims relative to actual events bounded by time, space, and circumstance (Figure 7.3). This is part of the necessary mindwork that carries fieldwork beyond the reactive experience of moving your body around an interesting place and taking in what is offered and toward a more proactive stance of sustained, intentional inquiry.

INVOLVEMENT

The concept of *involvement* takes us back to the types of practical and ethical questions raised in the discussion of Patrice's research that prefaced Part Two. How might your perceptions of what is, and your feelings about what could be or should be, affect your decision to share something openly with study participants or keep it to yourself? How much do you share with study participants about your aims as a researcher?

Getting into place as a fieldworker, as Dolby (2000) reminds us, is more a social than a physical enterprise, an ongoing process of negotiating competing knowledge claims and moral positions, through which you locate yourself as a participant at some level in a setting (Rogers & Swadener, 1999). As a fieldworker, you will be caught up in how a place is represented to you. In turn, those whose experiences you are attempting to understand will be sorting through how you are representing yourself and your purposes in being there. This dual consideration of degree of involvement and portrayal of involvement is illustrated in Figure 7.4.

Degree of Involvement

As framed by Rossman and Rallis (2003), these two aspects of a fieldworker's intended involvement suggest movement along different continua of participation and openness. Degree of participation is characterized at one end of the continuum as being fully present as a human researcher, what Rossman and Rallis term "coparticipation." This level of participation,

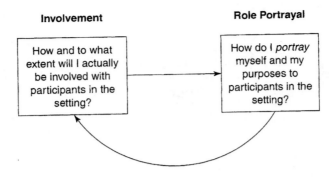

Figure 7.4
Fieldwork and Involvement

more than simply being immersed in a setting, entails the active collaboration of setting participants in shaping the agenda for inquiry, for example, by making observations, suggesting changes, and creating different avenues of questioning (Rogers & Swadener, 1999).

At the other end of the continuum, participation refers to the researcher being present as an engaged spectator who is experiencing, but is not overtly involved in, what is happening around him or her. Like Rossman and Rallis (2003), I believe all field-based researchers are, to varying extents, participants in settings. Consistent with this perspective, I, too, do not devote attention to the question of whether one is a participant observer or a nonparticipant observer. Sitting behind a two-way mirror and watching toddlers in a child-care facility, for example, is more accurately labeled *laboratory work*, not fieldwork. However, step into the room of children, even as a passive, but visible, observer, and you become a participant, at least in the sense that your presence and immediate responses have the potential to impact the natural behavior and activity of those in the room.

In between on the continuum are varied degrees of *immersion*—that is, "both being with other people to see how they respond to events as they happen and experiencing for oneself these events and the circumstances that give rise to them" (Emerson, Fretz, & Shaw, 1995, p. 2). This is accomplished through learning what is required to become a member of the participants' world, and approximating their experiences (by following local standards for behavior, moral conduct, and so on), but not actually becoming a member of that world (Emerson et al., 1995). Practical and ethical implications of partial engagement in a setting will factor into the discussion of trustworthiness in Chapter 8.

Several basic premises affect your role as a researcher regardless of where you locate yourself on this continuum of participation:

- Your participation on the continuum can, and probably will, change over the course of your inquiry. (Remember Bruce's advice to Patrice in the vignette that introduced Part Two.)
- Different degrees of participation can either help or hinder data collection; more participation does not necessarily facilitate your efforts, though it often does. (Here again, check to see if your level of participation is consistent with your research aims.)
- Amount of participation is a factor of time in the field; more involvement requires more time. (And more time and involvement likely translate into greater familiarity and trust between the researcher and participants in the setting.)

Portrayal of Involvement

Portrayal of involvement, according to Rossman and Rallis (2003), invites a twofold consideration: how to portray yourself and how to portray your research purposes to study participants. A basic concern in your code of ethics as a researcher is that people must be informed of who you are and what you want. One extreme of the continuum—in which your role as researcher is covert, participants do not know that research is being done, and you provide false explanations (or none at all) about why you are there—is an ethical violation. These days it is simply not acceptable. Acceptable portrayal of involvement ranges on a continuum from complete openness (participants know that research is going on and that you are doing it) and full explanation (participants are fully informed about the study's purposes) to partial sharing or being "truthful, but vague" (Taylor & Bogdan, 1984, p. 25).

When might you choose not to disclose fully your specific aims as a researcher? The answer turns on both ethical and pragmatic concerns. Foremost among these is the researcher's judgment that participants' awareness of details might make them particularly self-conscious. The core concern is that, if participants were aware of the specific research focus, they might adjust their behavior and actions to fit their understanding of the researcher's purposes and expectations.

For example, although she was conceptually focused on implicit class issues associated with providing services to families impacted by poverty, Patrice chose to convey her aims to participants in terms of understanding the experiences of families *in general* served by Early Head Start. She did not want to draw undue attention to a characterization ("being poor") that might hold entirely different meanings to study participants. If she turned poverty (or any topic) prematurely or inaccurately into a sensitive issue, she risked transforming her research agenda into something of a self-fulfilling prophecy (see the related discussion of role awareness later in this section).

We will revisit relational issues and ethical dilemmas tied to informing others of one's research purposes in the discussion of trustworthiness in Chapter 8.

FAMILIARITY

The concept of *familiarity* returns us to some of the basic concerns raised in the vignette that introduces Part Two and in Chapter 5's discussion of assumptions embedded within your research question. In a familiar setting, how do you handle the challenge of seeing too much in terms of your preconceived understandings or taking too much for granted and not seeing nearly enough? How do you take into account what you already know or assume about your study participants and their circumstances? How do you take into account what your study participants might already know or assume about you?

If we follow Patrice further down the path of inquiry to her preparations for fieldwork, it becomes apparent that the key challenge posed by familiarity was the ease with which she could become her own best source of information even before she entered the field. For example, in anticipation of questions that she might ask an Early Head Start home visitor in a preliminary interview, Patrice drafted the following, among others:

What happens to families when they sign up for Early Head Start?
How is an "ap" handled?

Both questions reveal Patrice's prior experiential knowledge regarding how Early Head Start works from the perspective of those who administer it. Because of the way these questions are phrased, we can anticipate that those being interviewed might presume (correctly) certain knowledge on Patrice's part and think it unnecessary to share particular information. The first question is embedded with the assumption that families simply "sign up" for the program. This has the effect of leap-frogging over the complex issues of how to make contact (do the families always take the first step?) and how it comes about that families seek services (or that the service providers seek the families) in the first place.

The second question, also assumption-bound, carries an added risk for Patrice. In using in-house slang ("ap," for application), Patrice may inadvertently convey to the person she is interviewing that she is already familiar with the processes involved in administering program services. That may suggest to the interviewee that it is all right to skip over seemingly insignificant, but potentially valuable, parts of his or her explanation.

Like the example of Tim and the assumptions underlying his initial research questions in Chapter 5, here is a consequence of the familiar being all too familiar. Patrice needed to anticipate this prior to entering the field and plan accordingly. Her best strategy in this regard was to make sure that the questions she planned to ask were not framed in terms of the way she already saw things. Instead, her questions should be set up as opportunities, or openings, for her vision of things to be discounted (whether or not it actually ends up being discounted). For this to occur, her questions need to be free from preconceptions and, at least initially, more open-ended. For example:

How is it that families and Early Head Start come to be linked up?
What needs to happen for this to occur?

Once you actually enter the field, familiarity will feed into the related consideration of *sense making*, as you work to maintain the important distinction between what you see or experience and what you infer or assume about an experience (Figure 7.5). Here you must be especially attentive to blind spots in your thinking that might stem from your preexisting knowledge of people, procedures, and happenings within the research setting. This means creating opportunities to have your preconceptions—what you thought you knew—disrupted by new information. As we have just seen in the illustration with Patrice, such opportunities can be realized, or missed altogether, in the deceptively straightforward task of constructing an interview question.

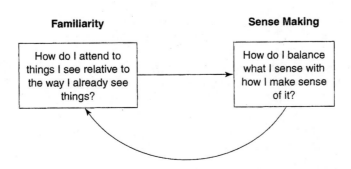

Figure 7.5
Fieldwork and Familiarity

ASIDE: Do You "Lead" with Your Social or Intellectual Self?

Considerations of involvement and familiarity raise a basic question you face as a field-worker: Can you be in role as a social being while being totally committed to your inquiry? The proper stance of the qualitative fieldworker was for many years portrayed as a shifting one: a researcher "poised on the interface between familiarity and strangeness" (Atkinson et al., 2003, p. 50). Classic formulations suggested that this marginal social position ideally paralleled the ability to be intellectually disengaged from a setting and its participants. This detachment was equated with the well-established analytic virtue of objectivity. In a sense, proper analysis was an act of estrangement, and the acknowledgment of difference and distance between researcher and study participants was a necessary condition for the disciplined, systematic reading of data.

What it means for a field researcher to sustain a marginal social position and a detached intellectual stance has shifted in more recent years. Relationships between researchers and study participants have become harder to define, but not because these relationships have become more complicated. Rather, we have become better at questioning assumptions about who we are relative to those with whom we interact in the field. *Othering*—a term that came to connote distancing ourselves from study participants by treating them as inherently different or exotic—is now intellectually and morally unacceptable. (In Patrice's study, hypothetically, "distancing" might be manifested by her decision to interpret the behavior of Early Head Start families solely in terms of what she knew, or thought was important to know, of values and beliefs shaped by people who are impacted by poverty.)

One lesson we can draw from discussions of involvement and familiarity is that *you are never simply a researcher.* Both you and your study participants develop multiple roles and relationships during fieldwork, bringing together aims and assumptions that can be mutually enriching, but can just as easily be misunderstood and at times may even be incompatible. In practical terms, this means you need to attend closely to the assumptions that underlie your relationships with others in the field. Foremost among these is that you, as researcher, are shaping relationships largely according to the intellectual (rather than social) needs you bring to the setting. You are there because you are a researcher conducting research; underlying even the most outwardly friendly interviews is the instrumental aim of persuading someone to provide you with data for your research (see Duncombe & Jessop, 2002). This does not mean the impact and the play of social relationships are not central to your work; they most certainly are. But your analytical intent—your explicit desire to make sense of things—introduces into these relationships the trust-building, distance-negotiating, disclosure-demanding process that field-based research entails.

POSITIONING

Positioning refers to the fact that you are working to get into place not only to gather but also to generate data—an analytic rather than social positioning. As suggested in Chapter 1, features that count in a setting do not simply announce themselves as significant and wait to be collected. Given some set of intentions and some frame of reference, you must see and make sense of what is to be seen. The operating assumption, as introduced in Chapter 3, is one of

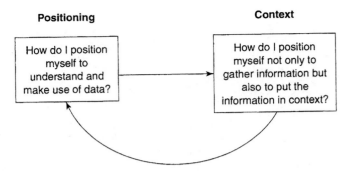

Figure 7.6
Fieldwork and Positioning

coherence: There is a way of thinking and seeing, a context for what's going on, in terms of which the information you gather will make sense in a particular way. Prior to actual field-work, you need to consider how you are situated to get the information (gather data) and then put the information in context (generate more data), as suggested in Figure 7.6.

A key element in considering this process is to recognize that behind every exploration made or question asked, there needs to be some sort of working hypothesis (Wolcott, 2005). By *working hypothesis* I mean an informed sense of potential significance, an as-sumption of coherence, that sets you up for more than gathering data simply for the sake of gathering data. As a qualitative researcher, you are not out to formalize or disprove hy-potheses, but neither are you in the business of picking up data in anticipation that an an-swer to your question is somewhere in the pile. The overarching theme of this chapter establishes itself more firmly and precisely: Look (think, check your reasoning) before you leap (ask, impose).

For Patrice, consideration of her positioning played into her decision to spend her first several months of fieldwork "peering broadly" at the overall dimensions of Early Head Start's home visitor program as a means to "nest" her subsequent and more extensive engagement with the families. This was no mere toss of the coin ("Well, I guess I'll talk to the home visi-tors first, then the families"). It was an approach Patrice determined to position her in time and circumstance relative to specific sources and types of data and based on the consideration that her research aims were best served if certain (context-heavy) information preceded other (nitty-gritty) information.

It is also important to keep in mind that the twofold task of gathering and generating data is in most cases *your* problem. You are the one trying to become competent enough to ques-tion and then figure out how things connect with each other and to a big picture. Things will continue to fit together for participants in the setting whether you are there or not and re-gardless of whether and how you make sense of it all.

At the same time, you will be in a setting doing something—observing, asking, docu-menting—that is not naturally or normally done there. Your sensitivity to the imposition of a research agenda onto the setting, even when accomplished under the most collaborative or co-participatory of terms, plays into the sixth and final strategic consideration discussed here, role awareness.

ROLE AWARENESS

"In the simple act of asking," writes Wolcott (2005), "the fieldworker makes a 180-degree shift from observer to interlocutor, intruding into the scene by imposing onto the agenda what he or she wants to know" (p. 95). In terms of actual practice, you might think of this distinction as the difference between what fieldworkers are up to when they engage in participant observation (self-consciously taking in information in the course of experiencing something) and interviewing (actively seeking information about something in particular). This is a deliberate and profound shift, and as such, it is something you should anticipate and plan for prior to entering the field. By anticipate I mean that:

- you need to be aware of which role you are emphasizing ("As a fieldworker, I know that sometimes I will simply be taking in whatever happens to come along; at other times, I will be making my presence felt by 'getting nosy' and making my personal and research preferences known").
- you need to consider the practical and strategic implications of this awareness ("In the former role, the agenda is laid before me and I can be nondirective; in the latter role, I take charge of the agenda").

The play of shifting roles feeds into consideration of *topic sensitivity* ("How much do I want to reveal of the fact that some issues or topics are of more consequence than others in my inquiry?"), as suggested in Figure 7.7. Your decision to reveal some issues as especially consequential—for example, through the questions you pose in an interview—imposes your agenda onto what might naturally be said or done. The inherent challenge is distinguishing between what you would like to know and how to go about making that interest known. Managing this distinction, which often turns on a split-second decision to ask a question or hold it for later, is not something for which you can explicitly plan. It does require that you bring to fieldwork the awareness that your role is not constant. You must understand that shifts in your role have implications for how, and how much, you influence the direction of your inquiry.

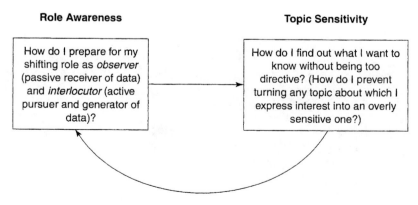

Role Awareness

How do I prepare for my shifting role as *observer* (passive receiver of data) and *interlocutor* (active pursuer and generator of data)?

Topic Sensitivity

How do I find out what I want to know without being too directive? (How do I prevent turning any topic about which I express interest into an overly sensitive one?)

Figure 7.7
Fieldwork and Role Awareness

ASIDE: Different Roles Imply Different Forms of Data

Distinctions between nondirective and directive roles also tie into distinctions you make between types of qualitative data. Broadly speaking, the ways you construct meaning as a qualitative researcher are linked to the forms in which data can occur. You produce textual sources for data through your creation of fieldnotes, interview transcripts, transcribed recordings of naturally occurring events or narratives, documents, and other graphic representations. As you consider how to work with these materials, it is helpful to take into account the distinction between naturally occurring and researcher-provoked data (Silverman, 2001).

Naturally occurring refers to data derived from activities or situations that occur spontaneously and "seem to exist independently of the researcher" (Silverman, 2001, p. 159). The researcher's role is nondirective, to the extent that we can speak of a researcher's ability to take in whatever happens to come along and then, for example, record it in his or her fieldnotes. *Researcher-provoked* refers to data which would "not exist apart from the researcher's intervention" (p. 159). This type of data might be generated, for example, from an interview or a multiple-choice questionnaire.

As already suggested around the issue of topic sensitivity, the emphasis you place upon making your personal and research preferences known has profound implications for how you and others regard the substance and meaning of your data. This, in turn, may impact the substance and persuasiveness of what you put forth as data. To adapt a specific illustration from Dey (1993, p. 16): If you ask me to describe my hair color, is my response less credible or less qualitative if I select "gray" from a list of alternatives that you have provided than if I write "gray" in a blank space? Alternatively, what if, without any prompting, I mention how I feel about my graying hair in a naturally occurring conversation to which you happen to be listening? This is a rather simplified illustration, but the underlying issue is crucial: How do you as a researcher determine the relative significance of the same information derived under such different circumstances? Exercise 7.1 starts positioning you to respond to this question.

Exercise 7.1

Preparing for How You Will Talk About Data

As you look ahead to the Research Procedures section of your research proposal, and specifically how you will justify what you select as potentially meaningful data, you should start thinking now about how you would respond to the questions listed in this exercise. At this point, you are not seeking absolute clarity on these issues but just a preliminary sense of how you stand as you anticipate your shifting roles during fieldwork. It is enough for now that you acknowledge your gut-level responses to some or all of these questions so that you can monitor how these initial feelings may shape the way you frame your approach to fieldwork.

I pose these questions with the aim of having them serve as small group discussion starters, although you might prepare for such exchange by tackling one or more of them in the form of an analytic memo to yourself. The eventual aim, targeted for your research proposal, is to be able to frame a thoughtful position about how you envision your researcher role and how you intend to construct meaning from your data.

1. Are spontaneous, naturally occurring statements more authentic and thus more meaningful than statements prompted by a researcher's question? Explain your reasoning.
2. What would be your argument for treating the statements you record during participant observation and the responses you prompt through interviews in the same way? Or, how would you argue for treating them differently?
3. How do you factor in your own input to an interview or conversation with a participant in terms of the meaning you attach to what is said? For example, if a participant incorporates your prompt or comment into his or her response, is the meaning of what is said a "shared" construction? If so, how would you convey that in what you eventually write up about what was said?

SUMMARY OF KEY POINTS

- Entering the field as a researcher reflects a deliberate choice informed by thoughtful consideration of the following question: Are you in the right place strategically to pursue a field-based inquiry?
- The critical role of researcher intent underscores your responsibility to revisit continually the question, "What's at issue here?" and to avoid the temptation to confuse where you are looking (locus) with what you are looking for (focus).
- Getting into place as a fieldworker entails consideration of how involved you plan to be in the setting and how you intend to portray that involvement.
- Questions of involvement may or may not entail risks posed by familiarity with the setting. That is, the more familiar you are with a situation, the greater the risk that your preconceptions will unduly influence what you see and experience and how you make sense of it all.
- Degree and portrayal of involvement necessarily play into your shifting roles in the field and how you go about making your research interests known to study participants.

RECOMMENDED READING

If you feel ready to grapple with some fairly heady but helpful discussions of familiarity, strangeness, rapport, and intimacy in fieldwork, the first two chapters in Atkinson, Coffey, and Delamont's (2003) book offer a wealth of thoughtful insights. It might also be instructive to take a look at Mitchell's (1991) discussion of secrecy and disclosure, particularly how the "paradox of intimacy" arises when affective, social relationships with study participants are developed more rapidly than the researcher's intellectual understanding of their practices.

Chapter 8

ESTABLISHING YOUR INQUIRY'S INTEGRITY

What can I do to ensure the credibility of my study, not only with respect to other researchers, policy makers, and practitioners, but also in the eyes of the study's participants? How do I maintain the integrity of my study, both methodologically and ethically?

This chapter prepares you to respond to the practical and ethical issues involved in establishing the *trustworthiness* of your study. This is the point at which the intellectual and conceptual coherence discussed in Chapters 3 and 4 is brought to bear on the overall integrity of your inquiry, as judged by standards for competent practice and ethical conduct.

How can you demonstrate that you and your account can be trusted, that you have the interests of your study's participants at heart, that you conduct your research ethically and with sensitivity to the politics of the topic and setting? These questions alert us to two necessary—and necessarily intertwined—dimensions of trustworthiness that contribute to your study's integrity. The first dimension, addressed in the following section as *practical considerations*, pertains to standards for competent performance as a fieldworker and reflects upon issues of researcher presence, the inevitable selectivity of fieldwork, and the play of subjectivity. The second dimension, *ethical considerations*, refers to standards for conduct based on moral principles and includes issues of posturing and role presentation, exchange and disclosure, making public the private, and building relationships amid expectations of eventual departure.

Thinking Ahead to Your Research Proposal. This aspect of your work takes shape in your eventual proposal in the Research Procedures section, where you address the relationship you hope to establish with research participants and especially as you make the case for the credibility and trustworthiness of your study. The distinctions I make in this chapter between and among practical and ethical considerations will tend to blur together in your final written proposal. This is to be expected: As you develop an increasingly complex picture of what your inquiry entails, the discrete elements you need to work through naturally become more integrated.

PRACTICAL CONSIDERATIONS

As a researcher you will face legitimate questions from readers and potential beneficiaries of your study that focus on the accuracy or plausibility of what you report and claim, how you generated the findings, and whether (and to whom) the study is useful. Rossman and Rallis (2003) describe these concerns in terms of a study's truth value, rigor, and significance or applicability. The challenges and dilemmas that overlap these concerns translate into several practical considerations you need to address as you seek to establish the integrity of your research. These considerations include presence, selectivity, and subjectivity (see Figure 8.1).

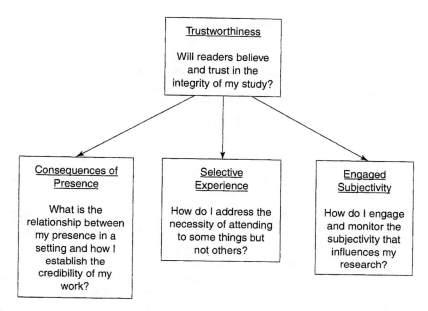

Figure 8.1
Practical Considerations in Establishing Trustworthiness

The first critical step is to make explicit the nature and implications of these concerns prior to entering the field. By doing so at this point I seek to establish them not as problems, but as perspectives that can help you proceed with your inquiry in a competent and credible fashion.

Consequences of Presence

What is the relationship between my presence in a setting and how I establish the credibility of my work?

The implications of "being there" and "seeing for myself" reflect in varying ways upon the truth value of one's work. This statement in no way asserts a direct relationship between presence and credibility. Being in a setting or interacting with people does not in itself provide the compelling authority for a credible account, given that the fieldworker's experience of that setting or with those people at best approximates rather than replicates participants' experiences (Bittner, 1988; Emerson et al., 1995). Patrice, for example, set for herself the task of engaging in the lives of families served by Early Head Start but did not (and could not) experience directly the day-to-day exigencies of membership in such a family.

It is inevitable, however, that a researcher's presence in a setting has implications for what takes place and how events are given meaning. Early on, Patrice expressed concerns that her presence might be viewed as a potentially contaminating influence on how participants talked or behaved ("They're going to say things because they think that's what I want or need to hear"). This type of influence, referred to as "reactivity" (de Laine, 2000; Maxwell, 2005) or "consequential presence" (Emerson et al., 1995), implies that fieldworker presence is a disruption or defect to be controlled or eliminated.

An alternative perspective suggests that relationships between field researchers and those in the setting help to reveal the underlying terms and bases on which processes and events occur. Proponents of this view claim that one's sustained presence can contribute to a fieldworker's heightened sensitivity to subtle understandings—for example, how meanings emerge through talk and action and how perspectives change over time—that are not readily available through detached or highly controlled observation or interview methods alone.

Rather than cast your understanding of presence one way or the other and hope for the best, recognize and harness what is fundamental to both perspectives: the inherent connection between what you come up with and how you go about doing it (Emerson et al., 1995). This means you come to terms with what you can and cannot accomplish as a researcher working within boundaries of time and circumstance. In terms of process, it means recognizing the necessarily interpretive nature of what you construct in the field.

Both aspects of fieldwork, practical constraints and interpretive necessity, turn on the same logic. Start with the practical. Whether observing, interviewing, experiencing, or pursuing some combination of strategies, you cannot be everywhere at once or take in every possible viewpoint at the same time. Instead, in conjunction with those in the setting, you develop certain perspectives by engaging in some activities or talking to certain people rather than others. Inevitably, whether by chance, deliberate choice, or the following of "political fault lines" in the setting, you are exposed to differing priorities and perspectives (Emerson et al., 1995). As a result, your task is not to assume there is one "natural" or "right" perception that determines "the truth," but to uncover any number of possible truths or meanings manifested in the experiences or words of participants (Mishler, 1979). You build assertions toward the never-quite-attainable goal of "getting it right," approximating realities but not establishing absolutes.

Your task, both derived from and constrained by your presence, is thus inherently interpretive and incomplete. The bottom line is that there is no bottom line: It is not necessary (or feasible) to reach some ultimate truth for your study to be credible and useful. To claim that something you have documented or described "rings true" is not incompatible with a recognition that your judgment or interpretation of it may be wrong or "off" a bit (Hammersley, 1990). Credibility does not demand certainty. This becomes more apparent as we consider the play of selectivity in the fieldwork experience.

Selective Experience

How do I address the necessity of attending to some things but not others?

It follows from our discussion of presence that qualitative fieldworkers cannot view their task simply as a matter of gathering or generating "facts" about "what happened." Nor can they too readily take one person's version of what happened, or what is important, as the "complete" or "correct" version of these matters. Rather, fieldworkers engage in an active process of interpretation and selection: noting some things as significant, noting but ignoring others as not significant, and missing other potentially significant things altogether (Emerson et al., 1995).

Addressing the necessity of attending to some things but not others filters down to questions of purpose. For example, if Patrice is going to describe a meeting between a home service provider and a family, it will make a considerable difference whether her interest is in what socioeconomic differences are revealed in the encounter, whose agenda is directing conversation, or how the immediate setting is influencing behavior, for example. Were Patrice to develop descriptions based on each of these various interests, they might overlap considerably, but they might also vary enough to suggest different meetings altogether.

That multiple descriptions of the same event are possible should not be construed as a challenge to the credibility of an account. The point is that each description needs to be an accurate or plausible representation of the phenomenon to which it refers (Hammersley, 1990; Schwandt, 2001) and that this representation accurately reflects the purposes and sensitivities of the researcher. Describing the same event for different purposes does not lessen the need to support one's findings with evidence or to establish that the evidence for your findings is more plausible and convincing than the evidence for alternative findings (Schwandt, 2001).

To claim that qualitative fieldwork is distinctively a matter of selective experience, then, is to acknowledge the practical necessity of reducing (not replicating) the lived complexity of social life. But choosing what to attend to is not a process of sampling according to some pre-determined principle. Rather, selectivity is

- **purposeful,** reflecting fieldworkers' need to attend to how their purposes, particular values, and biases influence the conduct and conclusions of the study.
- **circumstantial,** reflecting fieldworkers' understanding of findings as contingent upon the particular circumstances under which they elicit or construct them (and consequently reflecting the expectation that the findings cannot be absolute and unchanging).
- **intuitive,** reflecting fieldworkers' changing sense of what might possibly be important to a developing interpretation and what might be interesting or useful to readers of the study.
- **empathetic,** reflecting fieldworkers' sense of what is important or useful to study participants.[1]

All of these qualities feed directly into what is perhaps the most insistently present consideration of trustworthiness discussed in this section—how subjectivity plays out in the conduct of research.

Engaged Subjectivity

How do I engage and monitor the subjectivity that influences my research?

"The inescapable fact of our presence in research," write Jansen and Peshkin (1992), "means that we are present to make choices. Choices equal subjectivity at work" (p. 721). Although some of your choices about what to attend to and how to interpret it may be consciously made, others derive from personal qualities that come into play prior to and through your interactions with events and people in the field. This is the play of subjectivity.

At issue is the question of how and to what extent personal qualities or attributes, such as emotions or personal sensibilities, influence, or should influence, the research process (Jansen & Peshkin, 1992). Or, as Behar (1996) suggests more directly, how do you make the most of your own emotional involvement with the material?

---

[1]Further discussion of these and related ideas can be found in Creswell & Miller, 2000; Emerson et al., 1995; Glesne, 1999; Richardson, 2000.

For Patrice, this issue first took shape as an insight into the virtues of rigorous self-reflection as she took her early "reconnaissance" steps into the field. During some coding of preliminary data she noted:

> I have discovered that continuing to make sense of myself is a necessary part of the research . . . looking closely at the self who produces a document at a moment in time and thinking about how that self at that moment was constructed . . . taking the step of reflecting on my range of responses, thoughts, feelings recorded in my fieldnotes, my process journal, my memos. For example, "What had I read/heard/experienced that made me write that?"

The point is to suggest that aspects of the self can serve as important filters through which one perceives the topic or phenomena being researched. This does not mean you establish the goodness or rightness of your account in some private or personal sense. To the contrary, when you deliberately engage and monitor your subjectivity, you use your feelings and emotional responses as authentic points of departure, or cues, for inquiring into why you are perceiving and to what effect you are interpreting matters as you are (Glesne, 1999; LeCompte, Schensul, Weeks, & Singer, 1999; Peshkin, 1988, 1992).

Such a cue occurred for Patrice during one of the first times she accompanied an Early Head Start home visitor to the house of a family enrolled in the program. She noted in her field journal her surprise and discomfort as she observed the home visitor sit at a table with the family in adult-focused activity, with the child on the periphery. This contrasted sharply with her own early intervention experiences in the years prior to her research, when home visits consisted of sitting on the floor with the child in child-focused activity, with the adults on the periphery. Patrice noted her emotional response not as a judgment on what she was observing, but as a cue that prompted her to reexamine some of her assumptions and shape new questions regarding the context and dynamics of home visits. She actively sought in subsequent fieldwork to see what she was not seeing, to detect, for example, if more could or should be made of how and why people position themselves as they do during home visits.

Seen in this more "virtuous" light (Peshkin, 1985b), subjectivity becomes something to capitalize on rather than to discipline or exorcise, a means to enhance, not distort, the credibility of your study. In practical terms offered by Glesne (1999, p. 105):

> It is when you feel angry, irritable, gleeful, excited, or sad that you can be sure that your subjectivity is at work. The goal is to explore such feelings to learn what they are telling you about who you are in relationship to what you are learning and to what you may be keeping yourself from learning.

This goal—and, in particular, its dual focus on what you are learning and what you may be keeping yourself from learning—serves well to guide your consideration of subjectivity. Peshkin (1992) highlighted the need to explore what he called one's "null research behavior." That is, to help ensure that you don't "stack the deck" in favor of a particular perspective or unacknowledged bias that you bring to the work of generating data during fieldwork, keep interrogating yourself: Who am I not seeing? Where am I not going? What questions am I not asking? What am I hearing but not appreciating? Peshkin further noted the importance of looking for paradox, a strategy I also encourage for students so that they don't let their stake (Read: practical aims and emotional investment) in the research blind them to contradictions that characterize behavior and actions in the setting. Looking for paradox helps to expand the possibly narrowing impact of unexamined hidden agendas you might be carrying into your research.

ETHICAL CONSIDERATIONS

> In the process of negotiating relationships in the field, how quickly I have come to understand my position as one of privilege! It is so highly privileged because of the personal and delicate information I have that has the potential to harm relationships.
>
> Patrice, Reconnaissance Report I, July 2001

How does the way you enter into the world of your study participants impact your efforts to look systematically at what you are observing and experiencing? How do you feel about "examining" the lives of people with whom you will become involved and for whom, in many cases, you will come to care deeply? How do you reconcile your analytical work with the possibility that personal relationships with some people in the setting might become primary? Can you (and should you) endorse processes of friendship as part of your methods, as some researchers suggest (e.g., Tillmann-Healy, 2003)?

Ethical considerations are inseparable from your interactions with study participants in the field. Although ethical decisions are certainly not peculiar to qualitative inquiry, the negotiated and heavily contextualized nature of ethical dilemmas is a defining characteristic of qualitative fieldwork. In this section I address four key considerations in establishing the trustworthiness of your inquiry from an ethical standpoint:

- posturing and presentation of self
- disclosure and exchange
- making public the private
- disengaging and staying in touch

As in the previous section, my goal is to convey the nature and implications of these concerns as a means to anticipate and frame dilemmas, not necessarily to resolve them. My guiding questions adjust the focus on trustworthiness to reflect integrity in the particular context of relationships with study participants (see Figure 8.2).

Posturing and Presentation of Self

How do I balance my research commitments with my desire to engage authentically those who are participating in the study?

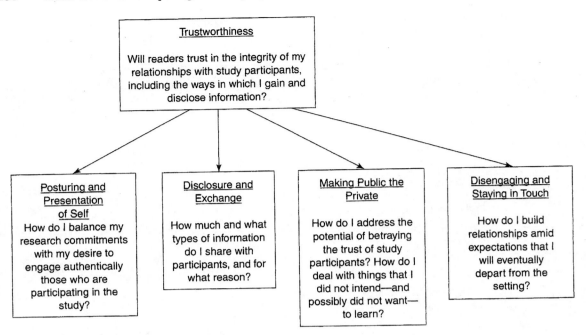

Figure 8.2
Ethical Considerations in Establishing Trustworthiness

A foremost consideration in establishing fieldwork relationships is your ability to maintain the distinct intentionalities embodied in your role as (take your pick) participant observer, resident visitor, friendly stranger, detached confidant, or neutral advocate, among others. Even under the most collaborative of circumstances with study participants, you and they are walking together on separate paths. Your dual responsibility as a researcher—to engage (walk together) with others while remaining faithful to the primary aim of conducting research—is a pairing of intentions separate from participants' everyday lives, although you hope they will understand and support your efforts.

Impression management (how you present yourself) of *posturing* thus becomes critical to the types and the integrity of relationships that you form in the field. The most commonly faced ethical decisions in this regard tend not to be about whether you present yourself in a false or affected way (posturing in a deliberately misleading and thus morally unacceptable sense). Rather, the key predicament lies in when and how you present and play out the genuine, multiple roles you bring to the field (posturing in a strategic sense). The kinds of roles you assume, far from being static, are evolving constantly.

A month or so after the initial meeting with her committee members to discuss her research, Patrice faced this predicament head on. She reflected on the questions raised during that meeting about the potentially conflicting expectations inherent in her current role as a researcher among families and her longtime professional role as a family interventionist. Recalling the specific question about observing a parent place Kool-Aid in her infant's bottle (see Part Two's introductory vignette), Patrice commented:

I undoubtedly will have an intervening effect on the families through my modeling of behavior and interactions. There is an arrogant assumption here, reflecting my professional interventionist self, that families might see in my actions the "right" way to do things. As a participant observer, I don't want families to copy me! This is why I first responded to the question about the Kool-Aid in the neutral way that I did. Now I think I would respond to the situation by explaining to the parent why a doctor or Early Head Start says not to put Kool-Aid in the infant's bottle. This might be slipping into my non-researcher professional role, but I see it more as a way to avoid saying what I personally would do. I don't want to be seen as the person who knows what is "right."

Intimate interactions like this hypothetical one around an infant's care pose ethical challenges for fieldworkers and suggest the heavy burden placed on them to express personal opinions, to act less like passive observers, and to expose their "true" selves. There are no easy answers to help you deal with such pressures. But it is crucial that, in your actions, you maintain the distinction between being something or someone you are not—generally regarded as an unethical ploy—and doing what comes naturally and seems appropriate to fit in and benefit your research aims. Consider Patrice's decision to dress a certain way for her fieldwork among families served by Early Head Start:

I have taken the designer label off the old, used backpack I carry. I bought white canvas sneakers at Wal-Mart (since my old sneakers say Adidas on the back) and . . . will go without a watch if I see few families wearing watches. When I go places with families, I want to try to fit in as much as possible with them. I envision joining the "circle of care" not as an interventionist, but as a free ride to town, as an extra set of hands when it's time to get food stamps or something like that.

Patrice's considerations reflect the range of intentions that, in varying degrees of emphasis, feed into a researcher's ongoing and ever-changing presentation of self in the field. These include:

- **rapport building,** or a process of establishing trust with participants that primarily serves the needs of the researcher; intention and purpose reside with the researcher. Fieldworkers manage their appearance and behavior in order to be acceptable to participants and foster continual access to information (Glesne, 1989; Wong, 1998).
- **friendship developing,** or the seeking of relationships founded on mutual affection and goodwill; friendship participants are equal actors in establishing, maintaining, and defining the duration, need, and ends of their relationship. "Friendship may bias data collection; but it may also contribute an even more potent voice than that gained through rapport" (Glesne, 1989, p. 53).

- **boundary spanning,** or developing relationships that transcend differences between groups or individuals within a setting, a need that is implied by the researcher's move from being strictly a passive observer to an active participant. Regarded by some as a form of cultural brokering (Goetz & LeCompte, 1984), boundary spanning often places the fieldworker in the delicate position of having to explain one group's actions to another, while avoiding being "marked" as an advocate for a particular group or perspective (Deyhle, Hess, & LeCompte, 1992).

Recent critiques of how rapport is gained and used in qualitative fieldwork question those who would automatically equate rapport with trust (see Duncombe & Jessop, 2002). They cite the development of techniques for "doing rapport" in the context of interviewing—for example, keeping eye contact, speaking in a friendly tone, and avoiding expressions of disapproval—as glossing over the ethical problem of "faking friendship" in order to encourage participants to open up. Even if you do not see matters in these exact terms, the fact that the researcher is the one working to establish rapport means that the social and interpersonal dynamics underlying rapport are usually imbalanced in the researcher-participant relationship. Other researchers, in contrast, promote "friendship as method" in qualitative inquiry, positing it as a kind of fieldwork in and of itself (Tillmann-Healy, 2003).

Elsewhere along a spectrum between the extremes of genuine empathy and elements of "faking" are those who raise practical concerns about the emergence of bias in developing friendships. Glesne (1989) describes three ways that friendship seems to bias one's inquiry. First, the researcher may unconsciously be tempted to talk primarily with persons he or she likes or finds politically sympathetic. Second, the researcher, although consciously aware of people who might be the best sources of information, may be denied access to them because of his or her friendship with others in the setting. Third, friends of the researcher in the setting may over-identify and, in so doing, act or respond in ways they think the researcher wants them to act or respond. Glesne concludes, "The case for cultivating research friendships under considered circumstances remains open, but, as a rule, I think we should give priority to developing and maintaining rapport, not friendships" (p. 50).

Glesne's advice serves you well at a practical level if you are clear in your own mind about what rapport is and is not, how it differs from friendship, and the extent to which elements of trust genuinely shape one or the other. I encourage you to explore how these issues are defined and debated in the writings of Burgess (1991), de Laine (2000), Duncombe and Jessop (2002), and Tillmann-Healy (2003). As a general rule, no matter how you define rapport or friendship, you need to pay careful attention to the assumptions that underlie your relationships with others. Foremost among these is that you, as a researcher, are shaping relationships largely according to the research needs you bring to the setting. In contrast, the cooperation of study participants tends to reflect less their estimation of the aims and merits of your research than their response to your personal attributes (Shaffir, 1991).

This leads me to another word of caution. All this talk of building rapport or developing relationships may suggest that you are relatively autonomous, assured, and self-directed as a fieldworker. Think again. Experienced researchers will be the first to tell you that the role you play in the field is not strictly and exclusively of your own choosing. Irrespective of your declared aims, participants in a setting naturally develop their own explanations for your presence. You may strive to present yourself as a friend, disinterested observer, or curious stranger in their midst, but participants "can and usually do reinterpret, transform, or sometimes altogether reject these presentations in favor of their own" (Mitchell, 1991, p. 101). What you present in the field is a *possible* self, subject to negotiation and variable "readings" by those in the setting. As noted in Chapter 3, qualitative fieldwork demands letting go of control of possible confounding variables, not the least of which is managing perceptions of your researcher role. How this plays out with respect to what researcher and participants ask and expect of each other is the next ethical consideration.

Disclosure and Exchange

How much and what types of information do I share with participants, and for what reasons?

A defining characteristic of relationships with fieldwork participants, in contrast to those with survey or questionnaire respondents or treatment groups, is the degree of personal disclosure that is both permitted and necessitated on the part of those involved (Deyhle et al., 1992). Tensions and dilemmas naturally emerge from the effort required to balance the level of shared knowledge necessary to establish rapport and the sense of responsibility that accompanies earned trust.

Your success as a fieldworker depends on being able to make requests of others. Typically, your requests (for information, for time, or simply to be present) fall outside the normal flow of events and must be negotiated and judged by participants to be appropriate or fair. This gives rise to a recurring ethical issue: How much information should you share in order to get the information you need from others? Ask yourself:

- Am I deceiving participants or putting them at risk if I deny them a complete account of my purposes? If people know fully or precisely what I am looking at or looking for, and why, will they be as forthcoming as I need them to be?
- How much should I tell participants about my preliminary sense of problem or conceptual context—that is, what I think may be going on?
- Should I let participants know in the (likely) event that my questions and focus of attention shift during the course of the study?

The answer that qualitative researchers would likely offer to any of these questions rests on a general concern to ensure that participants behave and respond in the most natural and genuine way possible. But implied in each case is the idea that the exchange of information in fieldwork unavoidably carries the potential for varying degrees of pretense and dissimulation— not to the unethical extent of lying, stealing, or breaking promises, but deception nonetheless.

Before you get too anxious over my use of the term *deception,* consider several ways it could be applied to your work as a researcher. In the course of fieldwork, you conduct numerous informal, conversational interviews. These often arise at times when, based on prior conversations and observations, you have determined that a particular line of questioning is relevant. In such instances, you may pretend to know less about a topic than you actually do. Some measure of deception characterizes this process. At other times, especially in the early stages of fieldwork, perhaps you make the decision to withhold information in order to gain what you think is a more valid and authentic data. For example, when I began fieldwork for my research into the learning and participation of Laotian students in a small high school (Schram, 1993, 1994), I initially told those in the setting that I wanted to understand the experiences of students in the school, and nothing more. I spoke truthfully but not fully about my intentions, basing my partial disclosure on a desire to ensure that participants acted and responded as naturally as possible. In yet other instances, you might pretend to participate more fully in a group's activities when in fact your aims are more in line with being a detached observer.

In none of these cases are your intentions to confuse or harm. In all of these cases you have made a pragmatic decision you believe addresses the needs of both researcher and participants in that your strategy yields fair and authentic representations of participants' natural behavior and circumstances. This rationale, however, does not lessen your responsibility to examine continually the basis of your decisions and to ensure that you do not step over the line toward more blatant and outright deception. Even if you take the pragmatic position, expressed by some researchers, that some "dissimulation is intrinsic to social life, and therefore, also to fieldwork" (Punch, 1994, p. 91; also see Shaffir, 1991), you are not off the ethical hook. You still find yourself in a discomforting, delicate, and ethically challenging position, one that clearly favors or privileges researcher needs and control of the relationship.

What is clear is that ethical standards and requirements of informed consent, avoidance of harm, and confidentiality are opposed to outright deception. Such standards make clear that it is unethical for researchers to:

- misrepresent their identity to gain entry into settings otherwise denied to them.
- deliberately misrepresent the purpose of their research.
- break promises made to people or otherwise act in ways that leave participants feeling cheated or put at risk (Glesne, 1999; Punch, 1994).

The principle of *informed consent* forms the basis of what is required by university human subject review committees for each dissertation and research proposal. In basic terms, it requires providing research participants with the opportunity to choose what shall or shall not happen to them. The most common concept of informed consent, based on the medical model, is a one-time, regulation-prescribed, written disclosure of required information about a study to a legally competent individual of majority age, based upon which he or she makes the decision to participate or not. This informed consent form or letter typically includes the following components (adapted from Rossman & Rallis, 2003): (a) the researcher informs participants as fully as possible about the study's purpose and audience, (b) participants are provided with enough information so that they understand what their agreement to participate entails, (c) participants give that consent willingly (and indicate so with their signature), and (d) participants understand that they may withdraw from the study at any time without prejudice or penalty.

Some qualitative researchers have argued against the implementation of what they deem the conventional biomedical model of informed consent in participant observation research (de Laine, 2000; Miller & Bell, 2002). They claim that, when conceived as a one-time provision of complete information about a prospective study, informed consent is inadequate or even unattainable, given the emergent nature and evolving relationships that characterize qualitative fieldwork. As Guillemin and Gillam (2004) assert, "Signed consent forms do not constitute informed consent, they merely provide evidence (perhaps of questionable value) that consent has been given" (p. 272). Another problem arises with the logistics of trying to obtain informed consent from everyone about whom researchers collect data in social settings where they have little control over who enters and exits the setting. Instead, they argue that informed consent should be viewed as more processual and dynamic—something that must be negotiated over and over again. It is a problematic issue: Informed consent presents participant observers with the dilemma of ensuring adequate disclosure to participants when what emerges is impossible to predict. Consent in such contexts is neither straightforward nor easily achievable.

Yet the principle of informed consent remains important. So you do your best to make your case for disclosure, honoring the trust on which your access to information is predicated and building on considerations of "doing good," not simply avoiding doing wrong. The call today for collaborative or participatory research encompasses the possibility that "collaboration in labor" contributes in unique fashion to establishing trust between researcher and participant, to greater mutuality in the interpretation of findings, and to more equalized power in research relationships (Zigo, 2001). This continues to be a promising approach to ethical responsibilities in research. But collaborative or otherwise, your challenge in initiating and sustaining the inquiry process is the same: convincing participants (as well as yourself) that the research is good and worthwhile, all the while making and honoring requests that jostle the balance of openness and trust.

Making Public the Private

How do I address the potential of betraying the trust of study participants? How do I deal with things that I did not intend—and possibly did not want—to learn?

Among the many implications of conducting oneself ethically as a fieldworker is the need to balance the requisites of gaining access and trust with the obligation to attend responsibly to the revelation and public sharing of knowledge that accompanies your eventual departure. With the access that participants grant you to trusted and privileged information and observations of unguarded behavior come the concerns about what you should disclose, at what cost, and for what audiences. Anticipation of this responsibility should inform every step you take toward and within the field.

The dialectic that informs much qualitative fieldwork—that is, unexpectedly acquired knowledge suggesting previously unforeseen questions leading to new directions for inquiry—heightens the risk of being misunderstood. For example, your attempt to reformulate an inadequate question based on feedback from the field—in your eyes a means for improving the credibility of your study—may be constructed by participants as changing topics in midstream in violation of a prior understanding. Or, in another twist on unintentional learnings, you may (and likely will) discover more than you want to learn, either in the form of information that is potentially dangerous to some people or that may be interesting but not of critical importance to your study. What to do?

The most basic advice I can offer is to always have in mind clear boundaries for your inquiry, and then have ways to convey those boundaries to those with whom you are interacting. The following guidelines highlight these points and provide a helpful summary of considerations to guide your conduct in the field (adapted from Rossman & Rallis, 2003; Wolcott, 2005; Zigo, 2001).

- Let participants know but also periodically remind them why you are there (either directly or, for example, by keeping your documenting activities and paraphernalia conspicuous).
- Remain aware of the boundaries you have established to define your purpose and focus so that you can convey those boundaries to participants. At the same time, be clear with participants about your need to remain flexible and open to the possibility that your focus will be refined or redirected.
- Set up opportunities to discuss fully the relative boundaries of power among all participants, recognizing and accepting the elusiveness of full equality in even the most well-intentioned partnerships.
- Be clear about your motivations and intentions when engaging with participants in activities that are, or that appear to be, other than for research purposes. Fieldwork does not preclude such shared and purposeful engagement (for example, babysitting children

so the mother can attend to errands). At the same time, participants will justifiably feel betrayed if knowledge gained under such circumstances is used to inform a published or otherwise shared account.

- Help participants maintain some sense of the nature and scope of what you intend to report (for example, by commending participant statements that are particularly helpful or informing a participant that a remark he or she just made is clearly outside the range of the study).

Attending responsibly to the manner in which you make your research public means following through with the assumption that you can and will do some good with what you have come to know. Patrice's research will not bring guarantees of infant well-being and greater equity to families served by Early Head Start; nor can she promise lifelong personal friendships to participants in her study. At the least, however, she can ensure that she will write honestly and cogently about what she has worked hard to understand, share the knowledge she has gained in a responsible and respectful fashion, and incorporate what she has learned into her own professional conduct.

Experienced fieldworkers readily note that a researcher is apt to receive more good from his or her research—status, attention, income—than study participants (Glesne, 1999; Rogers & Swadener, 1999). This is often unavoidable but not unethical, unless of course the researcher's concern fastens exclusively on personal gain. As conveyed in Patrice's prefacing statement to this section on ethical considerations, conducting fieldwork represents an assumption of privilege that researchers need to acknowledge (Emihovich, 1999). With that acknowledgment comes the obligation to attend responsibly to the ethical stance of not exploiting any person in any circumstances. This last point ties into a fourth ethical consideration: disengaging and staying in touch with study participants.

Disengaging and Staying in Touch

How do I build relationships amid expectations that I will eventually depart from the setting?

Leaving a field setting can place you in an uncertain and unsettling position. This is an ethical consideration because disengagement from a particular field situation is not simply a matter of wrapping up your study in anticipation of sharing your findings, but of dealing with a change in how you relate to study participants (Taylor, 1991). While it is true that many participants will neither want nor need to continue a relationship with you and some merely tolerate you while you are conducting your research, others can feel confused or exploited when you leave. You, in turn, will want to conclude your work on good terms with participants and leave the door open for future contacts. At the very least, you will feel you owe something to those people whom you have encouraged to open up and share with you.

You are probably wondering why I am talking about wrapping up your research now, well before you have even proposed your study. The reason is simple: beginnings affect endings. Initiating a field-based qualitative study puts you in the position of having to balance the requisites of gaining access to a research setting with the expectation of your eventual departure. This means, first, that you acknowledge how the process of disengaging from a field setting is directly related to the commitments you establish during the early phases of research; success at both ends depends on how you shape and sustain your relationships with others. Second, it means disabusing yourself of the notion that you can rely on institutional review boards and professional codes of ethics to make all your decisions for you. How you envision the establishment of relationships with study participants in this regard is an integral component of the research procedures you will outline in your proposal.

At a practical level, you want to leave doors open rather than closed at the conclusion of your fieldwork, especially the possibility of returning to the field to acquire data you may have missed earlier or perhaps to help spur a new initiative prompted by your research findings. Maintaining open doors—and doing so ethically—means fostering flexible relationships that acknowledge a spectrum of feelings, including guilt (yours, about having to leave), loss of interest (by participants), confusion (of participants about your aims), and ambivalence (on the part of everyone), among others. Be prepared to second-guess yourself: Have you assumed too much about how participants are defining the fieldwork situation and your relationship? Do participants actually have less (or more) concern about your presence than you thought? Anticipating such questions now helps you to make sound methodological and ethical decisions later.

Although there are no recipes for guaranteed success when it comes to engaging, disengaging from, and reengaging with study participants, we can look to several practical guidelines based in the experiences of other researchers to help get you started on the right foot (see Birch & Miller, 2002; Kaplan, 1991; Kleinman, 1991; Miller & Bell, 2002).

Take into account the fact that different people will regard your presence as a fieldworker differently. Especially if you are undertaking fieldwork for the first time, it is easy to over- or under-emphasize the impact of your presence upon a setting and its participants. This fieldwork that is so novel, so totally absorbing, and so central to you may not be so to those in the setting; they likely do not share the same level of excitement about your research that you do. Nor should you assume that your sudden and continued appearance on the scene necessarily fits into a pattern of behavior that is accepted routinely by a setting's participants. In short, you need to pay attention to the range of signals you receive from those in the setting about how you are being perceived.

In the early stages of my fieldwork among Laotian high school students and their teachers, I found myself being placed in number of categories: (a) I warranted casual indifference—in a social setting "characterized by disconnectedness," as one teacher tellingly noted, I was "just another person for someone not to connect with"; (b) I warranted grudging acceptance—with my focus perceived to be on the Laotian students, I was considered a contained curiosity rather than a broadly intrusive presence; (c) I warranted suspicion—"Does he work for the Immigration and Naturalization Service?" (students and their families) "Is he going to evaluate my teaching?" (teachers); (d) I warranted active cooperation—teachers who expressed feelings of guilt or frustration for their ineffectiveness in reaching out to the Laotian students believed I might be of some assistance. To base my actions on any one of these perceptions to the exclusion of others would have contributed to my intentions being misrepresented to those in the setting. It might even have led some in the setting to feel cheated or manipulated by what I did or did not do. And so we circle back to basic concerns addressed earlier: You need to be conscious of when and how you present and play out the genuine, multiple roles you bring to the field, and you need to acknowledge that these roles are evolving constantly.

Do not act as if your emotions have no effect on your fieldwork. Emotions express values, and values influence attitudes. Attitudes, in turn, affect how you choose to invest your time and effort in the field. You simply cannot afford to leave unexamined your emotional reactions to a setting and its participants. Kleinman (1991) has written in telling fashion of how her negative attitudes toward the actions of some study participants initially led her to assume a more judgmental stance, spend less time in the field, and have less enthusiasm for her research than she might have had otherwise. As she began to apply what she called the "fieldwork rule"—recognize your feelings and relate them to the phenomenon under study—she was able to attend more deliberately to how her emotions were shaping what she encountered and what she made of what she encountered.

Kleinman also points out that it is sometimes easier for others to push us to take our feelings into account than it is for us to do this ourselves. For this reason, she suggests talking to people you trust about your feelings and experiences, not only after you have data or manuscript in hand, but also, and especially, early on in the process. Actively seek their feedback on how to unravel those feelings and their real and imagined effects on how you conduct your fieldwork and analysis.

In sum, you need to commit yourself to documenting and examining the feelings you experience and encounter. This commitment should be reflected in the way you talk about your fieldwork procedures in your research proposal. Either as you introduce your proposed study or describe your procedures, make sure you write about why you chose the setting, how you see yourself as you initiate the research, and how your identity may impact your initial reactions to a setting and its participants. Later, as you move into fieldwork, continue to pay attention to how your attitudes may be affecting with whom you choose to hang around or interview and where you choose to invest your time and energy. "If you do not," cautions Kleinman (1991), "your feelings will still shape the research process, but you will not know how" (p. 184).

Question who is actually giving consent and to what, both at the outset and throughout your fieldwork. This is another way of saying you need to be aware of the differences between gaining access and consent. Confusing the two can set you up for serious misunderstandings and potential breakdowns between you and study participants. Moreover, as Miller and Bell (2002) caution, making decisions about access is not always in your hands, and even when it appears to be within your grasp, access can still be problematic.

Consider this example from my own fieldwork. As a discrete event, my initial entry to the setting of my research into the experiences of Laotian high school students reflected the problems and power differentials inherent in the hierarchical structure of a public school district. Any "halo effect" I might have hoped to achieve with an introduction by the "right person" lost its luster amid long-standing antagonism between the school's administrators and teachers. Suspicions directed by the faculty and students toward my first intermediary, a central office administrator—not my choice, but demanded by district protocol—translated into a cautious and questioning "Well, okay, we can see how it works" from those to whom I was introduced. It was a poor start—one I half anticipated—and I began hip-deep in a local history of teacher-administrator distrust, overcompensating to prove myself both nonthreatening and credible to those in the setting. The challenge I faced to disassociate myself diplomatically from the debilitating link with my administrative intermediary (while acknowledging the debt owed to that initial gatekeeper) demanded patience and perseverance.

More to the point, I clearly understood that those initial introductions and tepid responses accomplished nothing more than to point out potential routes of access to participants. Actual consent as an ongoing, negotiated, and renegotiated process between myself and research participants was going to play itself out throughout my fieldwork and extend into my write-up. The extent to which this process clearly defined where informed participation in my research began and ended would become apparent in how participants regarded my eventual disengagement from the setting.

To help ensure that you are continually reassessing such ethical considerations, Miller and Bell (2002) suggest using a research diary to document access routes and decisions you make throughout the research process around access, reaccess, and gaining consent. This is a practical strategy you can introduce in your research proposal when you discuss issues of credibility and trustworthiness.

In sum, attending responsibly to the manner in which you structure and sustain your relationships with study participants obligates you to act in ways that treat those relationships as ends as well as means (Rossman & Rallis, 2003). In part, this means behaving as you would want everyone else to behave in a given situation (with respect and dignity) and, conversely, not doing anything to others that you would not want them to do to you (e.g., exploit relationships or make promises you cannot keep). You cannot guarantee participants that their lives will be changed or improved by your efforts, but you absolutely do bear the responsibility to ensure that they are no worse off for having permitted you into their lives.

Exercise 8.1
Anticipating Ethical Challenges

In Chapter 9 I suggest that the Research Procedures section of your proposal—and, specifically, those portions in which you describe the relationships you hope to establish with study participants—is an appropriate place in which to address ethical issues that may arise in the conduct of your study. But prior to actually initiating your fieldwork, how do you meaningfully address these issues? What practical considerations can you offer to demonstrate that you are not simply proffering abstract assurances regarding what it means to be a researcher who is (take your pick) ethical, good, responsive, authentically engaged, moral, or honest? This exercise reflects the premise that it is never too early to anticipate and begin framing the ethical challenges your particular inquiry might pose.

Write an analytic memo in which you reflect upon how certain ethical issues are likely to manifest themselves in your proposed study. You might even regard this memo as the initial entry in a research diary of the sort noted in the previous section and/or as an outline of ethical issues you will address in your proposal. As you consider what you need to do to initiate and sustain your particular research activities and relationships, draft responses to some or all of the following questions (adapted from Miller & Bell, 2002) to help frame your ethical stance.

1. How am I envisioning routes of access into the setting of my research?
2. How am I distinguishing between gaining access and obtaining consent, given what I currently know of the study participants with whom I hope to be working and the local circumstances (political, social, cultural) in which I will be engaging these participants?
3. Are those individuals ("gatekeepers") through whom I will gain initial access in positions of some power over participants I hope to engage in the study? How am I taking this possibility into account?
4. In what ways might gender, ethnicity, or social position affect who I am able to engage in my research?

5. Will my use of formal methods of gaining consent (e.g., informed consent letter) risk excluding those individuals or groups who are difficult to access by such means?
6. How am I anticipating the need to negotiate and renegotiate consent with study participants?
7. How complete an account of my purposes do I plan to offer study participants initially?
8. How much do I plan to tell participants about what I think may be going on?
9. How will I document and assess decisions that I make throughout the research process (e.g., a research diary or journal, regular debriefings with peers)?

SUMMARY OF KEY POINTS

- Entering the field as a researcher reflects a deliberate choice informed by thoughtful consideration of the following questions:
  - Are you prepared to respond to practical questions about the trustworthiness of your fieldwork?
  - Are you in place ethically to do right by study participants?
- This chapter introduced issues that affect the trustworthiness, or overall integrity, of your study. Key issues that define *practical* aspects of trustworthiness include:
  - the influence of researcher presence, highlighting the link between what you come up with and how you go about doing it
  - the inherent selectivity of qualitative fieldwork, highlighting the task of reducing (not replicating) lived experience
  - the play of researcher subjectivity, highlighting the need to attend to how aspects of the self may be helping you to learn—or keeping you from learning—certain things
- Key issues that define *ethical* aspects of trustworthiness include:
  - posturing and role presentation, highlighting your dual responsibility to engage participants authentically while remaining faithful to your aim of conducting research
  - disclosure and exchange, emphasizing tensions that emerge from the uneasy balance between the level of shared knowledge necessary to establish rapport and the sense of responsibility that accompanies earned trust
  - making public the private, focusing on the consequences of revelation and, in particular, the risk that some participants may feel misunderstood or even betrayed by what a study reveals
  - disengaging and staying in touch, highlighting the need to anticipate how your initial encounters and commitments will influence the success of your exit and return strategies

RECOMMENDED READING

The first two chapters of Emerson, Fretz, and Shaw (1995) provide a practical discussion of how ethnographic participation ties into procedural matters of constructing and making meaning from fieldnotes, including their insightful notion of "participating in order to write." Peshkin's early writings (1985b, 1988, 1992) on subjectivity, feelings, and bias continue to hold relevance, practical value, and points to debate for many students. Mauthner, Birch, Jessop, and Miller's (2002) edited text on ethics in qualitative research works well as a supplemental text if you want to delve more deeply into issues that include informed consent, rapport, tensions in the researcher role, and so on from perspectives rooted in feminist ethics of care. Guillemin and Gillam (2004) provide a helpful discussion of ethical tensions that are part of the everyday practice of doing research. They make a useful distinction between what they call "procedural ethics" and "ethics in practice," and also help to clarify the notion of *reflexivity*.

Chapter 9

WRITING YOUR PROPOSAL

How do I transition from conceptualizing to proposing a study? How do I convey to others that my study is worthwhile and that I am capable of conducting it? How do I use features of my conceptualization to inform and shape the structure of my proposal? What actually goes into my research proposal?

This final chapter offers some practical guidelines and advice on how to make the shift from conceptualizing your inquiry to proposing a study. My less explicit, but no less important, aim is to ensure that you understand the important distinctions between these two tasks. Overall, if you have done a thorough and thoughtful job on the conceptualizing end of things, you will find that crafting a proposal is the easier task of the two.

FROM CONCEPTUALIZING TO PROPOSING

When . . . you think of Things, you find sometimes that a Thing which seemed very Thingish inside you is quite different when it gets out into the open and has other people looking at it.

— Winnie-the-Pooh

A research proposal represents the point at which you present and justify your research ideas in a manner that takes into account others' (a faculty committee's or funding agency's) collective judgment about what constitutes a coherent and worthwhile study. This is a decisive shift from all that you have been doing up to this point. You are stepping out of a process characterized by relative independence of judgment and an exploratory mind-set that enabled you to tack creatively between focus and breadth, observation and intuition, theory and Theory. Now you must consider how to reduce the iterative and interactive process in which you have been engaged into a product—a document—that others can understand and value.

"Each piece of your proposal," writes Maxwell (1996), "should be a clear answer to a salient question about your study" (p. 102). Viewed in this manner, your proposal highlights the decisions you have made to determine and justify the what, why, and how of your inquiry (Marshall & Rossman, 1999). A well-conceived proposal includes attention to some form of the following questions (adapted from Marshall & Rossman, 1999; Piantanida & Garman, 1999; Rossman & Rallis, 2003):

- What is the focus of your inquiry?
- What are the aims of your inquiry?
- How and why is your inquiry worthwhile and important?
- Does the way you plan to proceed with your inquiry make sense?

- Is it clear that you know what you're up to in conducting the inquiry?
- Is there an overall coherence to the reasoning that underlies your inquiry?

In transitioning from conceptualizing to proposing, you adjust your aims as a writer. The emphasis now is on presentation, not discovery; communication, not just coming to terms. In constructing your proposal you are not writing to inquire but writing to convince. Figure 9.1 portrays the processes and products that inform and distinguish these two tasks. Figures 9.2 through 9.7, with accompanying text, will unpack this first figure, clarify key linkages, and highlight the conceptualizing pieces that feed into each component of the proposal.

ARGUING FOR YOUR STUDY

Rather than provide a merely descriptive specification of what you will do, a qualitative proposal should present a clear, contestable argument that explains and justifies the logic of your study (Maxwell, 2005; Piantanida & Garman, 1999). Along the same lines as the generative and selective process that characterized the construction of your conceptual context and theoretical orientation (Chapter 4), you now make the case for the coherence, feasibility, and relevance of your inquiry in its entirety. The selective aspect of the process stands front and center in that your task at this point is one of getting down to essentials: how each choice you have made flows logically into others, and how all fit together as a coherent whole. Maxwell (2005) offers perhaps the best and most pointed advice I have encountered on this issue:

> Your proposal should be about *your study,* not the literature, your research topic, or research methods in general. You should ruthlessly edit out anything in the proposal that does not directly contribute to the explanation and justification of your study. (p. 119)

Here again it is helpful to revisit some of the cautions and pivotal concerns noted in Chapter 4's discussion of how to construct an argument for your study. Now, as then, you do not want to replace the formative task of making a case for your study with a thinly veiled summative effort to convey how learned you have become in the process of conceptualizing and constructing it. A tedious and comprehensive display of your theoretical, methodological, and/or political savvy is *not* how to demonstrate you are capable of conducting your research. Instead, continue to emphatically embrace pivotal concepts like the following:

- **Ownership.** Bear in mind Maxwell's advice to keep your proposal a matter of *your* study. Make sure the concepts and theories upon which you draw are serving your purposes and not the other way around.
- **Focus.** Stay directly and meaningfully engaged with your problem and purpose. Draw upon relevant and supplementary information on a "this-helps-me-make-my-case" basis rather than on a "see-how-much-I-know" basis.
- **Purposefulness.** Do not confuse the clarity and definition you seek in a proposal with the deceptive ease of a neat, tidy, and potentially self-fulfilling explanation or defense of some anticipated conclusions. You need not (and should not) avoid all that wonderful complexity with which you've come to terms, but you do need to be purposeful, particularly in terms of building your argument toward a meaningful, well-defined, and clearly justified research question.

CONCEPTUALIZING	PROPOSING
Problem finding and entry-level theorizing	**Title** • Contains conceptual points of reference • Orients and tracks your perspective
Situating your problem	
Clarifying practical and personal purposes	**Introduction** • Orients readers to purpose of your inquiry • Provides preview of research questions and type of study • Begins to frame the inquiry
Clarifying research purposes	
Clarifying your intellectual orientation and moral stance	**Conceptual Context and Theoretical Orientation** • Clarifies relevance and significance of your inquiry • Gives readers a clear sense of your theoretical approach • Establishes a basis for your research question
Constructing a conceptual argument	
Forming and justifying research questions	**Research Questions** • Clarifies focus and logic of your research questions
Choosing a reasearch approach	**Research Procedures** • Provides rationalization for methodological decisions and chosen mode(s) of inquiry • Explains and justifies particular strategies and methods • Addresses practical aspects of credibility and ethical considerations
Anticipating fieldwork strategies and procedures	
Establishing practical and ethical integrity	
Conducting a pilot study	**Significance and Implications** • Addresses "so what?" questions regarding your proposed inquiry • Reaffirms your purposes • Clarifies your claims
	Appendixes • Timetable for research • Tentative outline of chapters • Consent forms, IRB approval

Figure 9.1
From Conceptualization to Proposal

STRUCTURING YOUR PROPOSAL

A proposal requires structure. In this case, the term *structure* refers to the interrelation of parts and how their relative positioning contributes to the shape and substance of the whole. This understanding does not necessitate a rigid framework or formulaic outline, but it does encompass the need for clear definition and cohesiveness.

The proposal format outlined on the right side of Figure 9.1 and detailed in the following sections is certainly not the only way to structure a proposal, but it does reflect features generally regarded as consistent with the nature and design of a qualitative study. Your particular needs and style may demand variations on this structure. Where applicable, I have included student examples that illustrate contrasting ways to format the various sections.

If you conducted a prior pilot study that has direct implications for your study, you will need to incorporate discussion of that into your proposal. Your decisions about where and how to do so depend on your specific purposes for conducting a pilot study in the first place (see Chapter 2). For example, if a primary aim of the pilot study was to hone your skills as an interviewer and try out different questions and questioning strategies, then it makes sense to incorporate what you learned into your Research Procedures section. If your aim was to clarify the meaning and significance of pivotal concepts orienting your inquiry, then weave these insights directly into your Conceptual Context section or into a separate Pilot Study section immediately before or after your Conceptual Context section. If your pilot study played a significant role in defining or reconfiguring the shape of your research question(s), then describe how it did so in the Research Questions section of your proposal.

The key consideration in any case is to emphasize the specific and formative role of your pilot study in helping to shape one or more dimensions of your larger study. You do not need to provide all the details about what you did or what you derived from your pilot work. In a manner that mirrors your use of the literature and prior research, you draw upon your pilot study only to the extent needed to help clarify and justify the research decisions that underlie your inquiry.

Title

Key Concerns: Conceptual Significance, Perspective

Focus and Purpose of the Title

The title of your proposal deserves careful consideration. It conveys, if not the conceptual essence, at least conceptual points of reference for your study. Some researchers claim that each word in the title should relate to a key concept in your study, adding that each concept should then be explained in the proposal's text (Piantanida & Garman, 1999). Whether or not you push your title-building efforts to this level of precision, the basic message is that the title should flag what is under study and foreshadow the perspective that is orienting your approach to the topic. To this end, you will draw most substantially on your prior work in constructing a conceptual argument and clarifying your intellectual orientation as a researcher (see Figure 9.2). Another criterion for an effective title might include whether it conveys sufficient information to catch the attention of possible readers and to enable your work to be cataloged in an appropriate category based on the title alone (Wolcott, 2001).

Chapter 4's brief discussion of Working Through Titles (pp. 66–67 also see Exercise 4.1) should alert you to the potential and ongoing role of the title in terms of how you develop and

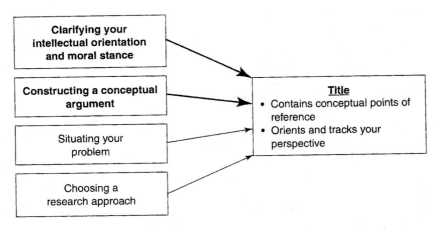

Figure 9.2
Constructing a Title

conduct your inquiry. If you systematically reflect upon your changing titles as your study evolves, they can be a means of tracking the evolution of your perspective and focus as a researcher. In effect, your successive title drafts serve as a way to highlight, address, and defend your emerging insights as a researcher throughout fieldwork, analysis, and write-up.

Introduction

Key Concerns: Purpose, Preview, Personal Connection

Focus and Purpose of the Introduction
The introduction section of your research proposal serves several major purposes. First, it orients readers to the purpose of your inquiry. Second, it provides a brief preview of your main research questions and the kind of study you are proposing. Third, it begins to frame your study by explaining what has led you to focus on the topic of your inquiry, conveying a personal and overall sense of its context and significance. A number of prior conceptualizing tasks, most prominently those of situating your problem and clarifying your research purposes, feed into the crafting of the Introduction (Figure 9.3).

In the example that follows, Patrice crafted the first paragraph of her Introduction with an eye toward purpose and preview:

> This proposed research is an anthropological field study of families who participate in an Early Head Start Program. I come to this study with two questions: What is the meaning of infant well-being from the perspective of families who participate in Early Head Start, and what is the experience of families who participate in Early Head Start? I ask the questions in this way because my broader goal is to understand the complexity of the social context of infants who are growing up in poverty and to understand the home visiting relationship when families receive support services. Of particular interest to me is what happens when a middle-class home visitor meets a low-income family in the home visiting relationship.

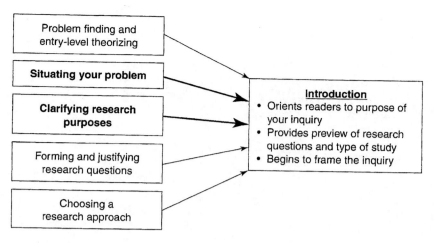

Figure 9.3
Crafting an Introduction

In this introductory paragraph, Patrice clearly and succinctly presents the purpose of her study in conjunction with a preview of her main research questions. Her opening sentence conveys in general terms the kind of study she will undertake. She wastes no words in getting to the point of her inquiry, effectively forestalling that most humbling of reader queries: "So, [insert your name here], tell me again—*why* am I reading all this stuff?"

Full details and discussion surrounding your research questions, conceptual or theoretical context, and research procedures are best left for subsequent sections of the proposal, as detailed in the following portions of this chapter. A fuller presentation and justification of research questions, in particular, is most effectively placed after the section of your proposal in which you lay out the conceptual and theoretical underpinnings of your inquiry. This is not a hard and fast rule, but as discussed earlier, this placement more accurately represents the thinking that actually went into the formation of your questions. More importantly, it enables you to build a case that supports the logic and rationale for your questions.

As for the rest of your Introduction, which normally ranges from three to four double-spaced pages, use it to frame your study with an explanation of what has led you to focus on the topic of your inquiry, conveying a personal and overall sense of its context and significance. The following section, supplemented by Example 9.1, describes one way to approach this task.

Addressing Personal Context in the Introduction

Piantanida and Garman (1999) suggest that providing contextual background from a personal perspective can be an effective way to help frame your study in the Introduction. They propose two questions you might address: "What brought me to this study?" and "Why do I find it compelling?" Preliminary memos you developed during your initial efforts at problem finding and entry-level theorizing can directly and logically feed into this portion of your Introduction.

For her Introduction, Patrice made the decision to clarify the focus of her inquiry in relation to her personal experience and context, reflecting a practice that is increasingly the norm (but is certainly not a requirement) in qualitative research proposals. As illustrated in Example 9.1, she began to address her personal connections to the topic in the second paragraph of her Introduction, eventually (but only briefly at this point) extending these connections into broader areas of concern and general references to pertinent literature.

EXAMPLE 9.1 Addressing Personal Context in the Introduction

The following excerpt from Patrice's proposal begins with the second paragraph of her Introduction. Her opening paragraph, as already noted, oriented readers to the nature and purpose of her inquiry and provided a brief preview of her guiding research questions. She then continued:

> My questions are prompted by my experience as a home visitor in early intervention for families with infants and toddlers with developmental delays and disabilities. Many of the families with whom I have partnered are socially and economically different from myself, and I question how these differences may implicitly impede the home visiting partnership and how my understanding of infant well-being may be different from families who live in circumstances entirely different from my own.
>
> In my privileged role as a home visitor for early intervention programs, I became a part of the lives of many families with diverse goals and priorities for their children in a range of contexts. I often felt comfortable in social and economic settings similar to that of my own childhood and my own parenting experience, and it was easier to relate to families who had a similar interaction style and who shared goals and priorities for their children like my own. It was the feeling of distance and disconnection, however, that intrigued me about my relationships with families who lived in circumstances different from my own. How could I support the father of a newborn infant and a toddler, both with fetal alcohol syndrome, whose alcoholic girlfriend (and the children's mother) had recently died from alcohol poisoning? What are the priorities of a family who are perpetually homeless when their goals do not seem to include housing? How could I emotionally connect with and be effective with families whose circumstances were outside my realm of experience?
>
> The current literature on infant development, although supported by increasing amounts of cross-cultural research, does not reflect a notion of infant well-being that takes into account the social and economic diversity of our society. Professionals in the field of infant development apply concepts of emotional health and development that have been created outside the social and economic contexts of the families to whom they are often applied. This is particularly evident in the process of determining eligibility for human service programs such as early intervention.

Patrice's second paragraph directs us to the experiential roots of her research questions and provides further definition of her research purposes. In the following paragraph, she begins to uncover the personal significance of her inquiry. Her narrative foreshadows broader concerns like the play of social and economic difference within relationships, while conveying the personal relevance of her inquiry through several very specific questions arising out of her own experience. Some of her statements are drawn directly from memos she had crafted in earlier phases of conceptualizing her inquiry (see Chapters 2 and 3).

Note that Patrice's final paragraph shifts from the personal realm to establish a link between her immediate interests and broader discussions in the literature and elsewhere. Piantanida and Garman (1999) remind us that such "conceptual bridgework" is necessary when starting with an account of one's personal engagement in the topic in order to avoid the risk of appearing naïve or unduly concerned with oneself at the expense of the bigger picture being addressed. Patrice's single paragraph is informative and serves the purpose of hinting at issues to be addressed in later sections of the proposal. Others might prefer to add more about the broader context within the Introduction, drawing further on information that fed into their initial efforts to situate the problem (see Chapter 2).

What, Why, Who, Where, When, and How

The approach described in the preceding section worked well in Patrice's case, but different studies will require different amounts of information to orient readers to the purpose of a study. If we examine the entirety of Patrice's Introduction, it is apparent that she has addressed the *what*, the *why*, and in a general sense, the *who* of her study.

At some point, readers will need a straightforward accounting that details key procedural and contextual issues, including the setting (where), participants (who), timeline for research (when), and specifics regarding the research approach (the nitty-gritty of the how, unpacking her general claim to be conducting an "anthropological field study"). Most of these details are properly addressed in a Research Procedures section of the proposal. You should revisit the why of your study in a later Significance and Implications section by extending into the broader arena of research and practice some of the "conceptual bridgework" (see Example 9.1) touched upon in your Introduction.

In sum, the Introduction should draw readers into your inquiry while orienting them in general terms to its nature and purpose. Its focus is appropriately on the what and why of your study. Keep in mind that you are merely setting the stage for explaining and justifying your research. It is sufficient that your audience members have a sense of what might appear on that stage, not be required to read the entire script, assured that details and dialogue will follow.

Conceptual Context and Theoretical Orientation

Key Concerns: Coherence, Relevance, Orientation

Focus and Purpose of the Conceptual Context and Theoretical Orientation

Your task as you consider this section is driven by the same question that guided your earlier efforts at constructing a conceptual context (see Chapter 4 and Figure 9.4):

> What do I need by way of theory—or, more modestly, by way of concepts—to help me develop a sound argument for what I am doing, how I am going about it, and what I am choosing to attend to in my fieldwork?

Labeling both conceptual context and theoretical orientation as complementary components lets you establish a level of emphasis for each with which you are most comfortable. As discussed in Chapter 4, thinking in terms of a conceptual context for your study allows you to be relatively modest when making claims about the ideas you are weaving into your work, while also inviting consideration of how these ideas may fit into some broader theoretical scheme. The fundamental assumption remains that of coherence, as defined in Chapter 4. Now, as then, you are constructing a way of thinking and seeing, an orientation in terms of

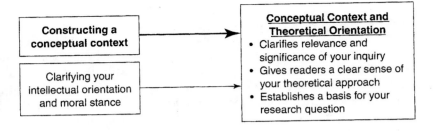

Figure 9.4
Constructing a Conceptual Context and Theoretical Orientation

which your inquiry and your reasons for pursuing it make sense. In basic terms, you are setting up the reader to understand how and why your research questions are the appropriate questions to be asking.

This means that you must establish the conceptual territory (not the entire landscape) in which your research is justified and makes sense. Your job at this point is essentially one of reframing or reducing your earlier conceptual argument in order to present it to an audience of others. Two helpful questions in this regard are those posed by Wolcott (2001) in describing the "tightening up" process in one's writing:

- Do you have everything you need?
- Conversely, do you need everything you have?

A common misstep in this section of the proposal is to go beyond what you need to make a sound argument for your inquiry. That is, you fall prey to the temptation to "load up" your proposal in an attempt to account for a full range of anticipated conclusions or analytical possibilities that your data may present. Bear in mind that your task in establishing the coherence of your conceptual framework is to make the case for your questions, not to preset the parameters of your answers. Just because a number of scholars have generated writings with potential relevance to your inquiry does not mean that you must account for every one of those perspectives in making the case for your research. If a particular perspective or set of findings contributes directly to the explanation and justification of your inquiry, then certainly incorporate it. If you are simply worried that not including a perspective suggests that you are failing to consider every possibility or that you are therefore prevented from drawing upon that perspective during your subsequent analytical work, then rethink your decision to include it in your proposal. Repeat the mantra of arguing for one's study: Ownership. Focus. Purposefulness.

Example 9.2 uses excerpts from Patrice's Conceptual Context section to portray the balance one seeks between situating the inquiry within an accumulating body of knowledge and making the case for orienting your inquiry along particular conceptual and/or theoretical lines. In general, the length of this section varies considerably among students, depending on the nature of the topic and the complexity of concepts requiring definition. It seems reasonable to expect that a sound conceptual argument for a qualitative research proposal can be made in 10 to 12 pages. Whether the length tends toward the shorter or longer end of this range depends on a number of factors, such as the amount of literature that actually exists around your topic and the extent to which you draw upon insights from a pilot study to inform your argument. The key is staying focused: Are you engaging directly with your problem by drawing on the relevant work of others only as needed to state your case, or are you parading everything you can find on your topic?

EXAMPLE 9.2 Conceptual Context and Theoretical Orientation

As with her Introduction, Patrice got right to the issues at hand in this section of her proposal. She built her conceptual context and theoretical orientation around the three primary currents of thought she had earlier identified: infant mental health, early intervention, and culture theory. This first brief excerpt is her opening paragraph.

> This study is informed by the literature and theories related to infant development and early intervention, particularly with the ecological approach to working with families (Dunst, 2000; Dunst, Trivette, & Deal, 1994). In the field of infant development we know that healthy, secure infant attachment is necessary for appropriate overall development for all human babies (Shore, 1997; Small, 1998; Zeanah, 1993). In order for children to endure the challenge of development, which involves risk-taking and inevitable stress, they need to have caregivers who are sensitive and responsive, and who foster a "secure attachment" between infant and caregiver.

The following excerpt illustrates, in one instance, how Patrice perceived that her proposed research fit into (or, rather, addressed gaps in) what was already known in the literature. Again, her intent was not to summarize what had already been done but to ground her proposed inquiry in relevant previous work (Maxwell, 1996). The second paragraph that follows, in particular, exemplifies what was described in Chapter 4 as a meaningful conceptual linkage between a particular category of knowledge and the problem one was proposing to study. (Note: In the paragraphs preceding this excerpt Patrice had identified and defined the notion of "ecological framework.")

> An ecological framework used to understand infant development has proven useful for researchers who are conducting cross-cultural studies and challenging long-held beliefs about normal child development. Small (1998) notes, for example, that "perhaps the most startling finding of ethnopediatrics [anthropological studies of child development] so far is the fact that parenting styles in Western culture—those rules we hold so dear—are not necessarily best for our babies. The parental practices we follow in the West are merely cultural constructions that have little to do with what is 'natural' for babies" (p. xvi). Current researchers are supporting broader understandings of child development, while also challenging long-held assumptions. In particular, that which we know to be valid for many mainstream middle-class American families is not necessarily valid for all children and families, particularly in as plural a society as the United States (Applequist & Bailey, 2000; Halpern, 1993).
>   Small's claim about the findings of ethnopediatricians, however, rests in the context of infant studies across ethnic and racial boundaries. My proposed study questions how

our understanding of infant development can be extended even further across social and economic lines. If ethnopediatrics has uncovered assumptions about "mainstream middle-class American families" relative to ethnically and racially different families, I question the extent to which those same assumptions color our perceptions about the development of infants who grow up in environmentally or economically diverse settings.

Subsequent paragraphs in this section similarly build upon other conceptual linkages Patrice had identified in her earlier efforts to construct a conceptual context for her inquiry. She then concluded her Conceptual Context section with three paragraphs, each of which focused on a specific current of thought and its linkages to her overall inquiry. Together, these concluding paragraphs provided a bridge to the Research Questions section of her proposal by addressing the essential "so what?" question underlying her discussion thus far: "How does my conceptual context feed into and help to frame my research questions?" You will note in the following excerpts the direct influence of the if-then propositions she had developed previously (see Chapter 4). I have included only two of the three paragraphs here.

As my questions relate to infant mental health, I question the relationship between social context and infant development. If parents and social groups have differing goals for their children based on the socially determined competencies necessary for survival in a group, then I question what the values and behaviors are of families who live in chronic poverty that adults reward and pass on to their children. Specifically, for families who live in social and economic circumstances different from my own, how do they understand and perceive the well-being of their babies? Do they understand it differently than I do? And do the experiences of infants whose families live in poverty differ significantly from infants whose families do not?

As my questions relate to early intervention, I desire to understand "natural environments" as a function of the social context of early development, in addition to the more apparent physical environment. In order to increase their effectiveness, help givers need to align their efforts with the attitudes, values, and beliefs of the families with whom they partner (Dunst, 2000). The feelings of "disconnect" I personally have experienced partnering with families outside my social experience indicate that I probably do not understand them—I do not know life from their perspective. I desire to know how they perceive the world and, in particular, their relationships with the people who are there to "help" them.

Note that Patrice included elements of her personal and professional experience in her discussion. This can be a useful and engaging, but also difficult or even distracting, strategy when constructing your conceptual context. It appears to work in Patrice's case because of how clear the connections are between those experiences and the topics of broader conceptual significance on which she is focused. The key issue in such cases, as Maxwell (1996) reminds us, is not interest, style, or intent, but relevance.

The "Lit Review" Issue

This last point alerts us to a secondary assumption at play in this section of your proposal, also mirroring your previous context work: the need for your efforts to be generative and selective, rather than simply summative and descriptive. As before, you should think in terms of composing an argument, not presenting a review. To help position yourself for this task, revisit Chapter 4's discussion of pivotal concerns in developing a conceptual context, and particularly the guiding questions aligned with the authority, focus, ownership, and purposefulness of your writing.

In highlighting these pivotal concerns, I am not seeking to put you at odds with a faculty committee that may demand a traditional, comprehensive review of the literature. At the same time, experience suggests that expectations for the "lit" review generally do not reflect the insistence that you "plow through the entire history of your topic before you dare take a step of your own" (Wolcott, 2001, p. 73).

One of my students once offered this insightful analogy: "Does a restaurant chef demonstrate a command of cooking simply by dumping recipes, unmixed ingredients, and cooking utensils on your table? Tell me, does that whet your appetite for what's being offered and instill confidence in what the chef can do?" Better at least to be one of those chefs who comes tableside to concoct the meal, all the while providing lively and precise narration about the selection and contribution of this or that ingredient and spice. That certainly appears the more persuasive way to make your case.

Like a growing number of researchers (Maxwell, 2005; Rossman & Rallis, 2003; Wolcott, 2001), I have become an advocate for critically uncovering rather than exhaustively covering what is relevant and what is problematic among the ideas circling around your inquiry. In a manner that reinforces Maxwell's "ruthless editing" caution near the start of this chapter, Wolcott (2001) likewise urges "sparing" use of citations "and only as the references are critical in helping you analyze and to situate *your* problem and *your* research within some broader context" (p. 75). In other words, make sure that the concepts and theories in the literature are serving your purposes, not the other way around.

Rossman and Rallis (2003) argue further that one's linkage with the literature need not be presented as a separate section of the proposal. "A more lively presentation," they write, "weaves the literature throughout a proposal, drawing on previous research or theoretical concepts to establish what your study is about and how it is likely to contribute to the ongoing discourse" (p. 123). They suggest building the framework that guides your inquiry within and throughout proposal sections that introduce the topic, situate the problem, and establish the study's significance. An especially creative and workable alternative to separating out one's conceptual argument as its own distinct section of the proposal is to weave it into the Research Questions section (described next) as a means to frame and justify those questions. In the following discussion of how to present your research questions in the proposal, I illustrate this strategy with excerpts from Jayson's proposal and compare it with Patrice's decision to construct a separate section to convey her conceptual and theoretical context.

Research Questions

Key Concerns: Focus, Logic

Focus and Purpose of the Research Questions Section

The Research Questions section is the heart of your proposal, the point at which you bring the *focus* and *logic* of your inquiry into clearest definition. Your proposal's Introduction

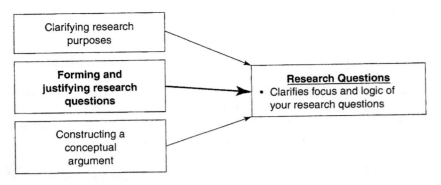

Figure 9.5
Constructing a Justification of Research Questions

provided a brief preview of your guiding questions, as already noted, and the preceding conceptual section has established a substantial foundation on which your questions can rest. Now is the time to reaffirm and explain the overall coherence of the questions guiding your inquiry. To this end, you will draw most substantially on your prior work in forming and justifying your research questions (Chapter 5). Your research purposes and the conceptual linkages identified in the preceding section serve as supplementary points of reference (see Figure 9.5).

In what follows, I suggest two possible ways of constructing this section of your proposal: (1) Patrice's strategy of getting right to the point based on her prior conceptual argument, and (2) Jayson's strategy of framing his conceptual argument within his presentation of research questions. There are certainly other strategies; I offer these two options to help illustrate approaches that have proven to be workable and effective.

Patrice's Strategy: Get Right to the Point Based on Your Prior Conceptual Argument
The key to this section's effectiveness is how clearly you connect your questions with each other and with the ideas that motivate and inform them. Let's first consider the format that Patrice employed in her proposal. To begin, she stated her questions:

> The specific questions guiding my research flow directly from the purposes and conceptual argument presented above and are central to my proposed inquiry:
>
> - What is the meaning of infant well-being from the perspective of families who participate in Early Head Start services?
> - What is the experience of families who participate in Early Head Start?

Patrice then offered concise explanations of the intentions and logic underlying each question:

It is important for me to understand infant well-being from the perspective of families because I make an assumption that families who live in social and/or economic circumstances unfamiliar to me value the well-being of their babies, but they value it in a way that I may not understand. This first question positions me to use a cultural interpretation to understand the context of infant development in socially and economically diverse settings. I hope to construct an understanding of how and why these families have the goals and priorities that they do. This understanding can inform service providers' efforts to become more effective helpers.

The second question relates more specifically to the relationship between home visitors and the families with whom they partner and who have different social and economic backgrounds. If families have different goals and priorities for their children based on culturally different ways of raising a baby, then understanding the experience of families' partnerships with home visitors from the perspective of families should illuminate factors that help or hinder these relationships. This knowledge can increase the effectiveness of home visitors as they partner with these families.

She got right to the point: "Here are my questions and this is how they make sense." You can stop at this point or extend your discussion by considering the play of additional subquestions. The power and logic of your central research question(s) can in many cases be enhanced by your ability to convey how they build upon or feed into relevant secondary or surrounding questions. Your basic criterion at this point is coherence, ensuring that your questions form a logically consistent whole, rather "a random collection of queries about your topic" (Maxwell, 2005, p. 124).

Patrice chose to continue her Research Questions section by connecting her primary research questions with sets of secondary questions (the topical questions she had earlier fleshed out, as portrayed in Figure 5.2 in Chapter 5). She wrote:

While there are two central questions driving my research, there are other secondary questions that contribute to my central focus. In order to understand how it is that families understand the well-being of their infants, I ask:

At this point she listed the four topical questions listed under her first research question in Figure 5.2. Then she did the same for her second guiding research question:

As I work to understand the experience of families in Early Head Start, my focus is aimed specifically at the relationship between home visitors and families during the process of a family's participation in services. In order to help me understand this relationship, I ask:

At this point she listed the four topical questions listed under her second research question in Figure 5.2.

My advice is to include consideration of such supplemental questions on a when- and-as-needed basis. Ask yourself: Do they contribute to a clear progression of thought, or will the additional questions simply generate separate (and potentially confusing) clusters of information (Piantanida & Garman, 1999)?

Patrice concluded her Research Questions section with a simple and concise statement of the connectedness among all her questions:

> The function of these secondary questions is to "build" an answer to my broader inquiry. While the central questions are grand in scale, the secondary questions pare down the larger questions and tie them more directly and explicitly to my purposes.

In sum, Patrice kept focus and logic in the forefront of her decisions about what and how much to include in the Research Questions section. The idea is to make sure that your questions and their respective justifications fit together, build upon one another, and fulfill the intent of your study.

Jayson's Strategy: Weave Your Conceptual Argument into Your Presentation of Questions

Now let's consider the format that Jayson employed in his proposal. He, too, kept focus and logic uppermost in his thinking, but chose to make his conceptual arguments specific to each of his research questions. As detailed in Chapter 5 (see Figure 5.3, in particular), Jayson generated one primary research question supported by two subquestions. Each of these three questions linked up with what Jayson termed *working hypotheses,* or tentative theories, he constructed about what he thought might be going on and why. In effect, each working hypothesis provided a concise abstract, or executive summary, for the more comprehensive conceptual argument that immediately followed it.

The following excerpt from his proposal demonstrates how this format looked for one of his two subquestions. I chose to use this question, rather than his primary question, for two practical reasons. First, it is the shortest of the three excerpts in this section of his proposal—brief enough to include here in its entirety, yet long enough to convey the essence of Jayson's approach to integrating a question with a conceptual argument. Second, this excerpt provides a clear and concise example of weaving an insight derived from his pilot study into the conceptual context. Like Patrice, he began by simply stating his research question. Then, in contrast to Patrice, he laid out a working hypothesis and conceptual context (argument, justification) specific to that question.

> *Question:* How is the construction of the adventure experience related to the institutional and social context in which it occurs?
> *Working Hypothesis:* First, participant experience is situated in a specific institutional context that is influenced by the values and meanings provided by Project

Adventure (which itself exists in a broader historical context), interpreted by a trainer, and enacted differentially based on specific forms of participation. Second, Project Adventure workshops involve socially and culturally situated actors. Actions and their meanings will be interpreted through broader cultural influences such as beliefs about the application of adventure techniques, gendered experience, and conflicts between a relational and individualist ontology. It is believed that the identity-conferring meaning enabled through the process of constructing "adventure" in Project Adventure workshops will interact with these cultural influences.

Jayson then proceeded into his more comprehensive conceptual argument focused on the need for research to take into account the ways in which local action is constrained by broader social conditions. In the first paragraph, he sets the stage for his argument by identifying a perceived problem or contradiction within prior research or theory. He then begins to make his case in the second paragraph, opening with the strong, clear claim from which he builds the justification for his question.

Adventure theorists generally have fallen into two camps, one concerned with specific programmatic elements of the adventure experience (e.g., Bisson, 1998; Gass & Priest, 1997; Joplin, 1981; Priest & Naismith, 1993), the other with the broader social context in which experience is located (e.g., Bell, 1997; Brookes, 2003; Mitten, 1985). Adventure theorizing and empirical studies of adventure educational practices have yet to transcend this macro-micro dichotomy, which is recognized in psychology and sociology as a weakness when seeking to understand social settings (Cole, 1995; Fine, 1991).

Outcome studies in adventure education that do not take into account the social and cultural location of programs remove learning from its context and fail to understand ways in which local action is constrained by broader social conditions. They therefore make a limited contribution to theorizing the relationship between experience and learning. As Fine (1991) states:

> Any approach to a social order must recognize that although actors themselves affect how they define their world, others—corporate, collective, imaginary, or metaphoric—considerably influence their choices. Our ethnographies, grounded in institutional realities and individual recognitions of these realities, demonstrate this, but our theory lags behind. (p. 165)

Fine's point is that any theory constructed with no account of how "macrosocial" conditions constrain "microsocial" activity (and vice versa) is inadequate since it is in the process of moving between local and distal influences where theories of social activity must be concerned. Similar to Lave and Wenger's (1991) proposition that learning can only be understood as movement within and among communities of practice, or Engestrom's (1987) assertion that the proper unit of analysis is the activity system, an adequate theory of practice for adventure education should explicate participation as being culturally and socially situated. Recent studies on adventure have begun to outline this (Brown, 2002; Hovelynck, 1999; Jonas, 1999; Kiewa, 2001), but as a theoretical perspective it is in its nascent stages. This study means to situate the adventure experience—and the learning that results from it—within a contextualized perspective.

Gender is one social structure that appears to impinge on participants' possibilities for interaction. Feminist scholars in adventure education have suggested that the adventure experience is a gendered experience (Bell, 1997; Warren, 1998; Warren & Reingold, 1993), but little empirical work exists to verify these claims. These feminist scholars criticize dominant theories of experiential education for assuming the universality of experience, while overlooking how experiences are perceived differently by women or other marginalized groups.

These scholars further assert that the organization of the adventure program will inevitably reflect a cultural orientation, and as a result will influence the experience of the participants. In other words, the very definition of adventure, as constructed through forms of action and dialogue, will likely represent gendered (or other) features that have an identifiable legacy. Lorraine Code's statement that, with respect to gender, "the world looks quite different from the way it might look from nowhere" (p. 20) is apt here. On this note, it is interesting that men in my pilot study workshop spoke of one particular event as "dysfunctional" rather than, as one woman described it, "isolating" (fieldnotes, 2/21/04; interview with "Gina").

On top of the singular incident during the pilot study in which gender appeared to play a strong role in the shaping of participant experience, common adventure discourses may reinforce and validate such activity. It is possible that gender, as one example, affects not only the actions within an experience, but also the interpretation of the experience, largely privileging certain forms of action and interpretation over others, despite the efforts of the trainer (see Hovelynck, 2001). Of particular concern in this study is how dominant cultural codes around gender, class, and other social structures manifest themselves in the actions and responses of participants during the adventure experience.

All told, this part of Jayson's proposal, in which he constructed conceptual arguments specific to his primary and two supporting research questions, accounted for roughly 9 pages, double-spaced. This is consistent with expectations for laying out one's conceptual context and theoretical orientation. The fact that Jayson located this dimension of his proposal in his Research Questions section does not fundamentally alter the task of conveying the conceptual argument that underpins one's inquiry; it merely suggests an alternative means of doing so. However you choose to proceed, your key challenge is to make sure that your questions and their respective justifications fit together, build upon one another, and fulfill the intent of your study.

Research Procedures

Key Concerns: Integrity, Credibility, Relationships

Focus and Purpose of the Research Procedures Section
This section of the proposal clarifies and justifies the particular procedural decisions you have made. Rossman and Rallis (2003) suggest that this section should accomplish three major purposes:

- It should present a particular course of action for the conduct of your study.
- It should demonstrate that you are capable of conducting the study.
- It should preserve the design flexibility that is characteristic of qualitative research.

Helping you to address these aims are the strategic, relational, and ethical considerations discussed in Chapters 6, 7, and 8, as well as the issues of perspective and stance described in Chapter 3 (see Figure 9.6). Given the scope and aims of this text, I am assuming that you are drawing upon additional educational experiences and resources, such as those recommended in Chapter 6, to learn of specific fieldwork methods needed to carry out your research and work with your data.

In suggesting the heading Research Procedures for this section of your proposal, I am following the lead of others (most notably Piantanida & Garman, 1999) whose concerns I share regarding the more common title for this section, Research Methodology or Research Methods. As discussed earlier, *methodology* refers to the theory and analysis of how inquiry does or should proceed and therefore is an inappropriate label for a section that addresses how you are actually going to carry out your study. The term *methods* commonly denotes specific techniques or tools used by the researcher to generate and analyze data. Using Methods as a title

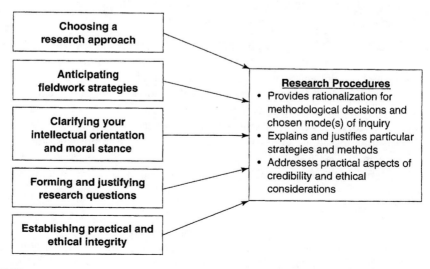

Figure 9.6
Constructing Research Procedures

is helpful and accurate to a point, but it does not encompass the range of logistical, relational, ethical, and credibility issues that you need to describe in this section of the proposal.

An understanding of your Research Procedures section as a *course of action* allows you to incorporate all of the following components:

Description of Setting or Social Context of Your Study. Although some choose to make it a separate section prior to Research Procedures, a description is an appropriate way to introduce this section and contextualize your choice of questions and methods. Your identification of the setting, population, or phenomenon of interest conveys the scope and boundedness of your study and thus provides an early indication of whether you are positioned to generate the amount and type of data you need to respond fully to your research questions.

Rossman and Rallis (1998) posit varying levels of constraint and types of obligations placed upon the researcher depending on whether one's research is site specific, population specific, or focused on a phenomenon.

Site-specific research represents a fairly constrained choice in that the study is defined by and closely linked to a particular place. This would have been the case had Patrice's study been focused on a specific Early Head Start center, keeping in mind that this decision would have been predicated on a different research question as well. This type of study requires that you provide significant detail regarding the setting as well as a rationale for why a selected setting might be more appropriate to your question than others.

A *population-specific* study is somewhat less constrained in that it could conceivably be conducted in any number of places. For example, Patrice's study was defined by and linked to participants in Early Head Start, a program with multiple locations and contexts. For this type of study the researcher needs to present a strategy for selecting participants from that population.

A study focused on a particular *phenomenon* is even less constrained by place or population. For example, Patrice might have kept her study at the level of inquiring into the notion of infant well-being without linking it to a particular group or location. This type of focus prompts the researcher to establish an understanding of how the concept or phenomenon of interest might exist across settings or contexts.

Rationale for Your Research Approach. It is usually necessary to provide a rationale for the research approach or tradition guiding your study. Although this argument can be woven throughout your proposal in ways both explicit (e.g., Patrice's opening statement in the Introduction) and implicit (e.g., Patrice's emphasis on cultural interpretation within her Conceptual Context), you need to convey how your overall approach is appropriate to your inquiry.

Carolyn, for example, chose to introduce the Research Procedures section of her proposal (a study of second language learning among adult Cambodian immigrants in rural New England) with statements aimed at justifying her selection of an ethnographic approach. I share her opening two paragraphs to illustrate several useful elements that she used to build her rationale. These include:

(a) making connections between her key conceptual concerns and the nature of her methodological perspective (her first paragraph)
(b) linking the particular aims of her inquiry to several fundamental assumptions that underlie an ethnographic approach (first part of the second paragraph)
(c) highlighting the capacity of her approach to account for the problematic nature of a pivotal concept in her inquiry (latter part of the second paragraph)

These two paragraphs do not contain her entire rationale—which, as I noted with Patrice, is conveyed in a variety of ways throughout her proposal—but they do convey several major considerations that contributed to her decision to proceed as an ethnographer.

> The conceptual and practical challenges inherent in my attempt to unravel relationships among self, identity, community, and "border-crossing" behaviors demands a methodological perspective that is both holistic and integrative. My decision to situate my questions within the particular context of contemporary Cambodian immigrant experience—real people and events bounded in time and circumstance—further extends the challenge I face in claiming to be both "specific and circumstantial" (Geertz, 1973, p. 23) and relevant in a broader context.
>
> In addressing these challenges through an ethnographic approach, I proceed from the assumption that the ways in which people construct and make sense of their lives are highly variable, locally specific, and capable of being abstracted from the researcher's direct experience with the naturally occurring complexity of those lives (Agar, 1996; Emerson, Fretz, & Shaw, 1995; Peacock, 1986). Emerson, Fretz, and Shaw (1995) suggest that, in conducting ethnographic work, I must "discern local knowledge not simply on the basis of people's talk but rather through their 'talk-in-interaction,' that is, [I] must notice what people do in relation to others in order to produce specific, situated meaning" (p. 133). This meaning-making aspect of the ethnographic process becomes especially relevant as I seek to make sense of something—a "Cambodian community"—that may or may not exist in a way I currently understand.

Carolyn then proceeded to discuss in more detail the methods and procedures that would contribute to her actual fieldwork, highlighting the relative play of participant observation and interviewing that she anticipated in light of the particular questions orienting her research. Further considerations about how to proceed with this section are addressed next.

Fieldwork Methods and Procedures.   In this part you need to explain how you will get the information you need to respond to your research questions. What kinds of interviews, observations, or other methods do you plan to use, and how will you conduct these? Think of this as the plan that will guide your decisions in the field. It is a demonstration of how you have thought through some of the complexities of fieldwork and formed your initial judgments about how to focus your efforts. This description should also indicate that you have considered the resource demands of specific decisions (i.e., "What do I need to accomplish this?").

The most common pitfall in constructing this part of your proposal is the tendency to present the nuts and bolts of gathering data as if such techniques existed in a vacuum without explicating the logical and empirical connections between your research questions, your approach, and your particular methods. "Except in the broadest of terms," cautions Wolcott (2005), "fieldwork techniques cannot be distilled and described independently from the questions that guide the research" (p. 148). You need to make clear to your readers the connections between particular methods and procedures and the data you need to address your questions.

To this end, a number of my students in recent years have found it helpful to construct some version of a data planning worksheet or data collection matrix as suggested by LeCompte and Schensul (1999; see also LeCompte & Preissle, 1993; Maxwell, 2005). As adapted for use by my students, the primary guiding component of the matrix—what the researcher needs to know—is constructed from topical subquestions that specify anticipated areas for inquiry (refer to Chapter 5 and the Research Questions section of this chapter). Table 9.1 is a hypothetical example of a data collection matrix for Patrice's study of Early Head Start families. (Patrice did not opt for this strategy herself.) For purposes of illustration, I have included an abbreviated sample of her topical questions pertaining to one of her two central research questions.

In developing the data collection section of your proposal, keep in mind that qualitative methods are no longer unknown or in need of exhaustive defense. You need not (and should not) provide a comprehensive and tedious review of the literature about such standard procedures as participant observation and interviewing. Be specific to your study and the significant linkages between your methods and your questions.

Ethical Concerns and the Relationship You Hope to Establish with Study Participants. Chapters 7 and 8 highlighted the importance of this dimension of your work, particularly as it pertains to degree and portrayal of involvement, consequences of presence, exchange, disclosure, and other ethical concerns. This is an appropriate section in which to discuss issues of ethics, including procedural matters like informed consent, and less straightforward matters pertaining to research relationships.

In his proposal, Jayson devoted a section to Ethical Concerns, in which he gave focused consideration to presentation of self, rapport building and reciprocity, and subjectivity and the researcher's perspective. I share the entirety of his narrative here to illustrate the effectiveness of his straightforward language, his sustained focus on the particularities of his study, and the useful ways in which he integrates insights gained from his pilot study. The first of his ethical concerns appeared under the subheading, *The Presentation of the Researcher:*

> Presentation must be considered in two ways: First, I will present myself to the facilitator, whom I will be interested in observing and interviewing. Second, I will present myself to the participants. I do not want to impact the actions of either the trainer or the participants to a great extent, since their actions form the basis of my inquiry. My involvement in their participation is inevitable to some extent, but I would like to mitigate it as much as possible. Therefore, to the participants, I will disclose that I am studying how group culture develops and how people learn in Project Adventure workshops. To the trainer, I will disclose the same information and I will also describe that I am interested in how they construct the flow of the workshop. Both statements are true, although they do not get into the complexities of the study. This presentation seemed to work well for the pilot study.

Jayson then continued his discussion of ethical concerns under the subheading, *Rapport Building and Reciprocity.* In these paragraphs he is more specific about decisions that stem from his pilot study. His final paragraph reveals his initiative in reaching out to an established scholar in his field for practical advice—a good habit to get into right from the start of your research career.

Table 9.1

A Data Planning Matrix[1]

Central Question: What is the experience of families who participate in Early Head Start?

What Do I Need to Know? (Topical Subquestions)	Why Do I Need to Know This?	What Kind of Data Will Answer the Question?	Whom Do I Contact for Access?[2]	Projected Timeline & Procedures
Are there implicit goals that home visitors bring to the relationship? If so, what are they?	To clarify values, assumptions, and personal factors on the part of home visitors that may be impacting the relationship	Formal and informal interviews with home visitors; observations of weekly staff meetings; home visitor questionnaire	Jill Smith, EHS Coordinator; EHS home visitors; Liz Jones, EHS administrative assistant	2001 March–June: Informal interviews; July–Aug.: In-depth interviews; Aug.–Oct.: Observations at EHS center; administer questionnaire
What is the process of relationship building that unfolds between home visitors and their partner families?	To understand how the process unfolds and determine the respective roles played by families and visitors in shaping the relationship	Observations of home visits; informal & formal interviews with families; informal & formal interviews with home visitors	Home visitors: Jan, Bev, Betty, Deb, Kim; Families: Andrews, Mills, Irvins, Gales, Williams	2001–02 Sept.–Jan.: Participant observation in family homes and at EHS center activities
What meaning do families ascribe to having a home visitor?	To clarify family perceptions and how they compare with visitor perceptions and stated program aims	Informal and formal interviews with families	Families: Andrews, Mills, Irvins, Gales, Williams	2001 Sept.–Jan.: Participant observation & interviews in family homes 2002 Jan.–March: Follow-up interviews

[1] Adapted from LeCompte and Schensul (1999). This example is based on a select sample of topical subquestions from Patrice's study of families who participate in Early Head Start. A complete matrix would include all of her topical subquestions.

[2] Pseudonyms used for illustrative purposes only.

While I will not be a full participant as either a facilitator or workshop participant, I want to be actively engaged with participants as much as possible. Given the context—a challenge course—it might be awkward to remain aloof, furiously jotting notes down while the rest of the group engages in their events. Therefore, I will take notes during most activities and will record virtually all reflection sessions. I may have more impact on the group's development if I stayed outside the group completely than if I participated slightly, especially at key times where my involvement would build trust and rapport.

During the pilot study I was able to differentiate to the participants my role as a researcher from just another participant or a co-facilitator. This has the added advantage of enrolling me in the process of cultural development so I can see meaning from the "emic" perspective as much as possible. Plus, I can also monitor my reactions at possibilities to get involved—for example, if I am not comfortable playing a game because of gender-biased language the group has begun to use, this would be helpful to note and would speak both to the development of the group in a particular direction as well as my orientation toward interpreting the data.

In a personal communication (November, 2003), Holyfield advised me that some sort of gift in exchange for being involved in the participants' experience is appropriate. She, for example, took a group picture of the workshop participants, which she later mailed to them. She indicated this was sufficient to acknowledge her gratitude under a limited budget.

Jayson concluded this section on ethical concerns with a focus on subjectivity and the researcher's perspective, framed by a straightforward acknowledgment of his own sensibilities and once again drawing upon insights gained from his pilot study.

My own sensibility as a trainer is around care and justice in facilitation, combined with the desire to work toward transformational social change. I can envision being drawn toward techniques or moments in the workshop where a trainer does something I would "approve" of, and being turned off by a trainer who preferences a way of acting that I may not find agreeable. However, such reactions, if I am able to diligently notice them, can serve as data since they inform the study as well as informing myself.

After the pilot study, I was struck by how extensively and frequently the trainer structured the experience for participants. It is likely that, in my own practice, I fell into some of the assumptions noted earlier, relating to the separation of trainer actions and participant experience. My strong reaction might have been a sort of coming to terms with my own assumption in this respect. I will need to monitor this sensitivity, since it would be easy to become inappropriately critical of the trainer. Additionally, I was struck by the role of gender during the events, and the extent to which it shaped women's experience of the workshop. I am interested in this for two reasons: first, it connected with my interest in feminist critiques of educational practice. Second, it caused me to reflect on my own facilitation and participation in adventure activities. My attention to gender will therefore remain heightened as the study progresses.

Finally, being a trainer for Project Adventure myself, I must remain vigilant to not take language or other cultural indicators for granted. I will attempt to keep my own location at the forefront, which will be manageable because, as a contract trainer and not a full-time employee, I am not a full "insider" at PA.

Jayson provided details regarding procedural matters of informed consent and the like in his proposal's Appendix, which included his approved application to the university's Institutional Review Board and a copy of his informed consent letter.

Credibility and Trustworthiness. In this section you address head on the manner in which you are responding to standards for competent performance as a fieldworker, highlighting such issues as researcher presence, the inevitable selectivity of fieldwork, and the play of subjectivity (see Chapter 8). You might use questions like the following to organize your ideas and proposed strategies:

- What are the primary ways in which I might be mistaken about what is going on?
- Why do I think that these particular challenges to the credibility of my research are especially serious?
- What do I plan to do to address these challenges and enhance the credibility of my account and conclusions?

Maxwell (2005) argues persuasively that, especially at the proposal stage, "it is often more important that your reviewers realize that you are *aware* of a particular problem, and are thinking about how to deal with it, than that you have an airtight plan for solving the problem" (p. 126). He goes on to point out that a critical issue in addressing the credibility issues in your proposal is indicating your openness to and strategies for the examination of competing explanations and discrepant data so that your research does not develop into a self-fulfilling description of events and ideas.

As addressed in Chapters 1 and 8, qualitative researchers tend to work from several assumptions regarding the nature of validity in their work:

(a) It is possible for there to be different, equally valid accounts from different perspectives.
(b) The possibility that there are multiple accounts of the same event should not be construed as a challenge to the credibility of one's own account.
(c) Not all possible accounts are equally useful, credible, or legitimate (see also Maxwell, 2002; Schwandt, 2001).

It is beyond the scope of this text to address the many and varied strategies for helping to ensure the credibility or validity of your research, such as member checks, triangulation, uncovering discrepant evidence, and establishing clear criteria for decisions about transcription. For specific, practical guidance on how to deal with challenges to validity, I highly recommend Chapter 10 in Creswell (1998), Maxwell (2002), Chapter 6 in Maxwell (2005), and Chapter 9 in Patton (2002). As a preliminary step, it is crucial that you come to terms in your own mind with how you are going to talk about notions of validity and credibility. In particular, when you make claims regarding the trustworthiness of your research, are you referring to your data, your data sources, your methods, the accounts you derive from your data, yourself as an interpretive filter? To help you sort these issues out, Maxwell (2002) offers an especially clear statement about how to think of validity in relation to methods, data, and accounts:

> . . . [A] method by itself is neither valid nor invalid; methods can produce valid data or accounts in some circumstances and invalid ones in others. Validity is not an inherent property of a particular method, but pertains to the data, accounts, or conclusions reached by using that method in a particular context for a particular purpose. To speak of validity of a method is simply a shorthand way of referring to the validity of the data or accounts derived from that method. (2002, p. 42)

Bear in mind that your basic aim is to generate a study that is useful and believable, not infallible and airtight. You are not expected to come up with guaranteed strategies that address every possible challenge to the credibility of your study, nor are you required to somehow match up your account against some ultimate, "correct" truth. As reflected in Maxwell's statements, this section of your proposal is well served by your ability to be as specific and as straightforward as you can, remembering—and reminding your readers—that you are taking particular actions in a particular context for a particular purpose.

Data Management and Analysis.   How to articulate at the proposal stage what you will do to make sense of the data you will collect is consistently a top-ranked concern of students. "How can I know now what 'chunks' of data are going to be meaningful?" "How can I talk now about my emerging understanding of what I will be learning?" "Won't my analysis take shape as I make decisions in the field and uncover important but unanticipated ideas?" All these questions reflect sound reasoning, but the fact remains that you are not a blank analytical slate, even at this preliminary point of inquiry. Decisions you have already made up to this point—about your approach, about connections between questions and methods, about linkages among your conceptual currents, even about your intended audience—all serve to foreshadow your analytical strategies. To illustrate, let's focus on two considerations—research approach and envisioned audience—and see how each can influence the way you talk about data analysis in your proposal.

Research Approach and Questions to Frame Your Analysis.   At the proposal stage, of course, you can't draw upon data you have yet to encounter to define how you are approaching your analysis. You can, however, use your selected research approach to suggest how particular methods of addressing your research questions likely translate into a particular way to make sense of what you uncover. Proceeding from an ethnographic stance, for example, Patrice might pose the following types of questions to frame her discussion of data analysis:

- How might ethnography's focus on cultural interpretation shape my interviewing methods and guide my decisions about what is significant in the analysis of interview data? What sorts of questions can I pose that will give priority to processes and meaning rather than to causes or internal psychological motives? On what basis will I distinguish culturally significant or patterned responses from idiosyncratic responses among my study participants?
- What will underlie my decisions about the relative significance of data generated through participant observation and data generated through interviews? In the case of

participant observation, what procedures will I use to determine whether or not and on what basis participants seem to attribute the same significance to events or incidents that I do?

- What types of questions might I ask in order to translate my fieldnotes into a data set? On what basis will I determine whether to preserve the storied quality of my data or engage in a process of coding and categorizing various data segments? Do I view the coding process as a means for developing interpretations and analytic themes or generating causal explanations?

Audience and Your Analytic Standpoint. How you choose to record, use, and write about your data is also linked to assumptions about the audience for whom you are writing (Emerson et al., 1995). Early on, you were probably shifting between yourself and other readers as actual and envisioned audiences, making moment by moment decisions about what is significant to include as aspects of your inquiry. In the conceptualization process, just as with your later fieldwork, that process of taking note and making note of some things to the exclusion of others implies decisions about *for whom* and therefore *from what analytic standpoint* you are writing up your ideas (Coffey & Atkinson, 1996; Emerson et al., 1995; Wolf, 1992). Analytic standpoint refers to having particular perspectives, emphases, and orientations that prompt you to construct your sense making in a particular way.

For her study of Cambodian adult learners, Carolyn identified her "disciplinary home" and envisioned at least one of the audiences as second language acquisition theorists. She worked initially, but still quite tentatively, from this analytic standpoint, and developed certain conceptual sensitivities as she read and learned about what researchers in this field had to say. For example, she was sensitive to the concept that a second language learner could gain access and power within the broader community through becoming fluent in the target language (English), but could also be inhibited by unequal power relations that characterized some social interactions. This conceptual sensitivity derived in part from her sense of audience or, specifically, her sense of what was a significant issue for an envisioned audience of second language theorists. As such, it served as a provisional point of reference as she anticipated her data analysis.

Let's consider a specific instance about the time that Carolyn was generating her proposal. During some preliminary exploration to decide on her field setting, she observed a community event that afforded a Cambodian adult learner the opportunity to practice some newly acquired literacy skills in a social situation outside the classroom. From her readings on second language acquisition theories, she recognized that this type of situation was potentially significant to her inquiry; she even had a hunch about how it might be so. With additional empirical instances like this one, she reasoned, her analysis might eventually take shape around this sort of focus: how it is through language that a person negotiates a sense of self and gains access to, or is denied access to, social networks that give learners the opportunity to speak.

This illustration bears a crucial point: The play of an envisioned audience in your analytical decisions is not definitive, prescriptive, formulaic, or even necessarily central to what you do. Rather, sense of audience is primarily a heuristic device, one among a range of conceptual tools to help you determine what among your potential data might be of real analytic significance. Coffey and Atkinson (1996) speak of this in terms of the "close, dialectical relationship between the kinds of analyses we produce and the kinds of texts we use as models and produce ourselves" (p. 120). How you conceptualize and represent your analytic work, they explain, turns in part on what you assume your readership will be:

> An audience of readers implies shared knowledge and assumptions about what is relevant to our own paper: past research, research methods, key authors, current debates, controversies, and fashions. The implied audience for our projected written work thus suggests lines of analysis and textual organization. (p. 120)

Significance and Implications

Key Concerns: Relevance, Claims-Making, Applicability, Generalizability

Focus and Purpose of the Significance and Implications Section

The explicit purpose of this section is to address the "So what?" and "What difference does it make?" questions that readers of your proposal might ask. A less explicit, but no less important, aim of this section is to reaffirm the purposes of your inquiry. Relative to the emphasis given to research purposes in your Introduction, this section of the proposal provides an opportunity to heighten emphasis on the practical aims of your inquiry (see Figure 9.7).

A third, more embedded aim of this section is to convey what you mean by your claims to be "getting at" the focus or topic of your inquiry. Piantanida and Garman (1999) speak of this in terms of students "owning their study," and define this in terms of "embrac[ing] more fully the epistemological assumption that the significance of their study lies not within the data per se but in the meaning they make of the data" (p. 145). In other words, maintain perspective on what you are claiming (portrayal of your experience with and understanding of a topic) and what you are not claiming (discovery or verification of "the truth" about a topic).

A significant dimension of your response to the "so what?" question is your effectiveness in discussing its potential relevance and implications for the broader field of ideas, research, and/or practice in which it is situated. Truth be told, we qualitative researchers would like to have our cake and eat it too: acknowledging the uniqueness of our particular inquiry, but claiming that it is "not so unique that we cannot learn from it and apply its lessons more generally" (Wolcott, 2005, p. 175). Wolcott goes on to highlight the logic and appeal of this

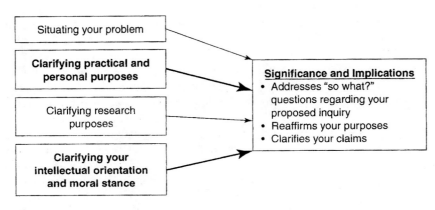

Figure 9.7
Constructing Significance and Implications

both/and stance in the context of providing some helpful advice on how qualitative researchers might respond to questions about the generalizability of their studies. For purposes of illustration, I am inserting Patrice's now familiar study into the guidelines suggested by Wolcott:

- I regard these particular families participating in Early Head Start to be families *in certain respects* like *all* other families participating in Early Head Start.
- I regard these particular families participating in Early Head Start to be families *in certain respects* like *some* other families participating in Early Head Start.
- I regard these particular families participating in Early Head Start to be families *in certain respects* like *no* other families participating in Early Head Start.[1]

This sort of thinking reflects the feeling among an increasing number of researchers that generalizability in qualitative research is best thought of as a matter of the "fit" between the situation studied and other situations to which readers might apply the concepts or theories generated through that study (Schofield, 2002). Generalization in this sense is based on the assumption that a theory generated from a qualitative study may be useful in making sense of similar processes or situations, including the possibility that the same process, in different situations, could lead to different results (Maxwell, 2002; see also Yin, 1994). To pose a hypothetical example, imagine that you are listening in as Patrice offers this explanation to her committee:

> My findings are not generalizable as descriptions of what other Early Head Start service providers do with their client families; but they are generalizable as descriptions of what any Early Head Start service provider, with his or her client families, *can* or *might* do, given that he or she is engaging a similar set of intentions and circumstances.

As Cronbach stated three decades ago when he argued that a top priority for the researcher is to do justice to the particular case, "When we give weight to local conditions, any generalization is a working hypothesis, not a conclusion (1975, pp. 124–125). Accordingly, what you are doing as a qualitative researcher is contributing knowledge that, "in a cumulative sense, builds general, if not necessarily generalizable, knowledge" (Patton, 2002, p. 583). Patton goes on to suggest that qualitative researchers use the term *extrapolations*, which he defines as "modest speculations on the likely applications of findings to other situations under similar, but not identical conditions" (2002, p. 584). You are going to encounter a range of similar terms suggested in the literature: transferability, fittingness, naturalistic generalization, to name a few. Ultimately, the precise term you use is not as crucial as articulating how the inquiry you conduct in your particular, purposefully selected research context carries the potential for broader relevance. This takes us back to issues of trustworthiness and validity, particularly in terms of your responsibility to provide the information and rich accounts necessary so that readers can make an informed judgment about the issue of fit.

---

[1]Wolcott specifically adapted a statement written decades ago (hence the outmoded gender language) by Kluckhohn and Murray to introduce their chapter on personality formation (1948, p. 35):

Every man is in certain respects

a. like all other men,

b. like some other men,

c. like no other man.

Appendixes

Key Concerns: Extension, Illustration

Appendixes should not simply be an afterthought. They extend and provide supplementary illustration for your proposal argument, without disrupting the flow of the main body of the text. Consider your need for some or all of the following components:

- **A timetable for your research.** This helps readers (and you) judge the feasibility of your proposed study and may suggest questions about logistics and practicality not immediately apparent in the body of your proposal. In some cases, a data planning matrix in the Research Procedures section (e.g., Table 9.1) can serve this purpose.
- **Copies of informed consent forms and/or letters of introduction.**
- **Copy of Institutional Review Board (or similar body) approval for your proposed study.** Requirements for this vary from institution to institution, as does the expectation that such approval precedes or follows the presentation and defense of your research proposal to a faculty committee or funding agency.
- **Detailed explanation or description of a particular data collection or analysis technique.** If full explanation of a specific method or technique would take up too much space or disrupt the narrative flow in the body of the proposal, include it as an appendix. This would also be the place for copies of proposed interview guides or questionnaires.
- **A tentative outline of chapters for your thesis or dissertation.** Nearly all my students have initially expressed shock at the suggestion of drafting a table of contents before they have even started their research (much as I responded when the chair of my dissertation committee at the University of Oregon, requested the same of me—complete with estimates of the lengths of each chapter!). Like my mentor, however, I have become convinced of the value of this exercise for several reasons (also see Wolcott, 2001). First, this initial attempt to structure what you think might be the account you want to develop reveals much about how tightly or loosely you are holding on to certain ideas, theories, and assumptions. To what extent might these ideas be dictating rather than serving your purposes? Second, a draft outline reveals how constrained (or not) you feel about the structure of the thesis or dissertation itself. Do you feel locked in to the traditional five or six chapter format, and is that format appropriate to the nature and direction of your inquiry? Third, and perhaps most importantly, working through drafts of the table of contents can serve, in similar fashion to the redrafting of titles discussed earlier, as a way to systematically monitor your emerging insights and evolving perspective as a researcher.

Additional Considerations

The framework I have presented in this chapter is geared toward proposals of roughly 25 to 30 double-spaced pages, not including appendixes and references (which should be limited to references actually cited in the body of your proposal). This is by no means the only way to organize and present a proposal, but it does respond to crucial concerns arising out of a thorough conceptualization process. I urge you to attend carefully to variations on this structure that reflect the expectations and requirements of your particular institution or situation.

CONCLUDING THOUGHTS AND ADVICE

COMING FULL CIRCLE

If you come away from this book with a sense that your conceptualizing efforts are, by nature and intent, more cumulative than conclusive, then you are well positioned to get on with the task at hand. You have come full circle, engaging with a sense of problem and purpose, communicating the focus of your aims in well-formulated questions, constructing conceptual linkages that lend coherence to your inquiry, arguing for ownership of your ideas, and, finally, staking your claim to follow through on what you want to accomplish.

Generating, accumulating, connecting, paring, and making your case. Together, these actions comprise an iterative process that prefigures your fieldwork and eventual write-up and reveals the inexhaustibility of the conceptualizing process. As suggested by the epigraph that prefaces this book, the real work of qualitative research—the essential mindwork that feeds and reflects back upon your research efforts—continues with no less intensity as you move into the field.

With an eye toward key lessons that might be derived from this book, I close with the following bits of advice, offered as a practical guide toward your next steps and ongoing decisions as a qualitative researcher.

SOME CLOSING ADVICE ABOUT PURSUING A QUALITATIVE STUDY

Do not confuse your proposed research with a personal crusade. "One of the worst things we can do as qualitative researchers," writes Gary Shank (2002), "is to be convinced that we are right about something before we begin. Even worse is the belief that doing the actual research is the best way to make sure that we were correct in the first place" (p. 186). As a qualitative researcher—or any type of researcher, for that matter—you should not be in the business of using research to deliver self-fulfilling prophecies or to safeguard the banner of some precious beliefs you may hold. It is one matter to build upon compelling interest in an issue, and even heartfelt advocacy for a perspective or cause, to drive one's research. It is quite another matter, as Shank cautions us, simply to "appropriate" research in order to further some other agenda. You need to allow research to be research and create the space for decisions that can take you in unanticipated directions, especially those directions that prompt you to reexamine or adjust prior beliefs. To this end, you need to be relentless in your efforts to uncover the influence of unexamined assumptions in your aims, questions, and tendencies as a researcher.

Creating the space for such inquiry necessitates looking beyond yourself for assistance and feedback. There is something of a therapeutic dimension to the task of bringing your assumptions, values, beliefs and modes of questioning to a level of awareness that permits you to perceive them as potential sources of bias, blindness, or single-mindedness in the research process. That is why you need to find a small support group—trusted peers at a similar point in the process who can bring a critical eye, a sympathetic shoulder, and stress-reducing humor to the process of talking about your research on a regular basis. Make it a priority from the start.

Go to original and firsthand sources to inform your methodological decisions. Once you have taken the opportunity to study and discuss some of the books that provide an overview of various research approaches, follow the references to their sources both in print and, when appropriate, in person (or via e-mail). You cannot build a viable rationale for a methodological choice based solely on someone's explanation of another person's approach. Nor can you do so based solely on reading a single text or taking a single research course. Start to establish your claim to be a contributing member of this or that qualitative conversation by attending conferences, e-mailing specific questions or comments to the author of a study that has particularly influenced your thinking, seeking feedback on your ideas, and reading completed studies. An increasing number of journals, such as *Anthropology and Education Quarterly,* now include the authors' contact information as an invitation for comments or dialogue.

The corollary caution is not to accept uncritically the first explanation of a research approach you encounter. There are different pathways to any particular approach, and you need to acknowledge, if not fully comprehend, the presence and influence of these options. For example, Kathy Charmaz's constructivist approach to grounded theory is currently finding an enthusiastic and growing researcher audience, and, given the exposure in the literature and at conferences that accompanies such appeal, hers may be the perspective through which you are introduced to grounded theory. But if you want to grasp the essence, nuances, and potential of her approach, you need at least a consumer's knowledge of grounded theory's roots in the work of Glaser and Strauss and its subsequent transformations in the work of others (as noted in Chapter 6).

Step back and take the opportunity to assess your conceptual understandings away from your immediate context, setting, or population of interest. I learned this valuable lesson as I was coming to terms with the conceptual underpinnings of my own dissertation study. I was pulling together the various components of my research proposal focused on a veteran teacher's entry and adjustment to a new work setting after 23 years in another school system. I was eagerly devouring all that the literature on teacher socialization had to offer, enthusiastically documenting the shift at that time toward a more interactive model of the teacher socialization process, and generally feeling rather smug about my grasp of the topic. I was particularly excited about the ways in which my focus on an experienced teacher was suggesting a needed alternative to the literature's predominant emphasis on the socialization of novice teachers.

That is, until my advisor asked me, "So, Tom, what does the notion of 'socialization' really have to offer us?"

"Well," I responded, "teacher socialization has been—"

"—I said *socialization,* not *teacher socialization.* Conceptually, where does that notion take us, how does it help our understanding? Why have you made it central to your inquiry?"

I realized that I was under Kaplan's proverbial street lamp (see Chapter 4), letting the literature of the day determine what I was looking for and why, and, in the process, becoming overly dependent on the illuminative power of a particular framework for my conceptual argument. So I stepped out from that circle of light (the teacher education literature) and sought out additional conceptual roots in sociology and anthropology oriented toward understanding the process of becoming a nurse, a canoe builder, an apprentice, a cocktail waitress, a tribal elder. This led to further steps toward exploring how the concepts of socialization and its (for me) newly rediscovered counterpart *enculturation* called attention to different facets of becoming whatever someone is becoming. This led me to the point where I wished I'd been from the start: realizing that simply putting a word to process—in this case, socialization or enculturation—would not dissolve its problematic character. I turned to the simple phrase *becoming a teacher* as a practical alternative that allowed me to assess a concept like socialization rather than simply adopt it, and, in so doing, create the capacity for more extensive and creative theory building.

This brief summary does not do justice to the insights gained from the straightforward advice to slow down and step off the conceptual train I was on in order to assess the viability, transferability, and potential constraints of the ideas with which I was working. This step did not add huge amounts of time to my proposal building but probably shaved weeks of wandering among superficial explanatory frameworks during my subsequent fieldwork and sense-making efforts. So, look up occasionally, see what street lamp you may be under, and consider what it may *not* be illuminating.

Do not equate mundane processes such as coding with the actual having of ideas. This is another way of cautioning you not to confuse a *way of looking* (directing attention to methods and procedures) with a *way of seeing* (directing attention to perspective and intent), a crucial distinction discussed in Chapter 6. Difficulties arise when you begin to define your conceptualizing and sense-making efforts according to a restricted or mechanistic set of procedures. This is illustrated most conspicuously in the fieldwork and analysis phase if the researcher uses computerized coding and data sorting programs simply to add another layer of "legitimacy" to what is an inherently complex process. It is one thing to regard the computer as a useful tool for preparing, organizing, retrieving, and displaying text, and quite another, as Fielding (2002) cautions, to concede it a major place in the analytic process. Shank (2002) frames such tendencies within what he calls the "sin of competitiveness," referring to the felt need among some, less confident qualitative researchers to establish the "fact" that their work is "just as valid" and "just as rigorous" as a quantitative study on the same topic (pp. 185–186). In such cases, he argues, an inordinate emphasis is placed on coding strategies and trying to account for each and every piece of information generated during the study—a neat and tidy (and often painstakingly detailed) methodological package, perhaps, but one ultimately defined by what others say it should be.

In short, don't be consumed by efforts to defend your methods, and by all means, remember that your intent and the questions you seek to answer determine what constitutes data in the first place. Data do not simply become ideas or emerge as concepts through a process of sorting and coding, and they do not speak for themselves. To claim that your data "speak" to you is merely convenient shorthand for the fact that you act upon the significance you've attached to those data and construct a reading of them relative to your ideas about them. How you organize, interpret, and bring data to bear on your ideas is more a matter how you *see* than how you *look at* something. Hold on to that distinction.

Devote time to practicing fieldwork skills. As noted in Chapter 2, the opportunity to practice interviewing and observation skills is one of the primary benefits of conducting pilot studies, but don't limit your skill development to your involvement in actual studies. The more you practice, the more you realize how much you can still do to improve. Embrace your mistakes, put them out on the table for others to examine and assess, seek feedback from experienced fieldworkers, and absolutely do not limit your preparation for fieldwork to reading books and articles about methods. Attend some of those preconference workshops on fieldwork methods, such as those offered at the Advances in Qualitative Methods hosted each February by the International Institute of Qualitative Methodology (www.ualberta.ca/iiqm/). You cannot assume that fieldwork simply requires a keen eye, a willing ear, and strong interpersonal skills. Practice, and then practice some more.

Be prepared to engage in the qualitative conversations touched upon by your own work. Once you begin to establish yourself as a qualitative researcher through your own fieldwork and writing, you may be asked or challenged to take a stand about any number of ethical, methodological, or political issues (alluded to in Chapter 1's selective summary of "qualitative conversations"). My advice to students and novice researchers, mirroring that offered by Wolcott (2005), is to be "informed as to the substance of these debates rather than to be drawn prematurely into them" (p. 151). To the extent that you can convey a thoughtful position with respect to how the issue at hand might pertain to your particular study, then by all means grab the opportunity to receive feedback on your ideas.

Be prepared to look more deeply at yourself. This final piece of advice is borrowed directly from Patton's (2002, p. 35) list of thoughtful considerations for prospective qualitative researchers, and is a natural extension of Chapter 8's discussion of how your emotions and mind-set affect, and are affected by, your fieldwork. The fact that you have chosen to invest your time and energy in qualitative research—and, particularly, the deep exploration of other people's lives and experiences—calls for a complementary openness to looking more deeply at yourself. Pay attention to what you can learn about who you are and how you change as a researcher and as a person through your engagement in this process.

References

Agar, M. H. (1994). *Language shock: Understanding the culture of communication.* New York: Morrow.

Agar, M. H. (1996). *The professional stranger: An informal introduction to ethnography* (2nd ed.). San Diego, CA: Academic Press.

Agar, M. H. (1999). How to ask for a study in qualitatisch. *Qualitative Health Research, 9*(5), 684–697.

Allen, D. (1995). *The tuning protocol: A process for reflection.* (Studies on Exhibitions, No. 15). Providence, RI: Coalition of Essential Schools, Brown University.

Andrews, M., Sclater, S. D., Squire, C., & Tamboukou, M. (2004). Narrative research. In C. Seale, G. Gobo, J. F. Gubrium, & D. Silverman (Eds.), *Qualitative research practice* (pp. 109–124). Thousand Oaks, CA: Sage.

Annells, M. (1996). Grounded theory method: Philosophical perspectives, paradigm of inquiry, and postmodernism. *Qualitative Health Research, 6*(3), 379–393.

Appadurai, A. (1988). Place and voice in anthropological theory. *Cultural Anthropology, 3*(1), 16–20.

Asmussen, K. J., & Creswell, J. W. (1995). Campus response to a student gunman. *Journal of Higher Education, 66,* 575–591.

Atkinson, P., Coffey, A., & Delamont, S. (2003). *Key themes in qualitative research: Continuities and changes.* Walnut Creek, CA: AltaMira Press.

Atkinson, P., & Hammersley, M. (1994). Ethnography and participant observation. In N. K. Denzin & Y. S. Lincoln (Eds.), *Handbook of qualitative research* (pp. 248–261). Thousand Oaks, CA: Sage.

Babchuk, W. A. (1997). The rediscovery of grounded theory: Strategies for qualitative research in adult education. Unpublished doctoral dissertation, University of Nebraska-Lincoln.

Barone, T. (2001). Science, art, and the predispositions of educational researchers. *Educational Researcher, 30*(7), 24–28.

Becker, H. S. (1993). Theory: The necessary evil. In D. J. Flinders & G. E. Mills (Eds.), *Theory and Concepts in Qualitative Research* (pp. 218–229). New York: Teachers College Press.

Behar, R. (1996). *The vulnerable observer.* Boston: Beacon Press.

Bell, D. (1980). *Brown v. Board of Education* and the interest convergence dilemma. *Harvard Law Review, 93,* 518–533.

Bell, D. (1987). *And we are not saved: The elusive quest for racial justice.* New York: Basic Books.

Benner, P. (Ed.). (1994). *Interpretive phenomenology.* Thousand Oaks, CA: Sage.

Berger, P., & Luckmann, T. (1967). *The social construction of reality.* New York: Anchor.

Birch, M., & Miller, T. (2002). Encouraging participation: Ethics and responsibilities. In M. Mauthner, M. Birch, J. Jessop, & T. Miller (Eds.), *Ethics in qualitative research* (pp. 91–106). Thousand Oaks, CA: Sage.

Bittner, E. (1988). Realism in field research. In R. E. Emerson (Ed.), *Contemporary field research: A collection of readings* (pp. 149–155). Prospect Heights, IL: Waveland.

Bogdan, R., & Biklen, S. K. (2003). *Qualitative research for education: An introduction to theory and methods* (4th ed.). Boston: Allyn and Bacon.

Brantlinger, E. A. (1999). Inward gaze and activism as moral next steps in inquiry. *Anthropology and Education Quarterly, 30*(4), 413–429.

Britzman, D. P. (1991). *Practice makes practice: A critical study of learning to teach.* Albany: State University of New York Press.

Brumann, C. (1999). Writing for culture: Why a successful concept should not be discarded. *Current Anthropology, 40*(1), 1–13.

Bruner, J. (1990). *Acts of meaning.* Cambridge, MA: Harvard University Press.

Burgess, R. G. (1991). Sponsors, gatekeepers, members, and friends: Access in educational settings. In W. B. Shaffir and R. A. Stebbins (Eds.), *Experiencing fieldwork: An inside view of qualitative research* (pp. 43–52). Newbury Park, CA: Sage.

Burke, K. (1935). *Permanence and change.* New York: New Republic.

Bushnell, M. (2001). This bed of roses has thorns: Cultural assumptions and community in an elementary school. *Anthropology and Education Quarterly, 32*(2), 139–166.

Carspecken, P. F. (1996). *Critical ethnography in educational research: A theoretical and practical guide.* New York: Routledge.

Carspecken, P. F. (2002). The hidden history of praxis theory within critical ethnography and the criticalism/postmodernism problematic. In Y. Zou & E. T. Trueba (Eds.), *Ethnography and schools: Qualitative approaches to the study of education* (pp. 55–86). Lanham, MD: Rowan & Littlefield Publishers.

Charmaz, K. (1990). Discovering chronic illness: Using grounded theory. *Social Science Medicine, 30,* 1161–1172.

Charmaz, K. (1991). *Good days, bad days: The self in chronic illness and time.* New Brunswick, NJ: Rutgers University Press.

Charmaz, K. (2000). Grounded theory: Objectivist and constructivist methods. In N. K. Denzin & Y. S. Lincoln (Eds.), *Handbook of qualitative research* (2nd ed., pp. 509–535). Thousand Oaks, CA: Sage.

Charmaz, K. (2002). Qualitative interviewing and grounded theory analysis. In J. F. Gubrium & J. A. Holstein (Eds.), *Inside interviewing: New lenses, new concerns.* (pp. 311–330). Thousand Oaks, CA: Sage.

Charmaz, K., & Mitchell, R. G. (2002). Grounded theory in ethnography. In P. Atkinson, A. Coffey, S. Delamont, J. Lofland, & L. Lofland (Eds.), *Handbook of ethnography* (pp. 160–174). Thousand Oaks, CA: Sage.

Clandinin, D. J., & Connelly, F. M. (2000). *Narrative inquiry: Experience and story in qualitative research.* San Francisco, CA: Jossey-Bass.

Clarke, A. E. (2003). Situational analyses: Grounded theory mapping after the postmodern turn. *Symbolic Interaction, 26*(4), 553–576.

Coffey, A., & Atkinson, P. (1996). *Making sense of qualitative data.* Thousand Oaks, CA: Sage.

Cohen, M., & Omery, A. (1994). Schools of phenomenology: Implications for research. In J. M. Morse (Ed.), *Critical issues in qualitative research methods* (pp. 136–156). Thousand Oaks, CA: Sage.

Collins, P. H. (1998). *Fighting words: Black women and the search for justice.* Minneapolis: University of Minnesota Press.

Copi, I. M., & Cohen, C. (1998). *Introduction to logic* (10th ed.). Upper Saddle River, NJ: Prentice Hall.

Cortazzi, M. (1993). *Narrative analysis.* Bristol, PA: Falmer Press.

Cortazzi, M. (2002). Narrative analysis in ethnography. In P. Atkinson, A. Coffey, S. Delamont, J. Lofland, & L. Lofland (Eds.), *Handbook of ethnography* (pp. 384–394). Thousand Oaks, CA: Sage.

Crepeau, E. B. (2000). Reconstructing Gloria: A narrative analysis of team meetings. *Qualitative Health Research 10*(6), 766–787.

Creswell, J. W. (1998). *Qualitative inquiry and research design: Choosing among five traditions.* Thousand Oaks, CA: Sage.

Creswell, J. W. (2002). *Educational research: Planning, conducting, and evaluating quantitative and qualitative research.* Upper Saddle River, NJ: Merrill/Prentice Hall.

Creswell, J. W. (2003). *Research design: Qualitative, quantitative, and mixed methods approaches* (2nd ed.). Thousand Oaks, CA: Sage.

Creswell, J. W., & Miller, D. L. (2000). Determining validity in qualitative inquiry. *Theory into Practice, 39*(3), 124–130.

Cronbach, L. (1975). Beyond the two disciplines of scientific psychology. *American Psychologist, 30,* 116–127.

Czarniawska, B. (1998). *A narrative approach to organization studies.* London: Sage.

Czarniawska, B. (2002). Narratives, interviews, and organizations. In J. F. Gubrium and J. A. Holstein (Eds.), *Handbook of interview research: Context and method* (pp. 733–749). Thousand Oaks, CA: Sage.

Daiute, C., & Lightfoot, C. (2004). Editors' introduction: Theory and craft in narrative inquiry. In C. Dauite and C. Lightfoot (Eds.), *Narrative analysis: Studying the development of individuals in society* (pp. vii–xviii). Thousand Oaks, CA: Sage.

DeCuir, J. T., & Dixson, A. D. (2004). "So when it comes out, they aren't that surprised that it is there": Using critical race theory as a tool of analysis of race and racism in education. *Educational Researcher, 33*(5), 26–31.

de Laine, M. (2000). *Fieldwork, participation and practice: Ethics and dilemmas in qualitative research.* Thousand Oaks, CA: Sage.

Delamont, S. (2004). Ethnography and participant observation. In C. Seale, G. Gobo, J. F. Gubrium, & D. Silverman (Eds.), *Qualitative research practice* (pp. 217–229). Thousand Oaks, CA: Sage.

Delgado, R. (Ed.). (1995). *Critical race theory: The cutting edge.* Philadelphia: Temple University Press.

Denzin, N. K. (1997). *Interpretive ethnography: Ethnographic practices for the 21st century.* Thousand Oaks, CA: Sage.

Denzin, N. K., & Lincoln, Y. S. (1994). Introduction: Entering the field of qualitative research. In N. K. Denzin & Y. S. Lincoln (Eds.), *Handbook of qualitative research* (pp. 1–17). Thousand Oaks, CA: Sage.

Denzin, N. K., & Lincoln, Y. S. (2000). Introduction: The discipline and practice of qualitative research. In N. K. Denzin & Y. S. Lincoln (Eds.), *Handbook of qualitative research* (2nd ed., pp. 1–28). Thousand Oaks, CA: Sage.

Dey, I. (1993). *Qualitative data analysis: A user-friendly guide for social scientists.* London: Routledge.

Dey, I. (2004). Grounded theory. In C. Seale, G. Gobo, J. F. Gubrium, & D. Silverman (Eds.), *Qualitative research practice* (pp. 80–93). Thousand Oaks, CA: Sage.

Deyhle, D. L., Hess, G. A., & LeCompte, M. D. (1992). Approaching ethical issues for qualitative researchers in education. In M. LeCompte, W. L. Millroy, & J. Preissle (Eds.), *Handbook of qualitative research in education* (pp. 597–641). San Diego, CA: Academic Press.

Dickens, D., & Fontana, A. (Eds.). (1994). *Postmodernism and social inquiry.* New York: Guilford Press.

Dolby, N. (2000). The significance of place: Fieldwork reflections on "South Africa" and "the United States." *Anthropology and Education Quarterly, 31*(4), 486–492.

Duncombe, J., & Jessop, J. (2002). 'Doing rapport' and the ethics of 'faking friendship'. In M. Mauthner, M. Birch, J. Jessop, & T. Miller (Eds.), *Ethics in qualitative research* (pp. 107–122). Thousand Oaks, CA: Sage.

Edson, C. H. (1988). Our past and present: Historical inquiry in education. In R. R. Sherman & R. B. Webb (Eds.), *Qualitative research in education: Focus and methods* (pp. 44–58). Bristol, PA: Falmer Press.

Edwards, R., & Mauthner, M. (2002). Ethics and feminist research: Theory and practice. In M. Mauthner, M. Birch, J. Jessop, & T. Miller (Eds.), *Ethics in qualitative research* (pp. 14–31). Thousand Oaks, CA: Sage.

Eisenhart, M. (1995). Research news and comment. *Educational Researcher, 24*(9), 32–33.

Eisner, E. W. (1997). The promise and perils of alternative forms of data representation. *Educational Researcher, 26*(6), 4–10.

Eisner, E. W. (1998). *The enlightened eye: Qualitative inquiry and the enhancement of educational practice.* Upper Saddle River, NJ: Merrill/Prentice Hall.

Eisner, E. W. (1999). Rejoinder: A response to Tom Knapp. *Educational Researcher, 28*(1), 19–20.

Eliot, T. S. (1950). *Selected essays.* New York: Harcourt Brace.

Emerson, R. M., Fretz, R. I., & Shaw, L. L. (1995). *Writing ethnographic fieldnotes.* Chicago: University of Chicago Press.

Emihovich, C. (1999). Studying schools, studying ourselves: Ethnographic perspectives on educational reform. *Anthropology and Education Quarterly, 30*(4), 477–483.

Erickson, F. (1984). What makes school ethnography ethnographic? *Anthropology and Education Quarterly, 15*(1), 51–66.

Erickson, F. (1986). Qualitative methods in research on teaching. In M. C. Wittrock (Ed.), *Handbook of research on teaching* (3rd ed., pp. 119–161). New York: Macmillan.

Esteva, G., & Prakash, M. S. (1998). *Grassroots postmodernism.* New York: Zed Books.

Farganis, S. (1994). Postmodernism and feminism. In D. Dickens & A. Fontana (Eds.), *Postmodernism and social inquiry* (pp. 101–126). New York: Guilford Press.

Ferrini-Mundy, J., & Schram, T. (Eds.). (1997). Recognizing and recording reform in mathematics education: Issues and implications. *Journal of Research in Mathematics Education,* Monograph No. 8. Reston, VA: National Council of Teachers of Mathematics.

Fielding, N. G. (2002). Computer applications in qualitative research. In P. Atkinson, A. Coffey, S. Delamont, J. Lofland, & L. Lofland (Eds.), *Handbook of ethnography* (pp. 453–467). Thousand Oaks, CA: Sage.

Fine, M., & Weis, L. (1998). *The unknown city: The lives of poor and working-class young adults.* Boston: Beacon Press.

Fine, M., Weis, L., Weseen, S., & Wong, L. (2000). For whom? Qualitative research, representations, and social responsibilities. In N. K. Denzin & Y. S. Lincoln (Eds.), *Handbook of qualitative research* (2nd ed., pp. 107–131). Thousand Oaks, CA: Sage.

Flinders, D. J. (1992). In search of ethical guidance: Constructing a basis for dialogue. *International Journal of Qualitative Studies in Education, 5*(2), 101–115.

Flinders, D. J., & Mills, G. E. (1993). *Theory and concepts in qualitative research: Perspectives from the field.* New York: Teachers College Press.

Flyvbjerg, B. (2004). Five misunderstandings about case study research. In C. Seale, G. Gobo, J. F. Gubrium, & D. Silverman (Eds.), *Qualitative research practice* (pp. 420–434). Thousand Oaks, CA: Sage.

Foley, D. E. (1995). *The heartland chronicles.* Philadelphia: University of Pennsylvania Press.

Foley, D. E. (2002). Critical ethnography in the postcritical moment. In Y. Zou & E. T. Trueba (Eds.), *Ethnography and schools: Qualitative approaches to the study of education* (pp. 139–170). Lanham, MD: Rowan & Littlefield Publishers.

Fontana, A. (1994). Ethnographic trends in the postmodern era. In D. Dickens & A. Fontana (Eds.), *Postmodernism and social inquiry* (pp. 203–223). New York: Guilford Press.

Fontana, A. (2002). Postmodern trends in interviewing. In J. F. Gubrium & J. A. Holstein (Eds.), *Handbook of interview research: Context and method* (pp. 161–175). Thousand Oaks, CA: Sage.

Fujimura, J. (1996). *Crafting science: A socio-history of the quest for the genetics of cancer.* Cambridge, MA: Harvard University Press.

Gee, J. P. (1996). *Social linguistics and literacies: Ideology in discourses* (2nd ed.). London: Taylor & Francis.

Gee, J. P. (1999). *An introduction to discourse analysis: Theory and method.* New York: Routledge.

Geertz, C. (1973). *The interpretation of cultures.* New York: Basic Books.

Geertz, C. (1984). On the nature of anthropological understanding. In R. A. Shweder & R. A. LeVine (Eds.), *Culture theory: Essays on mind, self, and emotion.* New York: Cambridge University Press.

Gharajedaghi, J., & Ackoff, R. L. (1985). Toward systemic education of social scientists. *Systems Research 5*(2), 21–27.

Giorgi, A. (1994). A phenomenological perspective on certain qualitative research methods. *Journal of Phenomenological Psychology, 25,* 190–220.

Giorgi, A. (1997). The theory, practice, and evaluation of the phenomenological methods as a qualitative research procedure. *Journal of Phenomenological Studies, 28*(2), 235–281.

Glaser, B. G. (1978). *Theoretical sensitivity.* Mill Valley, CA: Sociology Press.

Glaser, B. G. (1992). *Basics of grounded theory analysis.* Mill Valley, CA: Sociology Press.

Glaser, B. G. (Ed.). (1993). *Examples of grounded theory: A reader.* Mill Valley, CA: Sociology Press.

Glaser, B. G. (2002). Conceptualization: On theory and theorizing using grounded theory. *International Journal of Qualitative Methods, 1*(2). Article 3. Retrieved 03/09/03 from http://www.ualberta.ca/~ijqm/

Glaser, B. G., & Strauss, A. (1967). *The discovery of grounded theory.* Chicago: Aldine.

Glesne, C. (1989). Rapport and friendship in ethnographic research. *International Journal of Qualitative Studies in Education, 2*(1), 45–54.

Glesne, C. (1999). *Becoming qualitative researchers: An introduction* (2nd ed.). White Plains, NY: Longman.

Glesne, C., & Peshkin, A. (1992). *Becoming qualitative researchers: An introduction.* White Plains, NY: Longman.

Gobo, G. (2004). Sampling, representativeness, and generalizability. In C. Seale, G. Gobo, J. F. Gubrium, & D. Silverman (Eds.), *Qualitative research practice* (pp. 435–456). Thousand Oaks, CA: Sage.

Goetz, J. P., & LeCompte, M. D. (1984). *Ethnography and qualitative design in educational research.* New York: Academic Press.

Grant, J. (1993). *Fundamental feminism: Contesting the core concepts of feminist theory.* New York: Routledge.

Guba, E. G., & Lincoln, Y. S. (1994). Competing paradigms in qualitative research. In N. K. Denzin & Y. S. Lincoln (Eds.), *Handbook of qualitative research* (pp. 105–117). Thousand Oaks, CA: Sage.

Gubrium, J., & Holstein, J. (1997). *The new language of qualitative method.* Oxford, UK: Blackwell.

Gubrium, J., & Holstein, J. (2000). Analyzing interpretive practice. In N. R. Denzin & Y. S. Lincoln (Eds.), *Handbook of qualitative research* (2nd ed., pp. 487–508). Thousand Oaks, CA: Sage.

Guillemin, M., & Gillam, L. (2004). Ethics, reflexivity, and "ethically important moments" in research. *Qualitative Inquiry, 10*(2), 261–280.

Hamel, J. (1993). *Case study methods.* Newbury Park, CA: Sage.

Hammersley, M. (1990). *Reading ethnographic research: A critical guide.* New York: Longman.

Holstein, J. A., & Gubrium, J. F. (1994). Phenomenology, ethnomethodology, and interpretive practice. In N. K. Denzin & Y. S. Lincoln (Eds.), *Handbook of qualitative research* (pp. 262–272). Thousand Oaks, CA: Sage.

Holstein, J. A., & Gubrium, J. F. (2004). Context: Working it up, down, and across. In C. Seale, G. Gobo, J. F. Gubrium, & D. Silverman (Eds.), *Qualitative research practice* (pp. 297–311). Thousand Oaks, CA: Sage.

Husserl, E. (1967). The thesis of the natural standpoint and its suspension. In J. J. Kockelmans (Ed.), *Phenomenology* (pp. 68–79). Garden City, NY: Doubleday.

Jackson, M. (1996). Introduction: Phenomenology, radical empiricism, and anthropological critique. In M. Jackson (Ed.), *Things as they are: New directions in phenomenological anthropology* (pp. 1–50). Bloomington: University of Indiana Press.

Janesick, V. J. (1994). The dance of qualitative research design: Metaphor, methodolatry, and meaning. In N. K. Denzin & Y. S. Lincoln (Eds.), *Handbook of qualitative research* (pp. 209–219). Thousand Oaks, CA: Sage.

Jansen, G., & Peshkin, A. (1992). Subjectivity in qualitative research. In M. LeCompte, W. L. Millroy, & J. Preissle (Eds.), *Handbook of qualitative research in education* (pp. 681–725). San Diego, CA: Academic Press.

Josephson, J. R., & Josephson, S. G. (1994). *Abductive inference: Computation, philosophy, technology.* Cambridge, UK: Cambridge University Press.

Kaplan, A. (1964). *The conduct of inquiry.* Scranton, PA: Chandler Publishing.

Kaplan, I. M. (1991). Gone fishing, be back later: Ending and resuming research among fishermen. In W. B. Shaffir & R. A. Stebbins (Eds.), *Experiencing fieldwork: An inside view of qualitative research* (pp. 232–237). Newbury Park, CA: Sage.

Kellehear, A. (1993). *The unobtrusive researcher: A guide to methods.* Sydney: Allen and Unwin.

Kincheloe, J. L., & McLaren, P. L. (1994). Rethinking critical theory and qualitative research. In N. K. Denzin & Y. S. Lincoln (Eds.), *Handbook of qualitative research* (pp. 138–157). Thousand Oaks, CA: Sage.

Kincheloe, J. L., & McLaren, P. (2002). Rethinking critical theory and qualitative research. In Y. Zou & E. T. Trueba (Eds.), *Ethnography and schools: Qualitative approaches to the study of education* (pp. 87–138). Lanham, MD: Rowan & Littlefield Publishers.

Kitzinger, C. (2004). Feminist approaches. In C. Seale, G. Gobo, J. F. Gubrium, & D. Silverman (Eds.), *Qualitative research practice* (pp. 125–140). Thousand Oaks, CA: Sage.

Kleinman, S. (1991). Field-workers' feelings: What we feel, who we are, how we analyze. In W. B. Shaffir and R. A. Stebbins (Eds.), *Experiencing fieldwork: An inside view of qualitative research* (pp. 184–195). Newbury Park, CA: Sage.

Kluckhohn, C., & Murray, H. A. (1948). *Personality in nature, society, and culture.* New York: Alfred A. Knopf.

Knapp, T. R. (1999). Response to Elliot W. Eisner's "The promise and perils of alternative forms of data representation." *Educational Researcher, 28*(1), 18–19.

Kuper, A. (1999). *Culture: The anthropologists' account.* Cambridge, MA: Harvard University Press.

Labov, W., & Waletzky, J. (1997). Narrative analysis: Oral versions of personal experience. *Journal of Narrative and Life History 7*(1–4), 3–38.

Ladson-Billings, G. (1998). Just what is critical race theory and what is it doing in a "nice" field like education? *International Journal of Qualitative Studies in Education, 11*(1), 7–24.

Ladson-Billings, G. (2000). Racialized discourses and ethnic epistemologies. In N. K. Denzin & Y. S. Lincoln (Eds.), *Handbook of qualitative research* (2nd ed., pp. 257–277). Thousand Oaks, CA: Sage.

Lareau, A. (1989). *Home advantage: Social class and parental intervention in elementary education.* New York: Falmer.

Lather, P. (1991). *Getting smart: Feminist research and pedagogy with/in the postmodern.* New York: Routledge.

Lather, P. (1993). Fertile obsession: Validity after poststructuralism. *The Sociological Quarterly 34*(4), 673–693.

Laverty, S. M. (2003). Hermeneutic phenomenology and phenomenology: A comparison of historical and methodological considerations. *International Journal of Qualitative Methods, 2*(3). Article 3. Retrieved 10/07/03 from http://www.ualberta.ca/~iiqm/backissues/2_3/html/laverty.html

LeCompte, M. D., & Preissle, J. P., with Tesch, R. (1993). *Ethnography and qualitative design in educational research* (2nd ed.). San Diego, CA: Academic Press.

LeCompte, M. D., & Schensul, J. J. (1999). *Designing and conducting ethnographic research.* Walnut Creek, CA: AltaMira Press.

LeCompte, M. D., Schensul, J. J., Weeks, M. R., & Singer, M. (1999). *Researcher roles and research partnerships.* Walnut Creek, CA: AltaMira Press.

Lincoln, Y. S. (1995). The sixth moment: Emerging problems in qualitative research. *Studies in Symbolic Interactionism, 19,* 37–55.

Lincoln, Y. S., & Guba, E. G. (1985). *Naturalistic inquiry.* Beverly Hills, CA: Sage.

Lincoln, Y. S., & Guba, E. G. (2000). Paradigmatic controversies, contradictions, and emerging confluences. In N. K. Denzin & Y. S. Lincoln (Eds.), *Handbook of qualitative research* (2nd ed., pp. 163–188). Thousand Oaks, CA: Sage.

Macbeth, D. (2003). Hugh Mehan's learning lessons reconsidered: on the differences between the naturalistic and critical analysis of classroom discourse. *American Educational Research Journal, 40*(1), 239–280.

Magolda, P. M. (2000). The campus tour: Ritual and community in higher education. *Anthropology and Education Quarterly, 31*(1), 24–36.

Maguire, P. (1996). Considering more feminist participatory research: What's congruency got to do with it? *Qualitative Inquiry, 2*(1), 106–118.

Mandelbaum, D. G. (1973). The study of life history: Gandhi. *Current Anthropology 14*(3), 177–206.

Marshall, C., & Rossman, G. B. (1999). *Designing qualitative research* (3rd ed.). Thousand Oaks, CA: Sage.

Mattingly, C. (1998). In search of the good: Narrative reasoning in clinical practice. *Medical Anthropology Quarterly 12*(3), 273–297.

Mauthner, M., Birch, M., Jessop, J., & Miller, T. (Eds.). (2002). *Ethics in qualitative research.* Thousand Oaks, CA: Sage.

Maxwell, J. A. (1992). Understanding and validity in qualitative research. *Harvard Educational Review, 62*(3), 279–300.

Maxwell, J. A. (1996). *Qualitative research design: An interactive approach.* Thousand Oaks, CA: Sage.

Maxwell, J. A. (2002). Understanding and validity in qualitative research. In M. Huberman & M. Miles (Eds.), *The Qualitative Researcher's Companion* (pp. 37–64). Thousand Oaks, CA: Sage.

Maxwell, J. A. (2004). Causal explanation, qualitative research, and scientific inquiry in education. *Educational Researcher 33*(2), 3–11.

Maxwell, J. A. (2005). *Qualitative research design: An interactive approach* (2nd ed.). Thousand Oaks, CA: Sage.

Mayer, R. E. (2000). What is the place of science in educational research? *Educational Researcher, 29*(6), 38–39.

Melia, K. M. (1996). Rediscovering Glaser. *Qualitative Health Research 6*(3), 368–378.

Merriam, S. B. (1998). *Qualitative research and case study applications in education.* San Francisco: Jossey-Bass.

Metz, M. H. (2000). Sociology and qualitative methodologies in educational research. *Harvard Educational Review, 70*(1), 60–74.

Miles, M. B., & Huberman, A. M. (1994). *Qualitative data analysis* (2nd ed.). Thousand Oaks, CA: Sage.

Miller, S. M., Nelson, M. W., & Moore, M. T. (1998). Caught in the paradigm gap: Qualitative researchers' lived experience and the politics of epistemology. *American Educational Research Journal, 35*(3), 377–416.

Miller, T., & Bell, L. (2002). Consenting to what? Issues of access, gate-keeping and 'informed' consent. In M. Mauthner, M. Birch, J. Jessop, & T. Miller (Eds.), *Ethics in qualitative research* (pp. 53–69). Thousand Oaks, CA: Sage.

Mills, C. W. (1959). On intellectual craftsmanship. In C. W. Mills (Ed.), *The sociological imagination* (pp. 195–226). London: Oxford University Press.

Mills, G. (2000). *Action research: A guide for the teacher researcher.* Upper Saddle River, NJ: Merrill/Prentice Hall.

Mishler, E. G. (1979). Meaning in context: Is there any other kind? *Harvard Education Review, 49*(1), 1–19.

Mishler, E. G. (1986). *Research interviewing: Context and narrative.* Cambridge, MA: Harvard University Press.

Mitchell, R.G. Jr. (1991). Secrecy and disclosure in fieldwork. In W.B. Shaffir & R.A. Stebbins (Eds.), *Experiencing fieldwork: An inside view of qualitative research* (pp. 97–108). Newbury Park, CA: Sage.

Morrow, S., & Smith, M. (1995). Constructions of survival and coping by women who have survived childhood sexual abuse. *Journal of Counseling Psychology, 42,* 24–33.

Morse, J. M. (1994). Designing funded qualitative research. In N. K. Denzin & Y. S. Lincoln (Eds.), *Handbook of qualitative research* (pp. 220–235). Thousand Oaks, CA: Sage.

Morse, J. M., & Richards, L. (2002). *Readme first for a user's guide to qualitative methods.* Thousand Oaks, CA: Sage.

Moustakas, C. (1994). *Phenomenological research methods.* Thousand Oaks, CA: Sage.

Newman, I., & Benz, C. R. (1998). *Qualitative-quantitative research methodology: Exploring the interactive continuum.* Carbondale: Southern Illinois University Press.

Olesen, V. L. (2000). Feminism and qualitative research at and into the millennium. In N. K. Denzin & Y. S. Lincoln (Eds.), *Handbook of qualitative research* (2nd ed., pp. 215–255). Thousand Oaks, CA: Sage.

Page, R. N. (2000). The turn inward in qualitative research. *Harvard Educational Review, 70*(1), 23–38.

Patton, M. Q. (2002). *Qualitative research and evaluation methods* (3rd ed.). Thousand Oaks, CA: Sage.

Peacock, J. L. (1986). *The anthropological lens: Harsh light, soft focus.* New York: Cambridge University Press.

Peirce, C. S. (1992). *The essential Peirce: Volume 1 (1867–1893),* N. Houser & C. Kloesel (Eds.). Bloomington, IN: Indiana University Press.

Peirce, C. S. (1998). *The essential Peirce: Volume 2 (1893–1913).* The Peirce Edition Project (Eds.). Bloomington: Indiana University Press.

Peshkin, A. (1984). Odd man out: The participant observer in an absolutist setting. *Sociology of Education, 57,* 254–264.

Peshkin, A. (1985a). From title to title: The evolution of perspective in qualitative inquiry. *Anthropology and Education Quarterly, 16*(3), 214–224.

Peshkin, A. (1985b). Virtuous subjectivity: In the participant observer's I's. In D. Berg & K. Smith (Eds.), *Exploring clinical methods for doing social research* (pp. 267–282). Beverly Hills, CA: Sage.

Peshkin, A. (1988). In search of subjectivity—One's own. *Educational Researcher, 17*(7), 17–21.

Peshkin, A. (1992, January). *Experience subjectivity.* Keynote Address for the fifth annual conference of the Qualitative Interest Group, University of Georgia, Athens.

Peshkin, A. (2000). The nature of interpretation in qualitative research. *Educational Researcher, 29*(9), 5–9.

Piantanida, M., & Garman, N. B. (1999). *The qualitative dissertation: A guide for students and faculty.* Thousand Oaks, CA: Corwin Press.

Piantanida, M., Tananis, C., & Grubs, R. (2004). Generating grounded theory of/for educational practice: The journey of three epistemorphs. *International Journal of Qualitative Studies in Education, 17*(3), 325–346.

Pilcher, J. K., & Juneau, G. A. (2002). Authoring social responsibility. *Qualitative Inquiry 8*(6), 715–737.

Poggie, J. J., Jr., DeWalt, B. R., & Dressler, W. W. (Eds.). (1992). *Anthropological research: Process and application*. Albany: State University of New York Press.

Polkinghorne, D. E. (1988). *Narrative knowing and the human sciences*. Albany: State University of New York Press.

Polkinghorne, D. E. (1989). Phenomenological research methods. In R. S. Valle & S. Halling (Eds.), *Existential-phenomenological perspectives in psychology* (pp. 41–60). New York: Plenum.

Polkinghorne, D. E. (1995). Narrative configuration in qualitative analysis. In J. A. Hatch & R. Wisniewski (Eds.), *Life history and narrative* (pp. 5–23). Washington, DC: Falmer.

Porter, E. (1999). *Feminist perspectives on ethics*. New York: Longman.

Punch, M. (1994). Politics and ethics in qualitative research. In N. K. Denzin & Y. S. Lincoln (Eds.), *Handbook of qualitative research* (pp. 83–97). Thousand Oaks, CA: Sage.

Ray, M. A. (1994). The richness of phenomenology: Philosophic, theoretic, and methodologic concerns. In J. M. Morse (Ed.), *Critical issues in qualitative research methods* (pp. 117–133). Thousand Oaks, CA: Sage.

Reinharz, S. (1992). *Feminist methods in social research*. New York: Oxford University Press.

Richardson, L. (2000). Writing: A method of inquiry. In N. K. Denzin & Y. S. Lincoln (Eds.), *Handbook of qualitative research* (2nd ed., pp. 923–948). Thousand Oaks, CA: Sage.

Riessman, C. K. (1993). *Narrative analysis*. Newbury Park, CA: Sage.

Riessman, C. K. (2002a). Narrative analysis. In A. M. Huberman & M. B. Miles (Eds.), *The qualitative researcher's companion* (pp. 217–270). Thousand Oaks, CA: Sage.

Riessman, C. K. (2002b). Analysis of personal narratives. In J. F. Gubrium and J. A. Holstein (Eds.), *Handbook of interview research: Context and method* (pp. 695–710). Thousand Oaks, CA: Sage.

Robbins, T. (1980). *Still life with a woodpecker: A sort of love story*. New York: Bantam Books.

Rogers, L. J., & Swadener, B. B. (1999). Reframing the "field." *Anthropology and Education Quarterly, 30*(4), 436–440.

Rogers, R. A. (2002). Through the eyes of the institution: A critical discourse analysis of decision making in two special education meetings. *Anthropology and Education Quarterly, 33*(2), 213–237.

Rosaldo, R. (1989). *Culture and truth: The remaking of social analysis*. Boston: Beacon.

Rossman, G. B., & Rallis, S. F. (1998). *Learning in the field: An introduction to qualitative research*. Thousand Oaks, CA: Sage.

Rossman, G. B., & Rallis, S. F. (2003). *Learning in the field: An introduction to qualitative research* (2nd ed.). Thousand Oaks, CA: Sage.

Ryen, A. (2004). Ethical issues. In C. Seale, G. Gobo, J. F. Gubrium, & D. Silverman (Eds.), *Qualitative research practice* (pp. 230–247). Thousand Oaks, CA: Sage.

Salvio, P., & Schram, T. (1995). Making the familiar strange: Learning within and beyond one's cultural borders. *Teaching and Learning: The Journal of Natural Inquiry, 9*(3), 30–39.

Sanjek, R. (1991). On ethnographic validity. In R. Sanjek (Ed.), *Fieldnotes: The makings of anthropology* (pp. 385–418). Ithaca, NY: Cornell University Press.

Schensul, S., Schensul, J. J., & LeCompte, M. D. (1999). *Essential ethnographic methods: Observations, interviews, and questionnaires*. Walnut Creek, CA: AltaMira.

Schofield, J. W. (2002). Increasing the generalizability of qualitative research. In A. M. Huberman & M. B. Miles (Eds.), *The qualitative researcher's companion* (pp. 171–203). Thousand Oaks, CA: Sage.

Schram, T. (1993). Laotian refugees in a small-town school: Contexts and encounters. *Journal of Research in Rural Education, 9*(3), 125–136.

Schram, T. (1994). Players along the margin: Diversity and adaptation in a lower track classroom. In G. Spindler & L. Spindler (Eds.), *Pathways to cultural awareness: Cultural therapy with teachers and students* (pp. 61–91). Thousand Oaks, CA: Corwin.

Schram, T. (2000). *Extending ethnographic intent: What we do with what we know*. Paper presented at the annual meeting of the American Educational Research Association Annual Meeting, New Orleans, Louisiana.

Schutz, A. (1967). *The phenomenology of the social world*. Evanston, IL: Northwestern University Press.

Schutz, A. (1970). *On phenomenology and social relations*. Chicago: University of Chicago Press.

Schwandt, T. A. (1993). Theory for the moral sciences: Crisis of identity and purpose. In D. J. Flinders & G. E. Mills (Eds.), *Theory and concepts in qualitative research: Perspectives from the field* (pp. 5–23). New York: Teachers College Press.

Schwandt, T. A. (1994). Constructivist, interpretivist approaches to human inquiry. In N. K. Denzin & Y. S. Lincoln (Eds.), *Handbook of qualitative research* (pp. 118–137). Thousand Oaks, CA: Sage.

Schwandt, T. A. (1995). Thoughts on the moral career of the interpretive inquirer. *Studies in Symbolic Interactionism, 19*, 131–140.

Schwandt, T. A. (1997). *Qualitative inquiry: A dictionary of terms.* Thousand Oaks, CA: Sage.

Schwandt, T. A. (2000). Three epistemological stances for qualitative inquiry: Interpretivism, hermeneutics, and social constructivism. In N. K. Denzin & Y. S. Lincoln (Eds.), *Handbook of qualitative research* (2nd ed., pp. 189–214). Thousand Oaks, CA: Sage.

Schwandt, T. A. (2001). *Qualitative inquiry: A dictionary of terms* (2nd ed.). Thousand Oaks, CA: Sage.

Seale, C., Gobo, G., Gubrium, J., & Silverman, D. (Eds.). (2004). *Qualitative research practice.* Thousand Oaks, CA: Sage.

Seidel, J. (1992). Method and madness in the application of computer technology to qualitative data analysis. In N. G. Fielding & R. M. Lee (Eds.), *Using computers in qualitative research* (pp. 107–116). Newbury Park, CA: Sage.

Seidman, I. (1998). *Interviewing as qualitative research: A guide for researchers in education and the social sciences* (2nd ed.). New York: Teachers College Press.

Sevenhuijsen, S. (1998). *Citizenship and ethics of care: Feminist considerations of justice, morality and politics.* London: Routledge.

Shaffir, W. B. (1991). Managing a convincing self-presentation. In W. B. Shaffir and R. A. Stebbins (Eds.), *Experiencing fieldwork: An inside view of qualitative research* (pp. 72–86). Newbury Park, CA: Sage.

Shank, G. (2002). *Qualitative research: A personal skills approach.* Upper Saddle River, NJ: Merrill/Prentice Hall.

Silverman, D. (2001). *Interpreting qualitative data: Methods for analysing talk, text, and interaction* (2nd ed.). Thousand Oaks, CA: Sage.

Silverman, D. (2004). *Qualitative research: Theory, method, and practice* (2nd ed.). Thousand Oaks, CA: Sage.

Spindler, G., & Spindler, L. (1982). *Doing the ethnography of schooling.* New York: Holt, Rinehart and Winston.

Stake, R. E. (1995). *The art of case study research.* Thousand Oaks, CA: Sage.

Stake, R. (2000). Case studies. In N. K. Denzin & Y. S. Lincoln (Eds.), *Handbook of qualitative research* (2nd ed., pp. 435–454). Thousand Oaks, CA: Sage.

Stern, P. (1994). Eroding grounded theory. In J. M. Morse (Ed.), *Critical issues in qualitative research methods* (pp. 212–223). Thousand Oaks, CA: Sage.

Stewart, D., & Mickunas, A. (1990). *Exploring phenomenology: A guide to the field and its literature* (2nd ed.). Athens: Ohio University Press.

Strauss, A. (1987). *Qualitative analysis for social scientists.* New York: Cambridge University Press.

Strauss, A., & Corbin, J. (1994). Grounded theory methodology: An overview. In N. K. Denzin & Y. S. Lincoln (Eds.), *Handbook of qualitative research* (pp. 273–285). Thousand Oaks, CA: Sage.

Strauss, A., & Corbin, J. (1998). *Basics of qualitative research: Techniques and procedures for developing grounded theory* (2nd ed.). Thousand Oaks, CA: Sage.

Taylor, S. J. (1991). Leaving the field: Research, relationships, and responsibilities. In W. B. Shaffir & R. A. Stebbins (Eds.), *Experiencing fieldwork: An inside view of qualitative research* (pp. 238–247). Newbury Park, CA: Sage.

Taylor, S. J., & Bogdan, R. (1984). *An introduction to qualitative research: The search for meanings* (2nd ed.). New York: Wiley.

Tesch, R. (1990). *Qualitative research: Analysis types and software tools.* London: Falmer.

Thomas, G. (1997). What's the use of theory? *Harvard Educational Review, 67*(1), 75–104.

Tillmann-Healy, L. M. (2003). Friendship as method. *Qualitative Inquiry 9*(5), 729–749.

Tong, R. (1989). *Feminist thought: A comprehensive introduction.* Boulder, CO: Westview Press.

Van Maanen, J. (1988). *Tales of the field: On writing ethnography.* Chicago: The University of Chicago Press.

Van Manen, M. (1997). *Researching lived experience: Human science for an action sensitive pedagogy.* (2nd ed.). London, Canada: Althouse.

Watkins, J. M. (2001). Researching researchers and teachers: Comment on "not talking past each other." *Anthropology and Education Quarterly, 32*(3), 379–387.

Wax, M. L. (1982). Research reciprocity rather than informed consent in fieldwork. In J. E. Sieber (Ed.), *The ethics of research: Fieldwork regulation and publication.* New York: Springer-Verlag.

Willis, P. (1977). *Learning to labor: How working class kids get working class jobs.* Farnborough, England: Saxon House.

Wolcott, H. F. (1988). "Problem finding" in qualitative research. In H. Trueba & C. Delgado-Gaitan (Eds.), *School and society: Learning content through culture* (pp. 11–35). New York: Praeger.

Wolcott, H. F. (1990). Making a study more ethnographic. *Journal of Contemporary Ethnography, 19*(1), 44–72.

Wolcott, H. F. (1992). Posturing in qualitative inquiry. In M. LeCompte, W. L. Millroy, & J. Preissle (Eds.), *Handbook of qualitative research in education* (pp. 3–52). San Diego, CA: Academic Press.

Wolcott, H. F. (1994). *Transforming qualitative data: Description, analysis, and interpretation.* Thousand Oaks, CA: Sage.

Wolcott, H. F. (1999). *Ethnography: A way of seeing.* Walnut Creek, CA: AltaMira.

Wolcott, H. F. (2001). *Writing up qualitative research* (2nd ed.). Thousand Oaks, CA: Sage.

Wolcott, H. F. (2005). *The art of fieldwork* (2nd ed.). Walnut Creek, CA: AltaMira.

Wolf, M. (1992). *A thrice told tale: Feminism, Postmodernism, and ethnographic responsibility.* Stanford, CA: Stanford University Press.

Wong, L. (1998). The ethics of rapport: Institutional safeguards, resistance, and betrayal. *Qualitative Inquiry, 4*(2), 178–199.

Yin, R. K. (1994). *Case study research: Design and methods.* Thousand Oaks, CA: Sage.

Young, I. M. (1997). *Intersecting voices: Dilemmas of gender, political philosophy and policy.* Princeton, NJ: Princeton University Press.

Zigo, D. (2001). Rethinking reciprocity: Collaboration in labor as a path toward equalizing power in classroom research. *International Journal of Qualitative Studies in Education, 14*(3), 351–365.

Zou, Y., & Trueba, E. T. (2002). *Ethnography and schools: Qualitative approaches to the study of education.* Lanham, MD: Rowman & Littlefield.

Index